APIL MODEL PLEADINGS AND APPLICATIONS

APIL MODEL PLEADINGS AND APPLICATIONS

General Editors

Martin Bare
Partner, Morrish & Co

Richard Copnall
Barrister, Park Lane Chambers

Contributors

Andrew Axon
Barrister, Park Lane Chambers

Dominic Hughes
Solicitor, Morrish & Co

Simon Thorp
Barrister, Park Lane Chambers

JORDANS

Published by
Jordan Publishing Limited
21 St Thomas Street
Bristol BS1 6JS

British Library Cataloguing-in-Publication Data

A catalogue record for this book is available from the British Library.

ISBN 978 085308 949 0

Typeset by Etica Press Ltd, Malvern, Worcestershire
Printed and bound in Great Britain by Antony Rowe Limited, Chippenham, Wiltshire

FOREWORD

The art of litigation is practised best by lawyers who are well prepared and confident. As long as avoidable injuries occur victims will need expert legal representation to obtain justice. Whilst the modern trend is towards cooperation in dispute resolution, the threat of proceedings is the best incentive for encouraging defendants to settle claims. In the face of unmeritorious denials we must use the courts as a weapon.

In this work the authors explain the necessities of drafting pleadings and precedents, simultaneously educating us in the essential evidence to be captured at the outset of our instructions. They provide a clear and practical guide to solving the problem of defendants that have gone out of business or are threatening to do so. CPR only works if parties comply with the pre-action protocols and the precedent to enforce compliance is here. There is a comprehensive armoury of interlocutory applications. The reader is guided through the approach of the courts with helpful tips and appropriate warnings in a concise but readable way.

This is a book to read from cover to cover and then keep close to hand. It will be profitably read by the trainee and the most experienced. Enjoy!

Richard Langton
APIL President

February 2007

PREFACE

Claimant lawyers have always been under a duty to work as effectively and efficiently as possible. The arrival of CPR imposed further limitations on time and costs, and CFAs brought increased commercial pressures. For the minority of claims that do not settle or discontinue before issue, the margin between success and failure is often small and no opportunity to gain a proper advantage can be safely overlooked.

Our aim has been to guide readers towards using pleadings and applications in the most efficient and, crucially, effective way.

In the section on applications, we hope to have given much needed guidance on the often problematic area of insolvent defendants and, more generally, precedents that will allow the claimant's lawyer to be where they should be – in the driving seat, forcing the case forward to the earliest proper resolution.

Active case management by the court requires a pro-active claimant lawyer who, we hope, will now have a database of appropriate applications.

To those brought up in the tradition of 'prayers', 'aforesaids' and blunderbuss particulars, our approach to pleadings will be a revelation. We have deliberately removed legalese and verbiage to create an approach that is clear, precise, efficient and, above all, effective.

As with all precedents, it is important to use the documents in this book with care. Many areas of personal injury law are complex. The precedents are intended to be a useful addition to a sound understanding of the substantive law; they cannot replace it. Similarly, the variety of factual situations is limitless and each precedent should be carefully tailored to the circumstances of the case.

We have had considerable help from many people both in the preparation of this book and the work leading up to it. We would particularly like to thank, Andrew, Dominic and Simon for their contributions, inspiration and willingness to hold their own when we disagreed and Tony Hawitt at Jordans for his encouragement and patience.

Martin would like to thank his partners and staff for all their help, particularly Dominic Hughes and Tina Barker.

Richard would also like to thank Anne, Philippa and Isabel for sacrificing too many of their weekend plans and his colleagues at Park Lane Chambers for knocking the rough edges off his emergent ideas.

The law is, we hope, up to date as at 1 March 2007.

Marin Bare and Richard Copnall
Leeds
March 2007

ASSOCIATION OF PERSONAL INJURY LAWYERS (APIL)

APIL is the UK's leading association of claimant personal injury lawyers, dedicated to protecting the rights of injured people.

Formed in 1990, APIL now represents over 5,000 solicitors, barristers, academics and students in the UK, Republic of Ireland and overseas.

APIL's objectives are:

- to promote full and just compensation for all types of personal injury
- to promote and develop expertise in the practice of personal injury law
- to promote wider redress for personal injury in the legal system
- to campaign for improvements in personal injury law
- to promote safety and alert the public to hazards
- to provide a communication network for members

APIL is a growing and influential forum pushing for law reform, and improvements, which will benefit victims of personal injury.

Governed and monitored by an Academic Quality Council, APIL's accreditation scheme recognizes expertise and skills, and provides an independent, quality kitemark, which guides and informs the public. In addition, APIL offers cost effective, practical, specialist education and training for its members and other professionals.

APIL is also an authoritative information source for personal injury lawyers, providing up to the minute PI bulletins, regular newsletters and publications information databases and on-line services.

For further information contact:

APIL
11 Castle Quay
Nottingham
NG7 1FW

DX 716208 Nottingham 42
Tel: 0115 9580585
Email: mail@apil.com
Website: www.apil.com

CONTENTS

TABLE OF CASES

TABLE OF STATUTES

TABLE OF STATUTORY INSTRUMENTS

TABLE OF EUROPEAN LEGISLATION

Part I

PLEADINGS

Section 1

PLEADINGS – GENERAL INTRODUCTION

TERMINOLOGY

The Civil Procedure Rules 1998 (CPR) replaced a number of well-established legal terms. Some of these changes have been recognised as more easily understood by the layman and have been readily accepted by practitioners and the courts (eg 'Claimant' as opposed to 'Plaintiff'). The benefit of other changes has been less obvious. In particular, *'a statement of case'* is longer and perhaps no more informative to the layman than *'a pleading'*[1] and it also lacks a suitable equivalent verb. In order to reflect current usage, this book has retained the use of 'a pleading' and 'to plead'.

Until English develops a suitable alternative, we have avoided the 'his/her' formulation. Any references to the masculine includes the feminine and vice versa. This is in the interests of economy and elegance of language and no gender bias is intended.

THE AIM OF THIS SECTION

Historically, many practitioners favoured lengthy pleadings, packed with legalese and weighed down with scores of allegations of breach. These pleadings were impenetrable to laypeople, drew criticism from the courts and often hampered, rather than helped, the claimant towards a successful outcome.

Guidance towards an approach that is clear, concise and, most importantly, effective in maximising the claimant's prospects of success will be provided. This approach has the incidental benefit of being quicker, which is always welcome in the light of constant commercial pressure to be more productive and the court's objective of 'saving expense'.[2]

---

[1]   See CPR 2.3.

[2]   CPR 1.1.

1.   THE CLAIM FORM

The claim form is the document used to begin proceedings. Proceedings are begun when the court issues a claim form[3] at the request of the claimant and on payment of a fee.[4] It is an entirely formal document. Drafting is a matter of complying with the basic requirements of the rules, set out below.

The Basic Requirements

The claim form must:

(1) Contain a concise statement of the nature of the claim.[5]

(2) Specify the remedy that the claimant seeks.[6]

(3) Contain a statement of value.[7]

(4) If the particulars of claim are not included in the claim form, contain a statement that they will follow.[8]

(5) Contain a statement of truth.[9]

(6) Include an address at which the claimant resides or carries on business (even if the claimant's address for service is the business address of his solicitor).[10]

---

[3]   CPR 7.2.

[4]   Currently: up to £300 the fee is £30;

£300.01-£500 the fee is £50;
£500,01-£1,000 the fee is £80;
£1,000.01-£5,000 the fee is £120;
£5,000.01-£15,000 the fee is £250;
£15,000.01-£50,000 the fee is £400;
£50,000.01-£100,000 the fee is £700;
£100,000.01-£150,000 the fee is £900;
£150,000.01-£200,000 the fee is £1,100;
£200,000.01-£250,000 the fee is £1,300;
£250,000.01-£300,000 the fee is £1,500;
£300,000.01 or for an unlimited amount the fee is £1,700.
To issue proceedings where your claim is for something other than money the fee is £150.

[5]   CPR 16.2.

[6]   CPR 16.2.

[7]   CPR 16.2.

[8]   CPR 16.2.

[9]   CPR 22.1.

[10]   CPR 16 PD 2.

The Remedy

In most cases the appropriate remedy will be 'damages' but may occasionally include a 'declaration' (eg in a Motor Insurers' Bureau ('MIB') case). If the damages are 'provisional', 'exemplary' or 'aggravated', this must be stated in the particulars of claim, not the claim form.

The Statement of Value

The statement of value should be in the following form:[11]

(1)

    a) The Claimant expects to recover [not more than £5,000] /[more than £5,000 but not more than £15,000] / [more than £15,000];

    b) the Claimant cannot say how much he expects to recover.

(2) The Claimant expects to recover [*not more than £1,000*] / [*more than £1,000*] as general damages for pain, suffering and loss of amenity.

This statement of value is often seen in the following form:

    'The Claimant claims damages limited to £X,000.'

Such a construction does not comply with the CPR and should not be used. The 'statement of value' is a statement of the claimant's *expectation* at that particular time, not a limit.

The desire to 'limit' damages in the statement of value may be influenced by the County Court Fees Order 1999, which provides for a scale of fees by reference to the 'sum claimed'. Where the sum is 'not limited', the maximum fee (£1,700) is charged. If the court office is not prepared to accept the statement of value as the 'sum claimed', then practitioners should, for the avoidance of doubt, include a limit in addition to the statement of value. The figure in the statement of value may not be same as in the 'limit' as a claimant might have a current expectation of recovering, say, £5,000 but his evidence may be incomplete and he might not wish to limit himself to that figure for the future.

The Statement of Truth

All statements of case, including any amendments[12] and schedules of loss,[13] must be verified by a statement of truth.

There are only two possible forms:[14]

---

[11]   CPR 16.3.

[12]   CPR 22.1.

[13]   CPR 22 PD 1.4(3).

(1) When signed by the claimant:

   'I believe that the facts stated in this [*particulars of claim/reply etc*] are true'.

(2) When signed by the claimant's solicitor:

   'The Claimant believes that the facts stated in this [*particulars of claim/reply etc*] are true'.

Obtaining a statement of truth from the claimant provides an opportunity for practitioners to confirm that the Claimant agrees with the draft. A statement of truth from the Claimant's solicitor suggests to the reader a lack of organisation by the claimant or his legal team. Therefore, it should be used only if the delay in obtaining the claimant's signature would cause limitation problems.

2.   THE PARTICULARS OF CLAIM

The 'particulars of claim' are either contained within the claim form or, more usually, set out in a separate document. The examples in this book assume a separate document.

As with the claim form, the CPR provides various basic requirements for the particulars of claim. However, unlike the claim form, once the basic requirements are satisfied, there remains enormous scope for harming or enhancing a claimant's prospects of success when drafting the particulars of claim.

The Basic Requirements

Information Always Required

(1) A statement that the claimant is seeking interest and the enactment under which he claims.[15]

(2) A statement of truth.[16]

(3) The claimant's date of birth.[17]

(4) Brief details of the claimant's personal injuries.[18]

(5) Attached to the particulars of claim: a schedule of details of any past and future expenses and losses which he claims.[19]

---

[14]   CPR 22 PD 2. Alternative forms are available for corporate bodies

[15]   CPR 16.4. The *White Book 2005* at 7.022 (5), suggests that if the Claimant wishes the Court to depart from ordinary principles when awarding interest, he should say so in his particulars and set out the relevant facts.

[16]   CPR 16.4.

[17]   CPR 16 PD 4.

[18]   CPR 16 PD 4.

(6) Attached to the particulars of claim, or served with them where the claimant is relying on the evidence of a medical practitioner, a report from a (presumably meaning 'the') medical practitioner about the personal injuries which he alleges in his claim.[20]

(7) Sufficient information to identify the incident concerned.[21]

Information Required as Appropriate

(1) If the particulars of claim are not contained in claim form:[22]

    (i) The court name.

    (ii) Claim number.

    (iii) Title of proceedings.

    (iv) The claimant's address for service.

(2) If a claim is made for disadvantage on the labour market (*'Smith v Manchester'*), it is 'good practice' to plead this.[23]

(3) If a claim is made for aggravated or exemplary damages:

That aggravated or exemplary damages are claimed and the grounds for claiming them.[24]

(4) If a claim is made for provisional damages:[25]

    (i) That the claimant is seeking an award of provisional damages under either s 32A of the Supreme Court Act 1981 or s 51 of the County Courts Act 1984.

    (ii) That there is a chance that at some future time the claimant will develop some serious disease or suffer some serious deterioration in his physical or mental condition.

    (iii) The disease or type of deterioration in respect of which an application may be made at a future date.

(5) In a fatal accident claim

    (i) That it is brought under the Fatal Accidents Act.[26]

---

[19]   CPR 16 PD 4.2.

[20]   CPR 16 PD 4.3.

[21]   CPR 16 PD 4.3.

[22]   CPR 16 PD 3.3.8.

[23]   *Thorn v Powergen plc* [1997] PIQR Q 73.

[24]   CPR 16.4.

[25]   CPR 16.4, 16 PD 4.4.

[26]   CPR 16 PD 5.1.

(ii) The dependants on whose behalf the claim is made.[27]

(iii) The date of birth of each dependent.[28]

(iv) Details of the nature of the dependency claim.[29]

(6) Where a Conviction is Relied on[30]

    (i) That the conviction is relied on.[31]

    (ii) The type of conviction and its date.[32]

    (iii) The court that made the conviction.[33]

    (iv) The issue in the claim to which it refers.[34]

Information that is Advisable

(1)   Counsel's name.

Where pleadings are drafted by counsel, there is no longer a requirement for them to be named on the pleading.. However, there have been occasions when the defendant has been unaware of the identity of claimant's counsel, instructed the same counsel who has read the instructions before realising what has happened and then been required to withdraw, causing the claimant to lose his counsel of choice. Identifying specialist counsel on the pleadings also emphasises to the reader the strength of the claimant's representation.

Information that is never Required

The following are often found in particulars of claim, but are not required and should not be included.

(1) A statement of value[35].

---

[27]   CPR 16 PD 5.1.

[28]   CPR 16 PD 5.1.

[29]   CPR 16 PD 5.1.

[30]   Convictions are admissible as evidence in civil proceedings (see s 11 of Civil Evidence Act 1968). Although the existence of a conviction based upon those facts giving rise to the claim is not determinative of the issue of guilt, the legal burden of proof shifts to the Defendant to disprove those matters which constitute the offence.

[31]   CPR 16 PD 8.

[32]   CPR 16 PD 8.

[33]   CPR 16 PD 8.

[34]   CPR 16 PD 8.

[35]   This must appear in the claim form.

(2) A 'prayer' setting out the remedy sought[36]. (Note: aggravated, exemplary or provisional damages must be specifically pleaded in the particulars of claim).

(3) A summary of the submission that will be made at trial on the rate or period of interest, where a conventional approach is to be followed (if an unconventional approach is intended, the defendant should be given notice of it).[37]

(4) A 'backsheet'. This is a legacy from times when legal documents were folded in half, obscuring the front page. With modern filing, a backsheet is a waste of paper and ink and serves no useful function.

Beyond the Minimum Requirements

Presentation

There are is an infinite variety of layout, font, headings, numbering and other matters of presentation and no one approach stands out as the ideal. However, when choosing a form, the pleader should aim for one that is unobtrusive. Anything that draws the reader's attention away from the contents is to be avoided. This work adopts a conventional form of presentation and readers can be confident that it satisfies the requirement of being unobtrusive.

Style

A case that is set out in simple and clear terms is more likely to be attractive to its audience (judge, defendant, insurer, defendant's legal team) and more difficult to defeat. The requirements of good writing apply equally well to pleadings as elsewhere.

(1) Direct the writing at your readership: the judge, defendant, insurer and defendant's legal team.

(2) Be clear. The meaning should be immediately apparent to all readers

(3) Be efficient. Use as many words as are needed to convey the point but no more.

(4) Use simple vocabulary where possible. Foreign (including Latin), archaic or technical terms should be avoided, provided that this does not prevent compliance with (2) and (3) above. However, where a legal concept has no recognised English label (eg '*volenti non fit injuria*') the foreign term should be used in the interests of clarity and efficiency.

(5) Where alternatives to words are clearer and more efficient, use them. For example, identifying a defective part of a machine or the location of a defect in a highway using a plan or photograph is often preferable to a written description.

---

[36] The remedy sought must be set out in the claim form.

[37] CPR 16.4. The *White Book 2005* at 7.022 (5) suggests that if the Claimant wishes the court to depart from ordinary principles when awarding interest, he should say so in his particulars and set out the relevant facts.

(6) Order the point logically. Narrative should usually be chronological. Allegations should be in descending order of importance. The most important allegation is (all things being equal) that with the lowest standard of proof. A claimant who is unable to overcome a lower standard is unlikely to overcome a higher one.

In general, therefore, the strict duties come first, followed by those limited by reasonable practicability and then those limited by reasonableness. A departure from that order will be required, when two or more allegations are part of a larger regulatory scheme. For example: a number of regulations require employers to avoid a risk, but to minimise the risk when it cannot be avoided.[38] Allegations based on such pairs of duties should follow one after the other.

(7) Avoid including different types of information in the same paragraph; such as: facts, allegations and statements of law.

(8) Avoid including controversial and uncontroversial items in the same paragraph. This will make it easier for the defendant to admit a whole paragraph and the reader (particularly the judge) to identify the items in issue

Content

Beyond the basic technical requirements set out above, the particulars of claim must contain:

(1) The breaches of duty relied on.

(2) The findings of fact that are required to support the allegations of breach.[39]

It is at this point that the question of pleading, in particular, and the tactics of the litigation, in general, become inextricably linked. The task of the pleader is to distil the essential elements of the claim so that all the superfluous is removed but all that is essential to the claim is retained. A practical test, when reviewing a draft, is to ask whether that particular part is likely to help the claimant to win the case. If not, it should be removed.

The Allegations of Breach

The pleading should always include the claimant's strongest allegations, that is, those on which he is most likely to win. The extent to which the claimant should also rely on the weaker allegations will inevitably depend on the evidence in any particular case. Striking the balance at the wrong point gives rise to the following risks.

Too Few Allegations

(1) May need to amend to allow for the emergence of new evidence.

---

[38]   For example, reg 4(1)(a) an (b)(ii) of the Manual Handling Operations Regulations 1992 and reg 7(1) of the Control of Substances Hazardous to Health Regulations 1999.

[39]   CPR 16.4(1)(a).

(2) Might encounter a trial judge/appeal court not attracted to the pleaded allegations but would have been attracted to an allegation which has not been pleaded.

Too Many Allegations

(1) Can create the impression that the pleader lacks experience, familiarity with the subject or confidence in his ability or the quality of the evidence.

(2) Greater chance of allegations being unsustainable by the time of trial causing either:

a)   An impression of lack of thought or weakness if the allegation is dropped;

b)   Irritation from the judge if it is not.

(3) Even if arguable, the weaker allegations risk irritating a Judge who wants to go straight to the 'heart' of the case.

(4) Increases the defendant's opportunities to further obscure the claimant's best points by adducing evidence and making submissions on the weaker ones.

(5) Increases the time needed at the hearing (particularly problematic with the CPR, which restricts the majority of trials to five hours).

(6) Increases the risk that the trial judge/ defendant/insurer/defendant's legal team will lose sight of the claimant's best points amongst a forest of weaker ones.

(7) Increases the risk that the trial judge/defendant/insurer/defendant's legal team will approach the case on the basis of the points with which they are more familiar rather than those on which the claimant's case is strongest.

(8) Increases costs (more allegations to investigate and prove).

(9) Fails to comply with the claimant's duty to help the court to save expense, and deal with the case in a way that is proportionate (CPR 1.1, 1.3).

Weaker allegations should be relied on only if they can be specifically justified. For example:

(1) Allegations would be strong if the law were interpreted in the claimant's favour but which rely on propositions of law that are controversial or without authority.

(2) The factual basis of the claim is fragile because the claimant's evidence is weak or there is powerful rebuttal evidence. This is often the case where the investigation has been hampered by the passage of time[40] or instructions close to the expiry of limitation.

(3) Where the absence of an allegation distracts from the claimant's strong points. This is a rare but not unknown situation. It occurs, for example, in employers' liability claims where (almost always) the claimant's strongest allegations arise under regulations, which impose duties more onerous than at common law.

---

[40]   See for example the asbestos claims: **P15** at p 60, **P17** at p 65 and **P18** at p 68.

However, the absence of an *allegation of negligence,* allows the defendant to argue that this implies the *absence of negligence.* Whilst manifest nonsense, experience suggests that it can beguile a sympathetic court and should be headed-off in the particulars of claim.[41]

'Speculative Allegations

At the time of pleading the particulars of claim, the information available will, inevitably, be incomplete. A possible allegation might have been identified, but further investigation may be required before deciding whether to pursue it at trial. In such circumstances, it is better not to plead such a speculative (and unparticularised) allegation: it is likely to prompt a P18 request (which the claimant will not be able to answer) and will tend to make the claim look weak or poorly thought through if later abandoned. It is better to apply to amend if and when the information becomes available: allowing the allegation to be properly particularised and a decision to be made to rely on the contention at trial.

'Quantitative' Allegations

Imprecise quantitative terms such as 'excessive', 'substantial', 'frequent', 'rapid' will often invite a Part 18 request for clarification and should be used only where the term is helpful[42] and a satisfactory response could be given to a Part 18 request.

Catch-all Pleadings

An example of a catch-all pleading is:

'In the premises failed to take reasonable care for the Claimant'.

This is not simply a weaker allegation but a wholly vacuous one. It serves no purpose, has no place in a pleading and should not appear. It simply invites a request for further particulars that will show it to be vacuous. The disadvantages of pleading weaker allegations apply with even greater force to the catch-all.

Res Ipsa Loquitur

This is no more than an 'exotic … phrase to describe … a common sense approach … to the assessment of the effect of evidence [where] … it is not possible for [the claimant] to prove precisely what was the relevant act or omission which set in train the events leading to the accident; but on the evidence [at the close of his case] … it is more likely than not that the effective cause of the accident was [the

---

[41]   See for example the manual handling pleading: **P1** and **P2**.

[42]   Contrast, for example, exposure to asbestos and exposure to noise. For noise to be dangerous, the exposure must be above a certain level: 'excessive' noise is therefore part of the Claimant's case and should be pleaded. By contrast, any asbestos exposure is dangerous and the Claimant's case does not depend on establishing a 'excessive' exposure (although the extent of the exposure may be relevant to the employer's state of knowledge of the risk).

defendant's negligence]'.[43] As such there is no requirement to plead it. However, a failure to give advanced notice of the argument to the judge and defendant may create the impression of a last minute act of desperation in a (by definition) weak case. Notice should, therefore, be given in the particulars.

A suitable phrase would be:

> 'The Claimant relies on the circumstances of the accident as evidence of the Defendant's negligence'.

This should be set out in a separate paragraph. It is not a 'particular of negligence' and should not be included under that heading.

Vicarious Liability

The fact that the tort-feasor was acting in the course of his employment with the defendant should be pleaded when setting out the circumstances of the accident. For example:

> On 1 June 2006, in the course of his employment with the Defendant, Paul Smith ('Smith') drove a fork-lift truck into collision with the Claimant at the Defendant's premises in Wakefield.

An appropriate form of words for the particulars of negligence would be:

PARTICULARS OF NEGLIGENCE

The Defendant, by its employee Smith, negligently:

a) drove into collision with the Claimant;

b) … etc.

A reference to 'vicarious liability' is superfluous in most cases and should not be made. However, in an exceptional case, where the Defendant is likely to dispute vicariously liability, even on the claimant's own version of events, 'vicarious liability' should be specifically pleaded to give the defendant and the court notice of the argument.

Responding to the Defendant's Case

The CPR's 'cards on the table' approach to pre-action correspondence[44] will often provide the claimant with some idea of the defendant's likely case. However, the defendant's pre-action correspondence is usually drafted by lay insurers and often with incomplete instructions from the insured. In general, attempting to pre-empt a defence in the particulars of claim creates only disadvantages:

---

[43]   *Lloyde v West Midlands Gas Board* [1971] 1 WLR 749 Megaw LJ at p 755. For example. *Majrowski v Guy's Hospital* [2005] EWCA Civ 251.

[44]   Pre-action protocol for personal injury claims para 2.4.

(1) It dilutes the impact of the statement of the claimant's own case.

(2) It may be misconceived: the defence may put forward a different case, particularly when solicitors are instructed.

(3) It may suggest to the defendant a point that it had not considered.

(4) It may confuse the burden of proof and the order in which the issues are to be determined. For example, contributory negligence is for the defendant to prove and should be considered after primary liability. Attempting to rebut it in the particulars of claim fails to make this clear.

The place to respond to the defence is in a reply.[45]

LIMITATION

The principal exception to this approach is the issue of limitation. If the defendant's case on limitation is apparent from pre-action correspondence, then the particulars of claim can deal with issues of date of knowledge and any alternative application under s 33 of the Limitation Act 1980. However, the defendant's position is often unclear until the defence has been served, and a positive pleading by the claimant runs the risk of alerting the defendant to an argument that it had not considered. If in doubt: it is better to await the defence. If the defence pleads limitation a reply to the defence will invariably be required to deal with the issue.

Points of Law

The claimant may, but is not required to, refer to any points of law on which he relies.[46] In general, points of law should be made in submission at trial and nothing is to be gained by giving the defendant advanced notice in the pleadings.

However, where the point of law is likely to be controversial or unexpected, consideration should be given to pleading it because:

(1) It will help the court in considering allocation and timetabling. For example: if the claim is for less that £15,000 but more than a day is required for trial (because of the issues of law). It will be easier to persuade a court to allocate to the multitrack and allocated sufficient court time if the issue is highlighted in the particulars of claim.

(2) It will help the court in allocating a suitable judge. A difficult and novel point of general importance may be better dealt with by the designated civil judge.

(3) It may help the defendant to accept a fundamental flaw in its case and lead to earlier settlement.

---

[45]   Where the Particulars have been drafted by counsel in anticipation that a Reply may be required, a short note to that effect can be included to avoid any possible confusion.

[46]   CPR 16 PD13.3(1).

(4) The trial judge will not appreciate having to determine a difficult point without having had some warning of it. The particulars of claim is as good a place as any to give that notice.

(5) Inclusion of the point in the particulars tends to suggest that it is a serious point that has been part of the claimant's argument from the outset rather than a last minute 'try-on'.

(6) The trial judge will expect the defendant to be fully prepared to meet the argument. Any weakness in the defendant's submissions will be seen as a weakness in its case rather than a reflection of lack of notice.

(7) It might save time and cost by narrowing the issues, if the defendant is prepared to concede the point.

If a point of law is to be pleaded, it should be in sufficient detail to satisfy all the points above but no more. The authorities and the pleader's thinking on novel points of law have a tendency to develop over time, and leaving 'room to manoeuvre' is often useful.

Naming the Parties

Children

Since CPR, anyone below the age of 18 is a 'child'[47] and must have a 'litigation friend' to conduct proceedings on his behalf.[48] The child must be referred to in the title to the proceedings as 'A.B. (a child by C.D. her litigation friend)'.[49]

Patients

A person who by reason of mental disorder is incapable of managing his own affairs within the meaning of the Mental Health Act 1983 is a 'patient'[50] and must have a 'litigation friend' to conduct proceedings on his behalf.[51] The patient must be referred to in the title to the proceedings as 'A.B. (by C.D. his litigation friend).'[52] It should be noted that the word 'patient' does not appear in the title.

The Deceased

Claims against the deceased must be brought against the personal representatives where a grant of probate or administration has been made.[53]

---

[47] CPR 21.1(2)(a).

[48] CPR 21.2(1).

[49] CPR PD 21 para 1.1.

[50] CPR 21.1(2)(b).

[51] CPR 21.2(1).

[52] CPR PD 21 para 1.2.

[53] CPR 19.8(2)(a).

Where a grant of probate or administration has not been made, the claim should be brought against the estate and an application made to the court to appoint a person to represent the estate.[54] The name of the defendant is 'the estate of A.B.'

Sole Traders

In general, sole traders should be sued in their own name. Occasionally, the circumstances of the claim might be made clearer to the reader by including the trading name in the title, in which case, the title is 'A.B. trading as C.D.'[55]

Partnerships

In general, claims against partnerships should be in the name of the partnership.[56] Although not provided for in the rules, it is normal practice to refer to the partnership in the title as 'A.B. (a firm).'

Limited Liability Partnerships

Limited liability partnerships are sued in their incorporated name. This will end with 'LLP'.

Companies

Companies are sued in their registered names. The title should include the abbreviations 'Ltd' for a limited company or 'plc' for a public limited company.

If a company has been removed from the company register, it must be restored[57] before commencing proceedings.

If the claimant's employment was transferred to a new employer after the accident, the claim must be made against the new employer.[58]

Great care must be taken when suing a company to ensure that the correct defendant is named. This is a trap for the unwary and particularly dangerous as the expiry of limitation looms. The relevant company may have sold its assets, goodwill, premises and 'transferred' its name to an entirely different company. The dangers of confusion can be further compounded when (not unusually) the registered office and directors are common to both the new and the old companies. It is therefore essential to perform and study a company search prior to issue in order to identify the relevant company.

---

[54]   CPR 19.8(2)(b).

[55]   CPR Sch.2 CCR Ord 5, r 10.

[56]   CPR Sch.2 CCR Ord 5, r 9(1).

[57]   Companies Act 1985 s 653.

[58]   *Martin v Lancashire CC* [2000] 3 All ER 544, Transfer of Undertakings (Protection of Employment) Regulations 1981.

Central Government

The relevant 'authorised' department[59] should be sued or, if there is no relevant 'authorised' department, the Attorney-General.[60]

The Police

The chief constable (or equivalent) is liable for the acts of police officers and should be sued accordingly. Police authorities are responsible for the premises and equipment.

Unincorporated Associations

One or more members of an unincorporated association should be sued on behalf of all those who were members *at the time of the accident*.[61] The title is 'A.B. and C.D. on behalf of all other members of the … Club on [date].'

3. PART 18 REQUEST

CPR Part 18 permits the court to order the defendant to provide clarification or additional information in relation to any matter that is in dispute.[62] Before the claimant seeks such an order, he must serve a written request.[63] The request must:[64]

(1) Be headed with the name of the court, title and number of the claim.

(2) (In the heading) state that it is a Part 18 request and identify the party by whom and to whom the request is made.

(3) Set out each request in a separate numbered paragraph.

(4) (Where the request relates to a document) identify the document and (if relevant) the paragraph or words to which it relates.

(5) State a date by which the response should be served, allowing a reasonable time to respond.

(6) Be concise and confined to matters that are reasonably necessary and proportionate to enable the claimant to prepare his case and understand the defendant's.

(7) (So far as possible) be made in a single document.

---

[59] See list at CPR 19 PD 7.

[60] The Crown Proceedings Act 1947 s 17(3).

[61] CPR 19.6.

[62] CPR 18.1.

[63] CPR 18 PD 1.1.

[64] CPR 18 PD 1.

If the Request has been prepared on computer, an electronic copy should be provided to the other party in order to minimise costs.[65]

The Part 18 request can be an extremely useful tool for the claimant and is substantially underused in practice. It is unusual for the costs of a properly conceived request to be disallowed. The failure to serve a request should never be allowed to go by default but must always be a positive decision by the claimant's legal team.

On the face of the CPR, it is clear that:

(1) A defendant who fails to respond to an allegation in his defence is taken to admit it.[66]

(2) A defendant who intends to advance a different version of events, must state his own version in his defence.[67]

Unfortunately, claimants rely on these rules at their peril. In practice, the courts often allow defendants to defend allegations not dealt with in the defence and to advance alternative versions of events not particularised in the defence. The courts are particularly ready to do so where the matter has been raised by the defendant in correspondence, witness statements, expert reports or is thought to be 'obvious'. This approach is all the more prevalent in fast track cases where the alternative of allowing the defendant to amend and the claimant an adjournment at the defendant's expense is often dismissed as disproportionate.

In addition to the requirements of the CPR, the defendant is also required (at common law) to plead those matters on which he relies, on issues where he has the burden of proof, such as the failure to mitigate or a reasonable practicability 'defence' to a breach of statutory duty. Again, a claimant should be wary of relying on this rule and even more so in fast track cases.[68]

Pre-CPR, there were occasions when the claimant could say nothing about an apparent omission in a defence, and then rely on that omission at trial. Post-CPR, such an approach is dangerous, if not foolhardy, especially in fast track claims. A claimant who does so may well be criticised by the court for taking a 'technical' 'pleading point', failing to comply with his duty to assist the court in achieving the

---

[65] CPR 1.1(2)(b), 1.3. This rule is almost never observed but is to be encouraged.

[66] CPR 16.5(5).

[67] CPR 15.5(2)(b).

[68] See for example *O'Neill v DSG* [2002] EWCA Civ 1139, where the Defendant had failed to plead the reasonable practicability 'defence' to reg 4(1)(a) of the Manual Handling Regulations, the Claimant's engineering expert had not dealt with the issue and Claimant's counsel had not raised the Defendant's failure to plead until his closing. The Court of Appeal found that the Defendant could rely on the 'defence' without having pleaded it.

overriding objective[69] and failing to seek clarification at an earlier stage. As well as being unsuccessful, this approach is likely to irritate and alienate the judge (which is always to be avoided if possible).

The claimant's task is, therefore, to avoid these problems before they occur. Whilst the courts will often allow a defendant to go beyond the contents of the defence, it will be far more reluctant to allow it to advance a case which contradicts or is otherwise inconsistent with its pleaded case. The claimant should, therefore, ensure that the defendant's pleaded case is not allowed to remain silent on any relevant issue. The Part 18 request is the mechanism for doing so.

The aims when drafting the request are:

(1) To ensure that the defendant is, as far a possible, limited to an unambiguous and expressly pleaded case from the outset and is not able to introduce new lines of defence at a later stage (without the permission of the court).

(2) To demonstrate to the defendant, his solicitors, insurers and the judge, the lack of substance in a particular line of defence. Generalised allegations are easy to make but may be seen to be misconceived when attempts are made to particularise them.

(3) To encourage a speedy resolution of the claim and allow the claimant to direct his resources most efficiently by identifying the issues that are genuinely in issue, at an early stage.

A failure by the defendant to answer clearly, or at all, should be met by a further request. If that second request fails to produce a clear answer, consideration should be given to a Part 18 application to the court.

The Essential Questions

(1) Where the defence does not deal with an allegation in the particulars of claim, does the defendant admit, not admit or deny the allegation?

(2) Where the defence (or Part 18 response) denies:

    a)   does the defendant intend to advance a positive case?

    b)   if so, what is that case?

(3) Where (if properly advised) the defendant might be expected to raise a positive 'defence' at trial (eg limitation, reasonable practicability, failure to mitigate) but has not done so in the defence:

    a)   does the defendant intend to advance a positive case?

    b)   if so, what is that case?

(4) Where a positive case is pleaded:

---

[69]   CPR 1.1, 1.3.

a) is the meaning clear? (For example 'failed to heed his training' is clear, 'failed to take reasonable care for his safety' is not). If not, what is meant?

b) is the allegation precise? (For example 'disobeyed the instruction to wear goggles delivered by Mr Jones during a toolbox talk in the canteen on 1 April 2004' is precise 'failed to heed his training' is not). If not, what details will the Defendant be relying on at trial?

c) is the relevance apparent?

Supplementary Issues

Where the defendant is advancing a positive case which is not supported by documents previously disclosed, and a P18 request is being made, a request should be included for any supporting documents to be disclosed.

The variety of possible requests is limitless and does not lend itself to model pleadings. An example of a defence and a Part 18 request in response can be found in Section 10 Miscellaneous below.

4.   CLAIMANT'S RESPONSE TO THE DEFENDANT'S PART 18 REQUEST

A well-represented defendant will attempt to lure the claimant into developing his case into a more extreme or narrower position which is then easier to defend, or attempt to gain an advantage by eliciting details of the claimant's evidence, prior to mutual exchange. Properly pleaded particulars of claim should not require a response to a Part 18 request and careful consideration should be given before providing any substantive response.

The following requests frequently appear:

(1) Attempts to shift the burden?

Many statutory duties impose a simple, but potentially onerous duty on a defendant but then provide a 'defence' of reasonableness or reasonable practicability.[70] It is not part of the claimant's case to show how the defendant could have complied with the duty.

(2) A proper alternative?

Whilst the claimant is required to demonstrate that his accident arose from the defendant's breach, he is not required to establish a particular way in which the accident should have been avoided. For example, if the accident was caused by an unsafe system, the claimant does not have to prove that a safe alternative

---

[70]   For example, providing suitable work equipment (reg 4 of Provision and Use of Work Equipment Regulations 1998) or maintaining the highway (Highways Act 1980, s 41).

existed. Similarly, if his injury was caused by lifting an excessive weight, he need not contend for a safe lesser weight.

However, although demonstrating that a safe alternative was available is not strictly relevant, it is an extremely useful tool. The court will be far keener to find against a defendant that has ignored a simple, cheap and readily available safe alternative. A request by the defendant for a safe alternative provides a useful opportunity to make that point at an early stage. A request for an alternative should be met with a response that the claimant 'does not contend for any particular safe system [etc]. However, by way of illustration, the defendant could have [specify safe alternatives] …'

(3) Requests for evidence.

The distinction to be drawn is between the allegation that is made and the evidence that will be used to prove it. For example: if the Claimant relies on verbal instruction, the defendant is entitled to know the words relied on and who spoke them but not the identity of any witnesses to the occasion.

5. REPLY

A reply is optional.[71] A decision not to file a reply does not imply an admission of the defence.[72] Similarly, if a reply is filed, the defendant is required to prove any matter in the defence that is not specifically dealt with in the reply.[73]

However, as with Part 18 requests, the right to serve a reply provides a valuable opportunity for the claimant which is all too often dismissed without much, or any, thought. It should be dispensed with only following positive consideration.

Having received the defence (and, if necessary, a response to a Part 18 request) the live issues in the case ought to be clear (or at least clearer). In particular, any positive case that the defendant intends to advance will now be apparent. The reply allows the claimant to take account of the contents of the defence and a second opportunity to ensure that his pleadings contain the essential elements of his case and all of the allegations on which he wishes to rely.

The reply provides an opportunity for the claimant to highlight the nature of any positive case he intends to advance in rebuttal. However, this is to be distinguished from an attempt by the claimant to alter his primary case: he cannot do so in a reply but must amend his particulars of claim.[74]

---

[71]   CPR 15.8.

[72]   CPR 16.7(1)

[73]   CPR 16.7(2)

[74]   CPR PD16, para 9.2.

A reply is likely to focus further attention on the key issues in the case, with the attendant benefits of reducing cost and delay and improving the prospects of early settlement.

A number of matters raised in defences will almost always call for a reply.

(1) Factual allegation that the claimant wishes to rebut with his own version of events.

(2) Points of law that the claimant wishes to rebut.

(3) Limitation.

(4) Contributory negligence.

A reply will often be useful in response to 'defences' such as 'reasonable practicability', limitation, *volenti* and *ex turpi causa*.

The reply can also help to underline where the burden lies on a particular issue and the order in which it falls to be considered by the court.[75]

---

[75] For example, in a manual handling case:

(1) The Claimant will assert (in his Particulars of Claim) that he was injured whilst undertaking a manual handling operation;

(2) The Defendant will often respond (in its defence) that it was not reasonably practicable to avoid the need for the Claimant to undertake the manual handling operation and that the risk had been reduced to the lowest level reasonably practicable.

(3) The Claimant might set out in his Reply that the task could, for example, be performed using a hoist and refer to HSE guidance on manual handling.

Section 2

EMPLOYERS' LIABILITY

COMMENTARY

The Purpose of the Regulations

The principal aim of both domestic and European legislation is to prevent accidents, rather than to determine liability after they have happened. The directives and regulations therefore contain many provisions which add little or nothing to a claim. The temptation to complicate pleadings with numerous allegations of breach, simply because a breach might be provable, should be avoided.

Only Employers?

Some of the regulations impose duties only on employers.[1] Most also impose similar duties on others in respect of matters within their 'control'.

Reasonable Practicability

(1) Many of the statutory duties placed on defendants are limited by the requirement of 'reasonable practicability'. The burden is on the *defendant*[2] to plead and prove that it was not reasonably practicable to comply with the requirements of the regulation. Accordingly, the particulars of claim should never refer to 'reasonable practicability'.

(2) If a defendant does raise 'reasonable practicability' in the defence, this will often be wholly or largely unparticularised and if so, a Part 18 request must be made. When the nature of the defendant's case on reasonable practicability is clear, the claimant must notify the defendant of any positive case he intends to advance to rebut the defendant's factual allegations This should be done in a reply.

(3) The defendant may serve a Part 18 request, inviting the claimant to set out the 'reasonably practicable' steps that the defendant ought to have taken. This is an attempt by the defendant to shift the burden, to which the claimant must not succumb. However, the claimant will often wish to provide examples, at trial,

---

[1]   Eg Manual Handling Operations Regulations 1992.

[2]   See eg *Nimmo v Alexander Cowan & Sons Ltd* [1968] AC 107.

of reasonably practicable steps that could have been taken to prevent the accident. If so, this should be made clear in the Part 18 response. For example:

> 'The Claimant does not contend for any particular steps, the Defendant was free to comply with its duty as it saw fit. However, by way of example, the Defendant could have ...'

Risk Assessment

(1) The decision to plead a failure to risk-assess, presents the practitioner with a potentially difficult balancing exercise.

(2) Employers must assess every risk to which employees are exposed at work[3] However, a failure to perform a risk assessment will not usually be the operative cause of an accident.

(3) The Manual Handling Regulations illustrate the point. The employer is under a duty to perform a risk assessment and to reduce the risk to the lowest level reasonably practicable. If the employer undertakes a risk assessment but fails to act on it to reduce the risk to the lowest level reasonably practicable, it is no defence for the employer to say that he performed a risk assessment. Conversely, if a risk assessment is not performed but the employer reduces the risk to the lowest level reasonably practicable, the failure to perform a risk assessment will not be causative of the accident and the claim will fail in any event.[4]

(4) However, a failure by a defendant to undertake a risk assessment is often useful to the claimant, both to explain the background to the claimant's accident and to illustrate the defendant's lack of attention to its health and safety obligations. There is a small risk that some courts might prevent questions about risk assessment if a breach is not pleaded.

(5) In cases involving established systems and a foreseeable risk, a failure to assess can only be helpful and should be pleaded. However, at the other extreme: relying on a failure to assess a one-off operation, devised by a low ranking employee giving rise to an obscure risk can give the impression of 'desperation' by a claimant and will be used by a well represented defendant to distract the judge away from the claimant's central (and much stronger) allegations.

(6) Practitioners will have to balance the risk of being prevented from asking question about risk assessment against the risks of appearing 'desperate' and the judge (with or without the defendant's help) being distracted from the key issue in the case.

(7) In summary: if the practicability and usefulness of a risk assessment are unlikely to be seriously in doubt, the defendant's failure should be pleaded.

---

[3] Management of Health and Safety at Work Regulations 1999 amended by the Management of Health and Safety at Work and Fire Precautions (Workplace) (Amendment) Regulations 2003 to allow civil liability from 27 October 2003.

[4] See eg *Hawkes v Southwark Borough Council* per Sir Christopher Staughton (CA) 20 February 1989.

However, if this is likely to be controversial; pleading risk assessment is likely to create more problems than it solves and it should be omitted.

(8) The manual handling pleadings (**P1** and **P2**) include, as examples, allegations of failures to risk-assess.

(9) Occasionally, the duty is not merely to perform a risk assessment but involves a prohibition on undertaking work until a risk assessment has been performed.[5] In those circumstances, a breach should, of course, be relied on.

Training and Information

(1) Care must be taken not to confuse cases based on the absence of a safe system with those based on an absence of training and information. If the claimant's case is that the defendant operated a safe system, but the Claimant failed to follow it through lack of information and training, then the failure to train and inform should be pleaded from the outset. More commonly, however: the claimant contends that he was following the defendant's system, but that the system was unsafe. In such cases training and information should not be raised in the particulars of claim.

(2) If the particulars of claim have not raised information and training, but the defence alleges that the claimant has acted negligently, or wholly caused the breach .[6], the claimant will wish to argue, in the alternative, a failure to train and inform and this should be pleaded in a reply.

Claims against Emanations of the State

(1) Domestic health and safety regulations purport to give effect to the Framework Directive[7] and its various 'daughter' directives.[8] The courts are required to interpret the domestic regulations to give effect to the directives.[9] However, this is not always possible and in such circumstances[10] the directive can be directly applied against an emanation of the state.[11] Where the wording of the directive appears more favourable than that of the domestic regulation both the directive and the regulations should be pleaded.

(2) On an ordinary reading of Art 5 of the Framework Directive, the employers have a duty to ensure the health and safety of workers.[12] Their duty includes

---

[5]   COSHH 1999 reg 6(1).

[6]   See eg *Boyle v Kodak* [1969] 2 All ER 439.

[7]   89/391/EEC.

[8]   Eg Work Equipment Directive (89/655/ EEC), Workplace Directive (89/654/EEC) etc.

[9]   See eg *Litster v Forth Dry Dock* [1990] 1AC 546.

[10]   Readers should refer to specialists texts for an exploration of the circumstances in which a provision may not be directly applicable.

[11]   Eg central government department, local authority, NHS trust etc.

[12]   Article 5.1.

the prevention of occupational risks[13] and it is responsible (unless parliament legislates to the contrary) where occurrences are unusual, unforeseen or beyond its control or due to exceptional events, the consequences of which could not have been avoided despite the exercise of all due care.[14] Although this duty has been held not to be absolute,[15] its precise scope has not yet been the subject of definitive guidance from the appeal courts[16]. Currently, claimants should always plead Arts 5 and 6.

Complaints

(1) Complaints by the claimant to his fellow employees are unlikely to be directly relevant[17] and should not be pleaded. Complaints to supervisors and other managers may be relevant where the extent of the defendant's knowledge of a problem is an issue. If so, they should be pleaded as part of the factual background, not as particulars of negligence.

---

[13]   Article 6.1.

[14]   Article 5.4.

[15]   *Green v Yorkshire Traction* [2001] EWCA Civ 1925.

[16]   See however the dicta of Lord Clyde in *Robb v Salamis* [2006] UKHL 56.

[17]   They may be indirectly relevant in providing corroboration of the Claimant's account and if so, they should not be pleaded.

PI

MANUAL HANDLING – PARTICULARS OF CLAIM

IN THE [   ] COUNTY COURT   No [   ]

BETWEEN:

[   ]

Claimant

-and-

[   ]

Defendant

PARTICULARS OF CLAIM

---

(1) On 1/4/06, in the course of his employment with the Defendant, the Claimant was using a shovel to spread grit onto the car park at the Defendant's depot ('the Manual Handling Operation'). As the Claimant did so, he suffered an injury to his back.

(2) The Manual Handling Operations Regulations 1992 ('the Manual Handling Regulations') applied.

(3) The accident was caused by the Defendant's breach of statutory duty and the negligence of the Defendant, its servants or agents.

Particulars of Breach of Statutory Duty

a)   Failed to avoid the need for the Claimant to undertake the Manual Handling Operation, contrary to reg 4(1)(a) of the Manual Handling Regulations;

b)   Failed to reduce the risk arising from the Manual Handling Operation to the lowest level, contrary to reg 4(1)(b)(ii) of the Manual Handling Regulations;

c)   Failed to make a suitable and/or sufficient assessment, contrary to regulations 4 (1)(b)(i) of the Manual Handling Regulations[18].

---

[18]   Care should be taken with allegations of failure to risk-assess. See Employers' Liability Commentary above.

Particulars of Negligence

d) Failed to provide the Claimant with a safe system of work: the action of twisting while supporting and accelerating the weight of the shovel and grit was liable to cause injury.

(4) As a result of the accident, the Claimant has suffered pain and injury, loss and damage. Please see the attached schedule of details of the claim for past and future expenses and losses.

Particulars of Injury

The Claimant (dob 1/1/70) suffered a soft tissue injury to the lower back. The Claimant is at a disadvantage on the open labour market. The Claimant relies on the report of [*expert*] dated [*date*].

(5) Interest is claimed on damages pursuant to s 69 of the County Courts Act 1984.

[NAME OF COUNSEL]

(6) I believe that the facts stated in these Particulars of Claim are true.

Signed ……………………………..

(Print name) ……………………….

Dated…………………………….

Claimant's address for service:

[Claimant's address for service]

P2

MANUAL HANDLING – EMANATION OF THE STATE – PARTICULARS OF CLAIM

IN THE [   ] COUNTY COURT   No [   ]

BETWEEN:

[   ]

Claimant

-and-

[   ]

Defendant

PARTICULARS OF CLAIM

---

(1) On 1/4/06, in the course of her employment as a nurse with the Defendant, the Claimant was pulling a bed away from a wall in order to change the bedding. As the Claimant did so, she suffered an injury to her lower back.

(2) The Defendant is an emanation of the state, to which the Framework (89/391/EEC) and the Manual Handling (90/269/EEC) Directives are directly applicable.

(3) The accident was caused by the Defendant's breach of statutory duty and the negligence of the Defendant, its servants or agents.

Particulars of Breach of Statutory Duty

a) Failed to ensure the Claimant's safety, contrary to Article 5 of the Framework Directive.

b) Failed to take to measures necessary for the safety and health protection of the Claimant contrary to Art 6 of the Framework Directive by avoiding and/or removing and/or reducing the risk of injury.

c) Failed to avoid the need for the Claimant to undertake the Manual Handling Operation, contrary to:

     i)   Art 3.1 of the Manual Handling Directive;

     ii)   Reg 4(1)(a) of the Manual Handling Regulations.

d) Failed to reduce the risk arising from the Manual Handling Operation, contrary to:

  i)   Art 3.2 of the Manual Handling Directive;

  ii)   Reg 4(1)(b)(ii) of the Manual Handling Regulations.

e) Failed to make the Manual Handling Operation as safe and healthy as possible, contrary to Art 4 of the Manual Handling Directive.

f) Failed to[19]:

  i)   evaluate the risk contrary to Art 6(2)(b) of the Framework Directive;

  ii)   assess the health and safety conditions contrary to Art 4(a) of the Manual Handling Directive;

  iii) make a suitable and/or sufficient assessment, contrary to reg 4(1)(b)(i) of the Manual Handling Regulations.

Particulars of Negligence

g) Failed to provide the Claimant with a safe system of work. The Manual Handling Operation was liable to cause injury.

(4) As a result of the accident, the Claimant has suffered pain and injury, loss and damage. Please see the attached schedule of details of the claim for past and future expenses and losses.

Particulars of Injury

The Claimant (dob 1/1/70) suffered a low back strain. The Claimant is at a disadvantage on the open labour market. The Claimant relies on the report of [*expert*] dated [*date*].

(5) Interest is claimed on damages pursuant to s 69 of the County Courts Act 1984.

[NAME OF COUNSEL]

(6) I believe that the facts stated in these Particulars of Claim are true.

Signed ....

(Print name) ....

Dated................................

Claimant's address for service:

[Claimant's address for service]

---

[19]   Care should be taken with allegations of failure to risk-assess. See Employers' Liability Commentary above.

P3

MANUAL HANDLING – EMANATION OF THE STATE – REPLY

IN THE [   ] COUNTY COURT   No [   ]

BETWEEN:

[   ]

Claimant

-and-

[   ]

Defendant

REPLY

---

(1) Except where specifically addressed in the Particulars of Claim or below, the Claimant takes issue with the contents of the Defence.

(2) The Claimant was following the Defendant's normal practice at the time of the accident.

(3) It is denied that the Claimant was aware of the Defendant's alleged system.

(4) If, which is denied, the Defendant establishes that it operated the system of work for which it contends; in addition to the particulars set out at paragraph 3 a) – g) of the Particulars of Claim the Claimant will rely on the following further particulars

Particulars of Negligence and Breach of Statutory Duty

h) Failed to ensure that the Claimant received proper training and information:

    i)   Contrary to Art 6.2 of the Manual Handling Directive;

    ii)   Negligently.

[NAME OF COUNSEL]

(5) I believe that the facts stated in this Reply are true.

Signed ……………………………..

(Print name) …………………….

Dated……………………………

P4

LIFTING OPERATIONS – PARTICULARS OF CLAIM

IN THE [   ] COUNTY COURT   No [   ]

BETWEEN:

[   ]

Claimant

-and-

[   ]

Defendant

PARTICULARS OF CLAIM

---

(1) On 1/4/06, in the course of his employment with the Defendant at its premises in Aberystwyth, the Claimant was assisting in the positioning of a metal beam on a storage rack using a crane being operated by his colleague, Mr. Evans ('the Lifting Operation'). As the Claimant turned to look towards Mr. Evans, the beam moved, crushing the Claimant's finger against the rack.

(2) The Lifting Operations and Lifting Equipment Regulations 1998 ('the Lifting Regulations') applied.

(3) The accident was caused by the Defendant's breach of statutory duty and the negligence of Defendant, its servants or agents.

Particulars of Breach of Statutory Duty

a) Failed to ensure that the Lifting Operation was carried out in a safe manner contrary to reg 8(c) of the Lifting Regulations.

Particulars of Negligence

b) By its servant Evans: lowered the beam onto the Claimant's hand.

c) Failed to provide the Claimant with a safe system of work: the proximity of the rack to the beam and the Claimant's hand gave rise to a risk of a trapping injury.

(4) As a result of the accident, the Claimant has suffered pain and injury, loss and damage. Please see the attached schedule of details of the claim for past and future expenses and losses.

Particulars of Injury

The Claimant (dob 1/1/70) suffered fractures to 1st, 2nd and 3rd fingers of the dominant right hand. The Claimant is at a disadvantage on the open labour market. The Claimant relies on the report of [*expert*] dated [*date*].

(5) Interest is claimed on damages pursuant to s 69 of the County Courts Act 1984.

[NAME OF COUNSEL]

(6) I believe that the facts stated in these Particulars of Claim are true.

Signed …………………………..

(Print name) ……………………….

Dated…………………………….

Claimant's address for service:

[Claimant's address for service]

P5

PERSONAL PROTECTIVE EQUIPMENT – PARTICULARS OF CLAIM

IN THE [   ] COUNTY COURT   No [   ]

BETWEEN:

[   ]

Claimant

-and-

[   ]

Defendant

PARTICULARS OF CLAIM

---

(1) On 1/4/06, in the course of his employment with the Defendant, the Claimant was cleaning a building occupied and owned by the Defendant when his helmet fell to the floor. The Claimant descended the ladder to retrieve the helmet. As the Claimant did so, his head collided with a vertical metal bar as illustrated in the attached photograph.

(2) The Claimant was wearing ear defenders, the head-band of which ran beneath his helmet, preventing it from fitting securely to his head.

(3) The internal headband of the helmet was split preventing it from being adjusted to fit the Claimant's head. The Claimant had reported the defective headband to the Defendant's foreman, Mr Jones on 1/3/04.[20]

(4) The Personal Protective Equipment at Work Regulations 1992 ('the PPE Regulations') applied.

(5) The accident was caused by the Defendant's breach of statutory duty and the negligence of the Defendant, its servants or agents.

Particulars of Breach of Statutory Duty

a)   Failed to provide the Claimant with suitable personal protective equipment contrary to reg 4 of the PPE Regulations;

---

[20]   Regulation 11 requires employees to report 'forthwith' any loss of, or obvious defect in, an item of PPE.

b) Failed to ensure that the helmet was compatible with the ear defenders and continued to be effective contrary to reg 5 of the PPE Regulations;

c) Failed to maintain the helmet in an efficient state, in efficient working order and in good repair contrary to reg 7 of the PPE Regulations;

d) Failed to ensure that the helmet and ear defenders were properly used by the Claimant contrary to reg 10 of the PPE Regulations: the head band of the ear defenders should have been worn outside the helmet;

Particulars of Negligence

e) Failed to provide the Claimant with a helmet that fitted securely.

(6) As a result of the accident, the Claimant has suffered pain and injury, loss and damage. Please see the attached schedule of details of the claim for past and future expenses and losses.

Particulars of Injury

The Claimant (dob 1/1/70) suffered a lacerated scalp. The Claimant relies on the report of [*expert*] dated [*date*].

Interest is claimed on damages pursuant to s 69 of the County Courts Act 1984.

[NAME OF COUNSEL]

(8) I believe that the facts stated in these Particulars of Claim are true.

Signed …………………………..

(Print name) ……………………….

Dated……………………………….

Claimant's address for service:

[Claimant's address for service]

P6

WORK EQUIPMENT – PARTICULARS OF CLAIM

IN THE [   ] COUNTY COURT   No [   ]

BETWEEN:

[   ]

Claimant

-and-

[   ]

Defendant

PARTICULARS OF CLAIM

---

(1) At approximately 10.50 pm on 1/4/06 the Claimant was driving a bus, in the course of his employment with the Defendant, on route 123 from Pontefract to Shafton. He stopped a South Elmsal to allow three passengers to alight. The third passenger attacked the Claimant, punching him to the face.

(2) The bus was usually fitted with a driver's safety screen. The screen had become cracked and had been removed by the Defendant on 1 March 2004, but not replaced.

(3) The Provision and Use of Work Equipment Regulations 1998 ('the Work Equipment Regulations') applied.

(4) The accident was caused by the Defendant's breach of statutory duty and the negligence of the Defendant, its servants or agents.

Particulars of Breach of Statutory Duty

a) Failed to maintain the Work Equipment in an efficient state, in efficient working order and in good repair, contrary to reg 5 of the Work Equipment Regulations: the screen should have been replaced;

b) Failed to ensure that the Work Equipment was suitable contrary to reg 4(1) of the Work Equipment Regulations: the absence of a screen rendered the Bus unsuitable;

c) Failed to ensure that the Work Equipment was used only under conditions for which it was suitable, contrary to reg 4(3) of the Work Equipment

Regulations. It was not suitable for use in the presence of the Claimant's assailant;

Particulars of Negligence

d) Negligently: failed to provide the Claimant with safe equipment and a safe place of work: the screen should have been replaced.

(5) As a result of the accident, the Claimant has suffered pain and injury, loss and damage. Please see the attached schedule of details of the claim for past and future expenses and losses.

Particulars of Injury

The Claimant (dob 1/1/70) suffered a fractured jaw and psychological injury. The Claimant is at a disadvantage on the open labour market. The Claimant relies on the reports of [*expert*] dated [*date*] and [*expert*] dated [*date*].

(6) Interest is claimed on damages pursuant to s 69 of the County Courts Act 1984.

[NAME OF COUNSEL]

(7) I believe that the facts stated in these Particulars of Claim are true.

Signed …………………………..

(Print name) …………………….

Dated……………………………..

Claimant's address for service:

[Claimant's address for service]

P7

WORK EQUIPMENT – EMANATION OF THE STATE

IN THE [　　　　] COUNTY COURT　　　　　　　　　　　　　　No [　　]

BETWEEN:

[　　　]

Claimant

-and-

[　　　]

Defendant

PARTICULARS OF CLAIM

---

(1) At approximately 5pm on　1/4/06, the Claimant was driving an HGV(OE51 HBL) comprising a Scania tractor unit and a curtain sided trailer ('the Work Equipment') along the M1, travelling north. The curtains were closed and the trailer was without a load. In the vicinity of junction 69, the Work Equipment was blown onto its side by a gust of wind,. .

(2) At approximately 3pm on the day of the accident, the Met Office issued a severe weather warning, covering the time and location of the accident, forecasting force 10 winds and advising against the use of high-sided vehicles.

(3) The Defendant is an emanation of the state, to which the Framework (89/391/EEC) and the Work Equipment Directives (89/655/EEC) are directly applicable.

(4) The Provision and Use of Work Equipment Regulations 1998 ('the Work Equipment Regulations') applied.

(5) The accident was caused by the Defendant's breach of statutory duty and the negligence of the Defendant, its servants or agents.

Particulars of Breach of Statutory Duty

a)　Failed to ensure the Claimant's safety, contrary to Art 5 of the Framework Directive;

b) Failed to take to measures necessary for the safety and health protection of the Claimant contrary to Art 6 of the Framework Directive by avoiding and/or removing and/or reducing the risk of injury;

c) Failed to ensure that the Work Equipment was used only under conditions for which it was:

    i)   Appropriate, contrary to Art 4 and Annexe I para 2.12 of the Work Equipment Directive;

    ii)   Suitable, contrary to reg 4(3) of the Work Equipment Regulations:

        it was not appropriate or suitable for use in high winds: unloaded and/or without a load or at all

d) Failed to ensure that the work equipment might be used by the Claimant without impairment to his health or safety, contrary to Art 3.1 of the Work Equipment Directive.

e) Failed to minimize the risks to the Claimant's health and safety arising from the use of the Work Equipment, contrary to Art 3.2 of the Work Equipment Directive.

Particulars of Negligence

f) Caused or permitted the Claimant to be driving at the scene of the accident notwithstanding:

    i)   The prevailing winds;

    ii)   The Met. Office severe weather warning;

    iii)   The curtains being closed;

    iv)   The trailer being without a load.

(5) As a result of the accident, the Claimant has suffered pain and injury, loss and damage. Please see the attached schedule of details of the claim for past and future expenses and losses.

Particulars of Injury

The Claimant (dob 1/1/70) suffered a Colles fracture of the dominant right wrist. The Claimant is at a disadvantage on the open labour market. The Claimant relies on the report of [*expert*] dated [*date*].

(6) Interest is claimed on damages pursuant to s 69 of the County Courts Act 1984.

[NAME OF COUNSEL]

(7) I believe that the facts stated in these Particulars of Claim are true.

    Signed …………………………..

    (Print name) ……………………….

    Dated………………………………

Claimant's address for service:

[Claimant's address for service]

P8

WORKPLACE TRIP – PARTICULARS OF CLAIM

IN THE [   ] COUNTY COURT   No [   ]

BETWEEN:

[   ]

Claimant

-and-

[   ]

Defendant

PARTICULARS OF CLAIM

---

(1) On 1/4/06, in the course of her employment with the Defendant, the Claimant was leaving the Defendant's Boston Store through the staff entrance ('the Traffic Route') when she slipped on a pool of water and caught her right foot on the door threshold causing her fall to the ground.

(2) The threshold was warped and split causing it to be raised above its previous height by approximately 20mm.

(3) The Workplace (Health, Safety and Welfare) Regulations 1992 ('the Workplace Regulations') applied.

(4) The accident was caused by the Defendant's breach of statutory duty and the negligence of the Defendant, its servants or agents.

Particulars of Breach of Statutory Duty

a) Failed to prevent the Claimant's fall contrary to reg 13(1) of the Workplace Regulations;

b) Failed to maintain the threshold in an efficient state, in efficient working order and in good repair, contrary to reg 5 of the Workplace Regulations;

c) Provided the Traffic Route whose surface was not suitable contrary to reg 12 of the Workplace Regulations. The threshold rendered it uneven so as to expose the Claimant to a risk to his health or safety;

d) Failed to keep the traffic route free from the raised threshold and the water, contrary to reg 12(3) of the Workplace Regulations;

Particulars of Negligence

e) Failed to provide the Claimant with a safe place of work.

(5) As a result of the accident, the Claimant has suffered pain and injury, loss and damage. Please see the attached schedule of details of the claim for past and future expenses and losses.

Particulars of Injury

The Claimant (dob 1/1/70) suffered a fractured right patella. The Claimant is at a disadvantage on the open labour market. The Claimant relies on the report of [*expert*] dated [*date*].

(6) Interest is claimed on damages pursuant to s 69 of the County Courts Act 1984.

[NAME OF COUNSEL]

(7) I believe that the facts stated in these Particulars of Claim are true.

Signed …………………………..

(Print name) …………………….

Dated…………………………….

Claimant's address for service:

[Claimant's address for service]

P9

WORKPLACE TRIP – EMANATION OF THE STATE –
PARTICULARS OF CLAIM

IN THE [   ] COUNTY COURT   No [   ]

BETWEEN:

[   ]

Claimant

-and-

[   ]

Defendant

PARTICULARS OF CLAIM

---

(1) Access to the Offices at the Defendant's Baker Street Station ('the Workplace') is gained by stairs. The foot of the stairs is adjacent to a low point in the floor where a drain is located. The drain was blocked causing a puddle to form.

(2) The Workplace was first used after 31/12/92.

(3) On 1/4/06, in the course of his employment with the Defendant, the Claimant approached the stairs. As he did so, his right foot slipped in the puddle, causing him to fall forward and land on his knee.

(4) The Defendant is an emanation of the state, to which the Framework Directive (89/391/EEC) and the Workplace Directive (89/654/EEC) are directly applicable.

(5) The Workplace (Health, Safety and Welfare) Regulations 1992 ('the Workplace Regulations') applied.

(6) The accident was caused by the Defendant's breach of statutory duty and the negligence of the Defendant, its servants or agents.

Particulars of Breach of Statutory Duty

a) Failed to ensure the Claimant's safety, contrary to Art 5 of the Framework Directive;

b) Failed to take to measures necessary for the safety and health protection of the Claimant contrary to Art 6 of the Framework Directive by avoiding and/or removing and/or reducing the risk of injury;

c) Failed to clear the blocked drain contrary to Art 6 of the Workplace Directive;

d) Provided a floor that was slippery contrary to Art 3 and Annexe I of the Workplace Directive;

e) Failed to prevent the Claimant's fall contrary to reg 13 of the Workplace Regulations;

f) Failed to maintain the drain in an efficient state, in efficient working repair and in good condition, contrary to reg 5 of the Workplace Regulations;

g) Provided a floor that was not suitable contrary to reg 12(1) of the Workplace Regulations. The floor was slippery and did not have effective means of drainage;

h) Failed to keep the floor free from the water, contrary to reg 12(3) of the Workplace Regulations;

Particulars of Negligence

i) Negligently failed to provide the Claimant with a safe place of work.

(7) As a result of the accident, the Claimant has suffered pain and injury, loss and damage. Please see the attached schedule of details of the claim for past and future expenses and losses.

Particulars of Injury

The Claimant (dob 1/1/70) suffered a fracture left patella. The Claimant is at a disadvantage on the open labour market. The Claimant relies on the report of [*expert*] dated [*date*].

(8) Interest is claimed on damages pursuant to s 69 of the County Courts Act 1984.

[NAME OF COUNSEL]

(9) I believe that the facts stated in these Particulars of Claim are true.

Signed ....

(Print name) ....

Dated.................................

Claimant's address for service:

[Claimant's address for service]

P10

CONSTRUCTION FALL BEFORE 6/4/05[21] – PARTICULARS OF CLAIM

IN THE [   ] COUNTY COURT   No [   ]

BETWEEN:

[   ]

Claimant

-and-

[   ]

Defendant

PARTICULARS OF CLAIM

---

(1) The Claimant was employed by the Defendant on a construction site at Kings Road, Knaresborough.

(2) On 1/4/05, in the course of her employment, the Claimant was climbing a ladder in order to gain access to the upper level of a scaffold when a hammer fell from that upper level. As the Claimant attempted to lean over to avoid the falling hammer, the hammer struck the Claimant and the ladder moved to one side causing the Claimant to fall approximately 3 metres[22] to the floor.

(3) The Construction, (Health, Safety and Welfare) Regulations 1996 ('the Construction Regulations') applied.

(4) The accident was caused by the Defendant's breach of statutory duty and the negligence of the Defendant, its servants or agents.

Particulars of Breach of Statutory Duty

a)   Failed to provide safe access to and egress from the Claimant's place of work and/or to make and keep the Claimant's place of work safe, contrary to reg 5 of the Construction Regulations;

---

[21]   From 6 April 2005, regs 6–8 are repealed and replaced by the Work At Height Regulations 2005. See example pleading at **P13** at p 52.

[22]   Specific provisions apply to falls of two metres or more: see reg 6(3).

b) Failed to prevent the Claimant's fall contrary to reg 6(1) of the Construction Regulations;

c) Provided for the use of a ladder as a means of access to the scaffold, contrary to reg 6(5) of the Construction Regulations;

d) Contrary to reg 6 and Sch 5 of the Construction Regulations, failed to:

    i)   Erect the ladder so as to ensure that it did not become displaced;

    ii)   Secure the ladder;

e) Failed to prevent the hammer from falling and from the Claimant being struck by it, contrary to reg 8 of the Construction Regulations;

Particulars of Negligence

f) Failed to provide the Claimant with a safe place, and system, of work. The ladder should have been secured and in a position where objects were not liable to fall from above.

(6) As a result of the accident, the Claimant has suffered pain and injury, loss and damage. Please see the attached schedule of details of the claim for past and future expenses and losses.

Particulars of Injury

The Claimant (dob 1/1/70) suffered a fractured pelvis and left heel. The Claimant is at a disadvantage on the labour market. The Claimant relies on the report of [*expert*] dated [*date*].

(7) Interest is claimed on damages pursuant to s 69 of the County Courts Act 1984.

[NAME OF COUNSEL]

(8) I believe that the facts stated in these Particulars of Claim are true.

Signed ....

(Print name) ....

Dated....................................

Claimant's address for service:

[Claimant's address for service]

PII

CONSTRUCTION, SAFE PLACE – PARTICULARS OF CLAIM

IN THE [   ] COUNTY COURT   No [   ]

BETWEEN:

[   ]

Claimant

-and-

(1) [   ]

(2) [   ]

Defendants

PARTICULARS OF CLAIM

---

(1) The Claimant was employed by the First Defendant on a construction site at Ottways Lane, Ashtead, at which the Second Defendant was the main contractor.

(2) On 1/4/06, in the course of his employment with the First Defendant, the Claimant was walking across the path to the site to the site office when he caught his leg on a nail, projecting from a piece of timber ('the Timber') and protruding from a refuse sack ('the Sack').

(3) The Claimant was a visitor to, and the Second Defendant the occupier of, the site within the meaning of the Occupiers' Liability Act 1957.

(4) The Construction, (Health, Safety and Welfare) Regulations 1996 ('the Construction Regulations') applied.

(5) The Second Defendant owed the Claimant a duty to comply with the Construction Regulations: the matters complained of at paragraph 6 a) to d) below were within the Second Defendant's control.

(6) The accident was caused by the Defendants' breach of statutory duty and the negligence of the First Defendant, its servants or agents.

Particulars of Breach of Statutory Duty

a) Failed to provide safe access to and egress from the Claimant's place of work and/or to make and keep the Claimant's place of work safe, contrary to reg 5 of the Construction Regulations;

b) Failed to prevent the Claimant's access to the Sack, contrary to reg 5(3) of the Construction Regulations;

c) Failed to keep the site in good order and clean, contrary to reg 26 of the Construction Regulations: the sack should not have been located in the vicinity of the path;

d) Allowed the timber to remain in a place where the nail might become a source of danger contrary to reg 26 of the Construction Regulations.

Against the Second Defendant:

e) Failed to take reasonable care for the Claimant's safety contrary to s 2 of the Occupiers' Liability Act 1957. The Second Defendant should have ensured that the sack was not present in the vicinity of the path.

Particulars of Negligence

Against the First Defendant:

f) Failed to provide the Claimant with a safe place of work: the bag with the nail should not have been in a position adjacent to the path.

(7) As a result of the accident, the Claimant has suffered pain and injury, loss and damage. Please see the attached schedule of details of the claim for past and future expenses and losses.

Particulars of Injury

The Claimant (dob 1/1/70) suffered a lacerated calf. The Claimant relies on the report of [*expert*] dated [*date*].

(8) Interest is claimed on damages pursuant to s 69 of the County Courts Act 1984.

[NAME OF COUNSEL]

(9)   I believe that the facts stated in these Particulars of Claim are true.

Signed ……………………………..

(Print name) ……………………….

Dated……………………………….

Claimant's address for service:

[Claimant's address for service]

P12

CONSTRUCTION, TRAFFIC ROUTES – PARTICULARS OF CLAIM

IN THE [   ] COUNTY COURT   No [   ]

BETWEEN:

[   ]

Claimant

-and-

(1) [   ]

(2) [   ]

(3) [   ]

Defendants

PARTICULARS OF CLAIM

---

(1) The Claimant was employed by the First Defendant on a construction site at 131 Derby Terrace, Beeston, Notts., at which the Second Defendant was the Main contractor and the Third Defendant was a sub-contractor.

(2) On 1/4/06, in the course of his employment with the First Defendant, the Claimant was walking along the roadway to the canteen ('the Traffic Route') when he was struck by a dumper truck driven by Ian Jones, in the course of his employment with the Third Defendant.

(3) The Claimant was a visitor and the Second Defendant the occupier of the site within the meaning of the Occupiers' Liability Act 1957

(4) The Construction, (Health, Safety and Welfare) Regulations 1996 ('the Construction Regulations') applied.

(5) The Second and Third Defendants owed the Claimant a duty to comply with the Construction Regulations: the matters complained of at paragraph 6 a) to c) below were within the Second and/or Third Defendant's control.

(6) The accident was caused by the Defendants' breach of statutory duty and the negligence of the First and Third Defendants, their servants or agents.

Particulars of Negligence and Breach of Statutory Duty

Against the First and Second Defendant:

a) Failed to provide safe access to and egress from the Claimant's place of work and/or to make and keep the Claimant's place of work safe, contrary to reg 5 of the Construction Regulations;

b) Failed to organize the site in such a way that the Claimant could move safely and without risks to his health, contrary to reg 15(1) of the Construction Regulations;

c) Provided the Traffic Route that was not suitable, contrary to reg 6(3) of the Construction Regulations.

Against the Second Defendant:

d) Failed to take reasonable care for the Claimant's safety contrary to s 2 of the Occupiers' Liability Act 1957. The Second Defendant should have provided a pedestrian route to the canteen that was separate from the vehicular traffic route.

Against the Third Defendant:

e) Failed to warn the Claimant that he might be endangered by the movement of the dumper truck, contrary to reg 17(2) of the Construction Regulations;

f) Failed drive the dumper truck in a manner that was safe, contrary to reg 17(3)(b) of the Construction Regulations.

Particulars of Negligence

Against the First Defendant:

g) Failed to provide the Claimant with a safe place, and system, of work: using a roadway as a pedestrian was liable to expose the Claimant to a risk of being struck by a vehicle.

Against the Third Defendant:

h) By its servant, Jones: negligently drove into collision with the Claimant.

(7) As a result of the accident, the Claimant has suffered pain and injury, loss and damage. Please see the attached schedule of details of the claim for past and future expenses and losses.

Particulars of Injury

The Claimant (dob 1/1/70) suffered a fractured clavicle. The Claimant is at a disadvantage on the labour market. The Claimant relies on the report of [*expert*] dated [*date*].

(8) Interest is claimed on damages pursuant to s 69 of the County Courts Act 1984.

[NAME OF COUNSEL]

(9) I believe that the facts stated in these Particulars of Claim are true.

Signed …………………………..

(Print name) …………………….

Dated……………………………

Claimant's address for service:

[Claimant's address for service]

P13

FALL FROM 6/4/05 – PARTICULARS OF CLAIM

IN THE [   ] COUNTY COURT   No [   ]

BETWEEN:

[   ]

Claimant

-and-

[   ]

Defendant

PARTICULARS OF CLAIM

---

(1) The Claimant was employed by the Defendant on a construction site at Kings Road, Knaresborough.

(2) On 1/4/06, in the course of her employment, the Claimant was climbing a ladder in order to gain access to the upper level of a scaffold when a hammer fell from that upper level. As the Claimant attempted to lean over to avoid the falling hammer, the hammer struck the Claimant and the ladder moved to one side causing the Claimant to fall approximately 3 metres to the floor.

(3) The Work at Height Regulations 2005 applied.

(4) The accident was caused by the Defendant's breach of statutory duty and the negligence of the Defendant, its servants or agents.

Particulars of Breach of Statutory Duty

a) Failed to ensure that the Claimant's work was carried out in a manner that was safe, contrary to reg 4 (1)(c) of the Work at Height Regulations;

b) Failed to ensure that the work was not carried out at height, contrary to reg 6(2) of the Work at Height Regulations;

c) Failed to prevent the Claimant falling a distance liable to cause personal injury, contrary to reg 6(3) of the Work at Height Regulations;

d) Failed to minimise the distance and/or consequences of a fall contrary to reg 6(5) of the Work at Height Regulations;

e) Failed to prevent the fall of the hammer contrary to reg 10(1) of the Work at Height Regulations;

f) Failed to prevent the Claimant being struck by the hammer contrary to regulation 10(2) of the Work at Height Regulations;

Particulars of Negligence

g) Negligently, failed to provide the Claimant with a safe place, and system, of work. The ladder should have been secured and in a position where objects were not liable to fall from above.

(6) As a result of the accident, the Claimant has suffered pain and injury, loss and damage. Please see the attached schedule of details of the claim for past and future expenses and losses.

Particulars of Injury

The Claimant (dob 1/1/70) suffered a fractured pelvis and left heel. The Claimant is at a disadvantage on the labour market. The Claimant relies on the report of [*expert*] dated [*date*].

(7) Interest is claimed on damages pursuant to s 69 of the County Courts Act 1984.

[NAME OF COUNSEL]

(8) I believe that the facts stated in these Particulars of Claim are true.

Signed …………………………..

(Print name) …………………….

Dated……………………………

Claimant's address for service:

P14

CHEMICAL BURNS – PARTICULARS OF CLAIM

IN THE [   ] COUNTY COURT   No [   ]

BETWEEN:

[   ]

Claimant

-and-

[   ]

Defendant

PARTICULARS OF CLAIM

---

(1) The Claimants was employed by the Defendant in the manufacture of industrial cables at its factory premises in Crossgates, Leeds.

(2) On 1/4/06, in the course of his work, the Claimant was required to pour nitric acid ('the Acid') into the stripping bath. As he did so, the Acid splashed into his face causing burns.

(3) The Control of Substances Hazardous to Health Regulations 2002 ('the COSHH Regulations') applied.

(4) The Acid was a 'substance hazardous to health' within the meaning of the COSHH Regulations.

(5) The Claimant's accident was caused by the Defendant's breach of statutory duty and the negligence of the Defendant, its servants or agents.

Particulars of Breach of Statutory Duty

a) Carried on work that was liable to expose the Claimants to the Acid without having made a suitable and sufficient assessment of the risks created and the steps that need to be taken, contrary to reg 6 of the COSHH Regulations;

b) Failed to prevent the Claimant's exposure to the Acid, contrary to reg 7 of the COSHH Regulations;

c) Alternatively, failed to adequately control the Claimant's exposure to the Acid contrary to reg 7 of the COSHH Regulations;

Particulars of Negligence

d) Negligently, failed to provide the Claimant with a safe place and system of work: the acid was liable to splash and, in the absence of an effective mask, come into contact with the Claimant's face.

(6) As a result of the accident, the Claimant has suffered pain and injury, loss and damage. Please see the attached schedule of details of the claim for past and future expenses and losses.

Particulars of Injury

The Claimant (dob 1/1/70) suffered chemical burns to his face and psychological injury. The Claimant is at a disadvantage on the open labour market. The Claimant relies on the report of [*expert*] dated [*date*].

(7) Interest is claimed on damages pursuant to s 69 of the County Courts Act 1984.

[NAME OF COUNSEL]

(8) I believe that the facts stated in these Particulars of Claim are true.

Signed …………………………..

(Print name) …………………….

Dated…………………………….

Claimant's address for service:

[Claimant's address for service]

Section 3

INDUSTRIAL DISEASE

COMMENTARY

(1) The pleadings included in this section cover the principal cases that will be encountered in practice – asbestos exposure; control of substances hazardous to health; deafness; vibration exposure; work related upper limited disorder; stress. Common issues may well arise in relation (for example) to: limitation; 'guilty knowledge' (of an employer); nature and levels of exposure; foreseeability; breach of duty (including statutory duty) and causation. All of these will need careful consideration.

(2) Before drafting the pleading it will often be necessary to have expert evidence that addresses, for example: the nature and extent of any hazardous substance or agent; the likely effect of such exposure; foreseeability and the precautions that should be taken. In cases involving work-related upper limb disorders expert evidence will also address the frequency and force of an action and in cases involving vibratory tools 'anger time'.

(3) An expert is often the best source of factual evidence in relation to the state of knowledge in a particular industry at the relevant time. Whilst the date on which a particular employer should have appreciated a risk is perhaps not, strictly, a matter for expert evidence, such opinions can be useful.

(4) If the defendant's case on limitation is apparent from pre-action correspondence, then the particulars of claim can deal with issues of date of knowledge and any alternative application under s 33 of the Limitation Act 1980. However, the defendant's position is often unclear until the defence has been served, and a positive pleading by the claimant runs the risk of alerting the defendant to an argument that it had not considered. If in doubt: it is better to await the defence. If the defence pleads limitation a reply to the defence will invariably be required to deal with the issue.

ASBESTOS – COMMENTARY

(1) Claims for a variety of conditions arising from asbestos exposure had been on the increase in recent years. Whilst claims for mesothelioma are not expected to peak until 2015-2020, claims for asymptomatic pleural plaques have (at least for the present) come to an end following the recent decision in *Rothwell v*

Chemical and Insulating Co Ltd [2006] 4 All ER 1161 (CA). At the time of writing, an appeal is pending to the House of Lords, and practitioners should check that decision before proceeding. In at least one case at first instance, the approach in *Rothwell* was applied to asymptomatic pleural thickening and asbestosis (*Owen v Esso Exploration* (16 November 2006, unreported): HH Judge S Stewart QC). The judge emphasised that the decision was based upon the evidence presented in that particular case; an appeal is pending.

(2) An increasing number of claims are made for more serious conditions. In some cases (especially mesothelioma) life expectancy will be relatively short and proceedings may need to expedited. Use may be made of the 'fast track' procedure operated by Master Whitaker in the High Court in London.

(3) There are numerous different circumstances in which asbestos may have occurred and each pleading will need to be carefully tailored to meet those circumstances. The pleadings included here cover three of the principal areas of exposure: ship building and ship repairing; construction work and exposure in factory premises. Specific statutory provisions apply to these areas, in particular in relation to: ventilation and control of dust; protective equipment and more general provisions in relation to a safe place of work. The provisions of the Asbestos Industry Regulations 1931 and the Asbestos Regulations 1969 are more specific, and consideration should be given to whether it is also necessary to plead breaches of these provisions. In relation to the 1931 Regulations, the case of *Shell Tankers UK Ltd v Dawson* [2001] PIQR P19 gives a reasonably wide application.

(4) It will often be the case that the claimant was exposed to asbestos in a number of employments. Employers may have ceased trading and/or may have been taken over by other organisations. Employers' liability insurers may or may not be located. A decision will need to be made in relation to which employers to bring into the action in cases of 'divisible' injuries (eg pleural thickening; asbestosis) where each employer will be responsible for only for that part of the loss that it has caused.

(5) Causation in mesothelioma claims is unusual in that the claimant is required to prove only that the defendant's breach contributed to the *risk* of his contracting the condition[1] and can recover in full against any liable employer, however small its contribution to the risk[2]. The pleading will reflect this.

(6) If the defendant's case on limitation is apparent from pre-action correspondence, then the particulars of claim can deal with issues of date of knowledge and any alternative application under s 33 of the Limitation Act 1980. However, the defendant's position is often unclear until the defence has been served, and a positive pleading by the claimant runs the risk of alerting the defendant to an argument that it had not considered. If in doubt: it is better

---

[1]   *Fairchild v Glenhaven Funeral Services* [2002] PIQR P28.

[2]   Section 3 of the Compensation Act 2006 reversing the effect of *Barker v Corus (UK) plc* [2006] 2 AC 572. The provision is retrospective.

to await the defence. If the defence pleads limitation a reply to the defence will invariably be required to deal with the issue.

P15

ASBESTOS – FATAL – PARTICULARS OF CLAIM – CLAIM ON BEHALF OF THE ESTATE

IN THE [   ] COUNTY COURT   No [   ]

BETWEEN:

[   ]

(Widow and adminstratrix of the estate of [ ] Deceased)

Claimant

-and-

[   ]

Defendant

PARTICULARS OF CLAIM

---

(1) The Claimant is the widow and administratrix of the estate of John Smith ('the Deceased').

(2) The Deceased was employed by the Defendant or its predecessor in title ('the Defendant')[3] between 1950 and 1966, in the course of which he was exposed to asbestos ('the Exposure').

Particulars

The Deceased was employed as a fitter. He worked for the Defendant at various shipyards. He was required to strip down turbines and steam engines. This work involved the removal of old asbestos lagging. The Deceased also worked alongside labourers who were stripping asbestos, and alongside laggers who were mixing, cutting and applying asbestos after repairs had been carried out.

The Deceased was not provided with any protective equipment.

---

[3]   Claims arising from exposure to asbestos typically arise decades after the initial exposure. Particular care should be taken to ensure that the correct defendant is identified: See Asbestos – Commentary above at p 57.

(3) The Defendant (by its officers, servants or agents) knew, or ought to have known, that the Exposure gave rise to a risk of injury to the Deceased.[4]

(4) The following applied:[5]

a) Shipbuilding Regulations 1931 and thereafter Shipbuilding and Ship Repairing Regulations 1960 ('the Shipbuilding Regulations');

b) Factories Act 1937 and thereafter Factories Act 1961 ('the Factories Acts').

(5) By reason of the Exposure the Deceased sustained injury and subsequently died.

(6) The Exposure and the Deceased's injury and death were caused by the Defendant's breach of statutory duty and the negligence of the Defendant, its servants or agents.

Particulars of Breach of Statutory Duty

a) Failed to protect the Deceased against inhalation of asbestos dust, whether by the use of exhaust appliances to prevent the entry of the dust into the air, or otherwise, contrary to regs 18 and 53 of the Shipbuilding Regulations 1931 and 1960 respectively;

b) Failed to secure or maintain adequate ventilation contrary to reg 48 of the Shipbuilding Regulations 1960;

c) Failed to provide and/or maintain approved breathing apparatus for the Deceased's use, contrary to reg 76 of the Shipbuilding Regultions1960;

d) Failed to secure and/or maintain the adequate ventilation of the workplace and/or to render the asbestos harmless, contrary to s 4 of the Factories Acts;

e) Failed to prevent the accumulation of, or to protect the Claimant from inhaling, dust, contrary to ss 47 and 63 of the Factories Acts 1937 and 1960 respectively;

f) Failed to provide and maintain safe means of access to the Claimant's place of work and to make and keep his place of work safe, contrary to s 29 of the 1961 Act.

Particulars of Negligence

g) Failed to provide a safe place and system of work:

　　i)　caused the Exposure;

---

[4]　If this is not admitted in the defence, a reply will be required. See pleading **P16** at p 63.

[5]　The Asbestos Industry Regulations 1931 may also apply. See *Shell Tankers UK Ltd v Dawson* [2001] PIQR P19. It may or may not be helpful to plead these Regulations depending upon the other statutory provisions which apply. See P18 for a pleading under the 1931 Regulations.

      ii)   failed to minimise the extent of the Exposure (by: ventilation, damping down, segregation of those areas where asbestos was being used, the provision of protective equipment or other measures of the Defendant's choosing);

h) failed to warn the Deceased of the dangers to his health caused by the Exposure.

(8) By reason of the above the Deceased suffered pain, injury loss and damage. He subsequently died on 1/2/06. The Deceased's estate has suffered loss and damage. Further, the Claimant has suffered loss and damage as dependent of the Deceased. Please see the attached schedule of details of the claim for past and future expenses and losses.

Particulars of Injury

The Deceased contracted mesothelioma. The Clamant relies on the report of [*expert*] dated [*date*].

(9) The Claim is brought under the Fatal Accidents Act 1976 and the Law Reform (Miscellaneous Provisions) Act 1934.

(10)

a) The Deceased's dependant is;[6]

    Joanne Smith (wife) dob 1/2/49;

b) The Deceased was was born on 12/5/37. He was in good health prior to developing mesothelioma. He was in receipt of a pension. He carried out DIY and gardening work at home.

(11)   Damages are claimed for bereavement.

(12)   Interest is claimed on damages pursuant to section 69 of the County Courts Act 1984.

[NAME OF COUNSEL]

(13)   I believe that the facts stated in these Particulars of Claim are true.

    Signed …………………………..

    (Print name) ……………………

    Dated……………………………..

    Claimant's address for service:

    [Claimant's address for service]

---

[6]   A list of the dependants and their dates of birth must be specifically pleaded (CPR Part 16 PD 5.1). This is because only one action may be brought on their behalf and they must all be included in the single action.

P16

ASBESTOS – FATAL – REPLY

IN THE [   ] COUNTY COURT   No [   ]

BETWEEN:

[   ]

Claimant

-and-

[   ]

Defendant

REPLY

---

(1) In the light of the Defendant's [*denial/failure to admit*] that it knew or ought to have known that the Exposure gave rise to a risk of injury to the Deceased, in addition to the particulars set out at paragraph 6 a)–h) of the Particulars of Claim, the Claimant relies on the following further particulars of negligence.

Particulars of Negligence

i)   Failed to identify that the Exposure gave rise to a risk of injury, whether by:

    i)   undertaking an assessment of the Deceased's work;

    ii) consulting the published warning of the risks of exposure to asbestos, including the reports from the Chief Inspector of Factories; a report of Merewether and Price (1930) and the Asbestos Industry Regulations 1931 (full particulars will be provided if so requested and/or upon disclosure of expert evidence);[7]

    iii) obtaining expert advice.

---

[7] There are numerous reports and other publications warning of the dangers of asbestos exposure. If details are required, refer to specialist materials in this field. If there is any dispute raised, expert evidence may be required.

(2) I believe that the facts stated in this Reply are true.

     Signed …………………………..

     (Print name) ……………………

     Dated…………………………….

P17

ASBESTOS – PLEURAL THICKENING – PARTICULARS OF CLAIM

IN THE [   ] COUNTY COURT   No [   ]

BETWEEN:

[   ]

Claimant

-and-

[   ]

Defendant

PARTICULARS OF CLAIM

---

(1) The Claimant was employed by the Defendant as a heating engineer from 1956 to 1968.

(2) In the course of the Claimant's employment he was exposed to asbestos ('the Exposure').

Particulars

The Claimant undertook work on heating and ventilation systems during the construction of various power stations and other industrial premises. He was involved in fabricating, cutting and installing asbestos lagging on pipes, turbines and boilers. He worked alongside laggers who were cutting, drilling and installing asbestos sheeting. Asbestos was released during the course of this work. Asbestos was present in the air and fell upon the Claimant from work carried out above him.

No extraction facilities were provided and the Claimant was not provided with respiratory protective equipment.

(3) The Defendant (by its officers, servants or agents) knew, or ought to have known, that the Exposure gave rise to a risk of injury to the Claimant.[8]

(4) The following applied:[9]

---

[8]   If this is not admitted in the Defence, a Reply will be required. See Asbestos – Commentary at p 57.

i)   Building (Safety, Health and Welfare) Regulations 1948 ('the 1948 Regulations') and thereafter the Construction (General Provisions) Regulations 1961 ('the 1961 Regulations');

ii) Construction (Working Places) Regulations 1966 ('the 1966 Regulations').

(5) By reason of the Exposure the Claimant sustained injury.

(6) The Exposure and the Claimant's injury were caused by the Defendant's breach of statutory duty and the negligence of the Defendant, its servants or agents.

Particulars of Breach of Statutory Duty

a)   Failed to prevent the inhalation of asbestos dust, contrary to reg 82 of the 1948, and reg 20 of the 1961 Regulations;

b)   Failed to secure and maintain adequate ventilation, contrary to reg 21 of the 1961 Regulations;

c)   Failed to provide and maintain safe means of access to the Claimant's place of work and to make and keep his place of work safe, contrary to reg 6 of the 1966 Regulations.

Particulars of Negligence

d)   Failing to provide a safe place and system of work:

   i)   caused or permitted the Exposure;

   ii)   failed to minimise the extent of the Exposure (by, for example, the provision of ventilation, damping down, segregation of those areas where asbestos was being used, protective equipment or other measures of the Defendant's choosing);

e)   Failed to warn the Claimant of the dangers to his health caused by the Exposure.

(8) By reason of the above the Claimant suffered pain, injury loss and damage. Please see the attached schedule of details of the claim for past and future expenses and losses.

Particulars of Injury

The Claimant (dob 12/5/33) developed pleural thickening causing breathlessness. The Claimant experiences significant anxiety and stress due to the knowledge of his condition and the knowledge that there may be a serious deterioration in his condition. There is a chance that at some future time the Claimant will develop a serious disease or suffer some serious deterioration (in respect of which an application may be made at a future date),[10] namely:

---

[9]   The Asbestos Industry Regulations 1931 may also apply. See *Shell Tankers UK Ltd v Dawson* [2001] PIQR P19. It may or may not be helpful to plead these Regulations depending upon the other statutory provisions which apply. See **P18** for a pleading under the 1931 Regulations.

[10] See CPR 16.4 (1)(d) and 16 PD4.4.

mesothelioma; lung cancer and asbestosis. The Claimant relies on the report of [*expert*] dated [*date*].

(9) Interest is claimed on damages pursuant to s 69 of the County Courts Act 1984.

(10)   An award of provisional damages is sought under s 51 of the County Courts Act.

[NAME OF COUNSEL]

(11)   I believe that the facts stated in these Particulars of Claim are true.

Signed …………………………..

(Print name) ……………………….

Dated…………………………….

Claimant's address for service:

[Claimant's address for service]

P18

ASBESTOS – MESOTHELIOMA – PARTICULARS OF CLAIM

IN THE [   ] COUNTY COURT   No [   ]

BETWEEN:

[   ]

Claimant

-and-

[   ]

Defendant

PARTICULARS OF CLAIM

---

(1) The Claimant was employed by the Defendant as a fitter at its factory premises at Princes Street, Cambridge between 1962 and1972.

(2) The Claimant was exposed to asbestos in the course of his employment with the Defendant ('the Exposure').

Particulars

The Defendant manufactured dry-cleaning presses. The Claimant was engaged in the sealing of platens on the presses in the course of which he mixed asbestos into a paste and applied it to the presses. Asbestos dust was released both during this process and when the paste became dry. Asbestos was present on the floor and on equipment within the premises. No exhaust equipment was provided. The Claimant was not provided with protective equipment.

(3) The Defendant (by its officers, servants or agents) knew, or ought to have known, that the Exposure gave rise to a risk of injury to the Claimant.[11]

(4) The following applied:

      i)   Asbestos Industry Regulations 1931 and thereafter Asbestos Regulations 1969;

      ii)   Factories Act 1961.

---

[11]   If this is not admitted in the Defence, a Reply will be required. See pleading **P16** at p 63.

(5) By reason of the Exposure the Claimant sustained injury.

(6) The Exposure and the Claimant's injury were caused by the Defendant's breach of statutory duty and the negligence of the Defendant, its servants or agents.

Particulars of Breach of Statutory Duty

a) The mixing and blending of asbestos was carried on without the dust being suppressed, contrary to reg 2 of the 1931 Regulations;

b) Failed to prevent asbestos dust entering the air contrary to reg 7 of the 1969 Regulations;

c) The floors, machinery, apparatus, work benches and other plant and equipment were not kept in a clean state and free from asbestos dust contrary to reg 7 of the 1931 Regulations and reg 9 of the 1969 Regulations;

d) Failed to secure and maintain the adequate ventilation of the workplace and render the asbestos harmless, contrary to s 4 of the Factories Act;

e) Failed to protect the Claimant against inhalation of dust and/or prevent its accumulation contrary to s 63 of the Factories Act;

f) Failed to provide and maintain safe means of access to the Claimant's place of work and to make and keep his place of work safe, contrary to s 29 of the Factories Act.

Particulars of Negligence

g) Failed to provide a safe place and system of work:

    i)   causing or permitting the Exposure;

    ii)   failing to minimise the extent of the Exposure (by, for example, the provision of ventilation, damping down, segregation of those areas where asbestos was being used, protective equipment, or other measures of the Defendant's choosing);

h) Failed to warn the Claimant of the dangers to his health caused by the Exposure.

(8) By reason of the above the Claimant suffered pain, injury loss and damage. Please see the attached schedule of details of the claim for past and future expenses and losses.[12]

Particulars of Injury

The Claimant (dob 1/3/40) developed mesothelioma. The Claimant relies on the report of [*expert*] dated [*date*].

(9) Interest is claimed on damages pursuant to s 69 of the County Courts Act 1984.

---

[12] It is likely that the Schedule will include claims for loss of earnings, care, aids and appliances and other items along with a claim for 'lost years'.

(10)   I believe that the facts stated in these Particulars of Claim are true.

Signed …………………………..

(Print name) …………………….

Dated……………………………

Claimant's address for service:

[Claimant's address for service]

COSHH – COMMENTARY

(1) Various statutory provisions may apply. Of particular importance are the Control of Substances Hazardous to Health Regulations 2002 (which replaced the Control of Substances Hazardous to Health Regulations 1999). These are likely to be construed strictly (see, for example, *Dougmore v Swansea NHS Trust* [2003] 1 All ER 333). Careful consideration should be given to the issue of which individual Regulations are relevant to a particular case. Other statutory provisions are likely to be of some assistance including the Workplace (Health, Safety and Welfare) Regulations 1992 and the Provision and Use of Work Equipment Regulations 1998.

(2) The duties under the Control of Substances Hazardous to Health Regulations 2002 apply to all employers,[13] not only the claimant's employer.

(3) The COSHH Regulations[14] provide rare example of a 'risk assessment' provision that is likely to provide a useful allegation of breach. There is an absolute prohibition on undertaking any work liable to expose employees unless he has first performed a risk assessment and complied with its findings.

(4) Regulation 7(1) requires the defendant to establish that it was not reasonably practicable to prevent exposure and, if it succeeds in doing so, that the exposure was 'adequately' controlled. The claimant should plead only that he was exposed to a substance to which the regulations apply.[15]

---

[13] Only the claimant's employer owes the duties in relation to health surveillance. The duties in relation to monitoring, information and training apply only to the claimant's employer and any employer who is undertaking work on the premises where the claimant is present.

[14] Regulation 6.

[15] *Bilton v Fastnet Highlands Ltd* 1998 SLT 1323, OH.

P19

ASTHMA – PARTICULARS OF CLAIM

IN THE [   ] COUNTY COURT   No [   ]

BETWEEN:

[   ]

Claimant

-and-

[   ]

Defendant

PARTICULARS OF CLAIM

---

(1) The Claimant was employed by the Defendant in the bakery at its supermarket at Bury between 1/12/02 and 3/2/06.

(2) In the course of the Claimant's employment with the Defendant he was exposed ('the Exposure') to flour and flour dust ('the Flour').

Particulars

The Claimant undertook various bakery tasks ('the Work') including tipping flour into mixers, mixing flour, kneading, dusting and baking. Flour was present in the air throughout the day. Flour was also released when it was cleaned from floors, surfaces, plant and equipment.

(3) The Defendant (by its officers, servants or agents) knew, or ought to have known, that the Exposure gave rise to a risk of injury to the Claimant.[16]

(4) Face masks were provided by the Defendant but it was normal practice amongst all employees (including the Claimant's supervisors) that such masks were not worn.

(5) The following applied:

  a) the Control of Substances Hazardous to Health Regulations 2002 ('the COSHH Regulations');

---

[16]   If this is not admitted in the Defence, a Reply will be required. See model pleading **P20** at p 75.

b) the Workplace (Health, Safety and Welfare) Regulations 1992 ('the Workplace Regulations');

c) the Provision and Use of Work Equipment Regulations 1998 ('the Equipment Regulations').

(6) The Flour was a substance hazardous to health within the meaning of the COSHH Regulations.[17]

(7) By reason of the Exposure, the Claimant developed occupational asthma.

(8) The Exposure and the Claimant's condition were caused by the Defendant's breach of statutory duty and the negligence of the Defendant, its servants or agents.

Particulars of Breach of Statutory Duty

a) Carried out the Work without having undertaken (or reviewed) a suitable and sufficient risk assessment and/or taken the steps needed to meet the requirements of the COSHH Regulations, contrary to reg 6 of the COSHH Regulations;

b) Failed to prevent the Exposure, contrary to reg 7(1) of COSHH Regulations;

c) Failed to adequately control the Exposure, contrary to reg 7(1) of COSHH Regulations;[18]

d) Failed to ensure that the Claimant wore a face mask, contrary to reg 8 of the COSHH Regulations;

e) Failed to ensure that local exhaust ventilation was maintained in an efficient state, in efficient working order, in good repair and/or in clean condition contrary to reg 9 of the COSHH Regulations;

f) Failed to ensure that local exhaust ventilation was maintained in an efficient state, in efficient working order and in good repair contrary to reg 5 of the Workplace Regulations;

g) Failed to ensure that the Claimant was under suitable health surveillance contrary to reg 11 of the COSHH Regulations;

h) Failed to provide the Claimant with suitable and sufficient information, instruction and training contrary to reg 12 of the COSHH Regulations: the Claimant should have been made aware of the nature of occupational

---

[17] If the Defence does not admit that flour and flour dust is a substance hazardous to health, a Reply should be served: see COSHH – Commentary at p 71.

[18] Reg 7(3) provides that where it is not reasonably practicable to prevent exposure, the employer shall comply with the duty to control by taking various specified measures including appropriate processes, equipment, ventilation, personal protective equipment etc. If the Defence suggests that the exposure was adequately controlled, a Reply should be served if the Claimant is to advance a positive case on equipment, ventilation etc.

asthma and that a failure to wear a mask at all times would make him liable to contract that condition.

Particulars of Negligence

i)   Failed to provide a safe place and system of work:

> i)   causing or permitting the Exposure;
>
> ii)   failing to minimise the extent of the Exposure (by, for example, effective extraction the use of protective equipment, or other measures of the Defendant's choosing);

j)   Failed to warn the Claimant of: the dangers to his health caused by the Exposure; the precautions to be taken by him and steps that he should take should he become aware of respiratory symptoms;

k)   Failed to undertake health surveillance.

(9) By reason of the above the Claimant suffered pain, injury loss and damage. Please see the attached schedule of details of the claim for past and future expenses and losses.

Particulars of Injury

The Claimant (dob 6/1/62) developed occupational asthma. He is at a disadvantage on the open labour market. The Claimant relies on the report of [*expert*] dated [*date*].

(10)   Interest is claimed on damages pursuant to s 69 of the County Courts Act 1984.

[NAME OF COUNSEL]

(11)   I believe that the facts stated in these Particulars of Claim are true.

Signed …………………………..

(Print name) ……………………….

Dated……………………………

Claimant's address for service:

[Claimant's address for service]

P20

ASTHMA – REPLY

IN THE [   ] COUNTY COURT   No [   ]

BETWEEN:

[   ]

Claimant

-and-

[   ]

Defendant

REPLY

(1) In the light of the Defendant's [*denial/failure to admit*] that it knew or ought to have known that the Exposure gave rise to a risk of injury to the Deceased, in addition to the particulars set out at paragraph 6 a) – k) of the Particulars of Claim, the Claimant relies on the following further particulars of negligence.

Particulars of Negligence

l)   Failed to identify that the Exposure gave rise to a risk of injury, whether by:

       i)   undertaking an assessment of the Deceased's work;

       ii)   consulting the published warning of the risks of exposure to flour including various reports from the Health and Safety Executive (including HSE guidance note MS25 (1991) and guidance in 1994 in the booklet *Preventing Asthma At Work*) and the fact that the Department of Social Security recognized flour and flour dust as a cause of occupational asthma in 1982. (full particulars[19] will be provided if so requested and/or upon disclosure of expert evidence);

       iii)   obtaining expert advice.

---

[19]   If further particulars are required, refer to the appropriate specialist publications. Expert evidence may be required.

[NAME OF COUNSEL]

(2)   I believe that the facts stated in this Reply are true.

     Signed …………………………..

     (Print name) …………………….

     Dated…………………………….

P21

DERMATITIS – PARTICULARS OF CLAIM

IN THE [   ] COUNTY COURT   No [   ]

BETWEEN:

[   ]

Claimant

-and-

[   ]

Defendant

PARTICULARS OF CLAIM

---

(1) The Claimant was employed by the Defendant as a production operative at the Defendant's factory premises at the High Street Trading Estate, Oxbridge between 1/12/02 and 4/2/06.

(2) In the course his employment, the Claimant was exposed ('the Exposure') to chlorotoluene, cyanimide and diphenyl ('the Chemicals'). The Claimant poured the Chemicals, in liquid form, from glass jars into a vat (together, 'the Work Equipment') ('the Work'). The Chemicals splashed onto the Claimant and soaked through his clothing.

(3) The following applied:

    a) the Control of Substances Hazardous to Health Regulations 2002 ('the COSHH Regulations');

    b) the Workplace (Health, Safety and Welfare) Regulations 1992 ('the Workplace Regulations');

    c) the Provision and Use of Work Equipment Regulations 1998 ('the Equipment Regulations').

(4) The Chemicals were substances hazardous to health within the meaning of the COSHH Regulations.

(5) By reason of the Exposure, the Claimant developed dermatitis.

(6) The Exposure and the Claimant's condition were caused by the Defendant's breach of statutory duty and the negligence of the Defendant, its servants or agents.

Particulars of Breach of Statutory Duty

a) Carried out the Work without having undertaken (or reviewed) a suitable and sufficient risk assessment and taken the steps needed to meet the requirements of the COSHH Regulations, contrary to reg 6 of the COSHH Regulations;

b) Failed to prevent the Exposure, contrary to reg 7(1) of COSHH Regulations;

c) Failed to adequately control the Exposure, contrary to reg 7(1) of COSHH Regulations;[20]

d) Failed to ensure that the Work Equipment was suitable and used only for operations for which and under conditions for which it was suitable, contrary to reg 4 of the Work Equipment Regulations;

e) Failed to monitor the Exposure contrary to reg 10 of the COSHH Regulations;

f) Failed to ensure that the Claimant was under suitable health surveillance contrary to reg 11 of the COSHH Regulations;

g) Failed to provide the Claimant with suitable and sufficient information, instruction and training contrary to reg 12 of the COSHH Regulations. The Claimant should have been made aware of the nature of dermatitis and that contact between the Chemicals and his skin was liable to cause that condition;

h) Failed to provide suitable or sufficient washing facilities, contrary to reg 21 of the Workplace Regulations.

Particulars of Negligence

i) Failed to provide a safe place and system of work:

    i)   causing the Exposure;

    ii)   failing to minimise the extent of the Exposure (by, for example, the use of protective equipment, washing facilities, replacing contaminated clothing with clean clothing or other measures of the Defendant's choosing);

j) Failed to warn the Claimant of: the dangers to his health caused by the Exposure; the precautions to be taken by him and steps that he should take should he become aware of symptoms.

---

[20] Reg 7(3) provides that where it is not reasonably practicable to prevent exposure, the employer shall comply with the duty to control by taking various specified measures including appropriate processes, equipment, personal protective equipment etc. If the Defence suggests that the exposure was adequately controlled, a Reply should be served if the Claimant is to advance a positive case on equipment etc.

(9) By reason of the above the Claimant suffered pain, injury loss and damage. Please see the attached schedule of details of the claim for past and future expenses and losses.

Particulars of Injury

The Claimant (dob 6/1/62) developed dermatitis to his hands and arms. Symptoms are likely to be permanent. The Claimant is at a disadvantage on the open labour market. He relies on the report of [*expert*] dated [*date*].

(10)   Interest is claimed on damages pursuant to section 69 of the County Courts Act 1984.

[NAME OF COUNSEL]

(11)   I believe that the facts stated in these Particulars of Claim are true.

Signed ………………………..

(Print name) ……………………

Dated……………………………

Claimant's address for service:

[Claimant's address for service]

P22

CHEMICAL BURNS – PARTICULARS OF CLAIM

IN THE [   ] COUNTY COURT   No [   ]

BETWEEN:

[   ]

Claimant

-and-

[   ]

Defendant

PARTICULARS OF CLAIM

---

(1) The Claimants was employed by the Defendant in the manufacture of industrial cables at its factory premises in Crossgates, Leeds.

(2) On 1/4/06, in the course of his work, the Claimant was required to pour nitric acid ('the Acid') into the stripping bath. As he did so, the Acid splashed into his face causing burns.

(3) The Control of Substances Hazardous to Health Regulations 2002 ('the COSHH Regulations') applied.

(4) The Acid was a 'substance hazardous to health' within the meaning of the COSHH Regulations.

(5) The Claimant's accident was caused by the Defendant's breach of statutory duty and the negligence of the Defendant, its servants or agents.

Particulars of Breach of Statutory Duty

a) Carried on work that was liable to expose the Claimants to the Acid without having made a suitable and sufficient assessment of the risks created and the steps that need to be taken, contrary to reg 6 of the COSHH Regulations;

b) Failed to prevent the Claimant's exposure to the Acid, contrary to reg 7 of the COSHH Regulations;

c) Alternatively, failed to adequately control the Claimant's exposure to the Acid contrary to reg 7 of the COSHH Regulations;

Particulars of Negligence

d) Negligently, failed to provide the Claimant with a safe place and system of work: the acid was liable to splash and, in the absence of an effective mask, come into contact with the Claimant's face.

(6) As a result of the accident, the Claimant has suffered pain and injury, loss and damage. Please see the attached schedule of details of the claim for past and future expenses and losses.

Particulars of Injury

The Claimant (dob 1/1/70) suffered chemical burns to his face and psychological injury. The Claimant is at a disadvantage on the open labour market. The Claimant relies on the report of [*expert*] dated [*date*].

(7) Interest is claimed on damages pursuant to s 69 of the County Courts Act 1984.

[NAME OF COUNSEL]

(8) I believe that the facts stated in these Particulars of Claim are true.

Signed ....

(Print name) ....

Dated..................................

Claimant's address for service:

[Claimant's address for service]

DEAFNESS PLEADINGS – COMMENTARY

(1) It will often be the case that the claimant has been exposed to excessive noise in a number of employments. It should be remembered that noise-induced hearing loss is a 'divisible' injury and that each additional exposure to excessive noise will cause further hearing loss. An employer will only be liable to compensate the claimant in respect of its own contribution towards his overall hearing loss, and not for hearing loss which has been caused by other employers/causes. This being so, consideration should be given to bringing proceedings against all employers who may be liable to the claimant (so long as there is sufficient evidence against any particular employer) – although low value claims arising from short periods of exposure may not be economically viable.

(2) In cases of exposure after 1/1/90 breach of the Noise at Work Regulations 1989 should be pleaded. The Control of Noise at Work Regulations 2005 are now in force. In practice, most claims relate to earlier exposure and for this reason, no pleading under these Regulations has been included.

(3) If the defendant's case on limitation is apparent from pre-action correspondence, then the particulars of claim can deal with issues of date of knowledge and any alternative application under s 33 of the Limitation Act 1980. However, the defendant's position is often unclear until the defence has been served, and a positive pleading by the claimant runs the risk of alerting the defendant to an argument that it had not considered. If in doubt: it is better to await the defence. If the defence pleads limitation a reply to the defence will invariably be required to deal with the issue.

P23

INDUSTRIAL DEAFNESS – FACTORY – PARTICULARS OF CLAIM

IN THE [   ] COUNTY COURT   No [   ]

BETWEEN:

[   ]

Claimant

-and-

(1) [   ]

(2) [   ]

Defendant

PARTICULARS OF CLAIM

---

(1) The Claimant was employed:

  i) by the First Defendant as a machine operator at its textile mill at Halifax during the period 1971-1978;

  ii) by the Second Defendant as a steelworker at its foundry in Sheffield during the period 1978-1986.

(2) The Factories Act 1961 applied.

(3) In the course of the Claimant's employment with the Defendants he was exposed to excessive noise ('the Exposure').

Particulars

FIRST DEFENDANT

The Claimant worked in the production area, 8 hours a day, 5 days a week with a 1 hour break for lunch. He was exposed to noise from spinning machines and twisting machines. The levels of noise were such that the Claimant and other employees were required to shout in order to hear one another.

SECOND DEFENDANT

The Claimant worked 7 hours a day 5 days a week. He was exposed to noise from foundry machinery, hammers, furnaces and other equipment. The level of noise was such that the Claimant and other employees were unable to communicate verbally.

(4) The Claimant was provided with no hearing protection by either Defendant.

(5) The Defendant (by its officers, servants or agents) knew, or ought to have known, that the Exposure gave rise to a risk of injury to the Claimant.[21]

(6) By reason of the Exposure the Claimant sustained injury.

(7) The Exposure and the Claimant's injury were caused by the Defendant's breach of statutory duty and the negligence of the Defendant, its servants or agents.

Particulars of Breach of Statutory Duty

a)   Failed to make and keep safe the Claimant's place of work contrary to s 29 of the Factories Act 1961:

    i)   causing or permitting the Exposure;

    ii)   failing to minimise the extent of the Exposure (by, for example: the use of hearing protection; job rotation; repairing or adapting the machinery; introducing sound absorbing material and barriers, or other measures of the Defendant's choosing);

Particulars of Negligence

b)   Failed to provide a safe place and system of work:

    i)   causing or permitting the Exposure;

    ii)   failing to minimise the extent of the Exposure (by, for example: the use of hearing protection; job rotation; repairing or adapting the machinery; introducing sound absorbing material and barriers, or other measures of the Defendant's choosing);

c)   Failed to warn the Claimant of: the dangers to his health caused by the Exposure; the precautions to be taken by him and steps that he should take should he become aware of symptoms;

d)   Failed to detect the onset of the Claimant's symptoms by regular testing.

(8) By reason of the above the Claimant suffered pain, injury loss and damage. Please see the attached schedule of details of the claim for past and future expenses and losses.

---

[21]   If this is not admitted in the Defence, a Reply will be required. See Deafness Pleadings – Commentary at p 82.

Particulars of Injury

The Claimant (dob 26/1/40) developed binaural noise induced hearing loss (assessed at 31dB) and tinnitus. The Claimant relies on the report of [*expert*] dated [*date*].

(9) The Claimant's date of knowledge (within the meaning of s 14 of the Limitation Act 1980) was 17/5/02, when he attended at his own doctors and was diagnosed for the first time as suffering from noise induced hearing loss.

(10) Interest is claimed on damages pursuant to s 69 of the County Courts Act 1984.

[NAME OF COUNSEL]

(11) I believe that the facts stated in these Particulars of Claim are true.

Signed ....

(Print name) ....

Dated................................

Claimant's address for service:

[Claimant's address for service]

P24

INDUSTRIAL DEAFNESS – CONSTRUCTION – PARTICULARS OF CLAIM

IN THE [   ] COUNTY COURT   No [   ]

BETWEEN:

[   ]

Claimant

-and-

[   ]

Defendant

PARTICULARS OF CLAIM

---

(1) The Claimant was employed by the Defendant between March 1980 and February 2000.

(2) In the course of the Claimant's employment with the Defendant he was exposed to excessive noise ('the Exposure') for most of the working day.

Particulars

The Claimant carried out general labouring and roadwork. He was exposed to noise from tools (used by him and by his fellow employees) including jack hammers, jigger picks, whacker plates, Stihl saws and concrete breakers.

(3) The Claimant was provided with no hearing protection.

(4) The Defendant (by its officers, servants or agents) knew, or ought to have known, that the Exposure gave rise to a risk of injury to the Claimant.[22]

(5) The following applied:

    a) The Construction (Working Places) Regulations 1966 and thereafter the Construction (Health, Safety and Welfare) Regulations 1996 ('the Construction Regulations');

---

[22]   If this is not admitted in the Defence, a Reply will be required. See **P25** for model pleading.

b) (from 1/1/90) the Noise at Work Regulations 1989 ('the Noise Regulations').

(6) By reason of the Exposure the Claimant sustained injury.

(7) The Exposure and the Claimant's injury were caused by the Defendant's breach of statutory duty and the negligence of the Defendant, its servants or agents.

Particulars of Breach of Statutory Duty

a) Failed to reduce the risk of injury to the Claimant to the lowest level, contrary to reg 6 of the Noise Regulations;

b) Failed to make and to keep safe the Claimant's place of work, contrary to regs 6 and 5 of the Construction Regulations 1966 and 1996 respectively;

c) Failed to reduce the Exposure to the lowest level, contrary to reg 7 of the Noise Regulations;

d) Failed to provide the Claimant with suitable or efficient personal ear protectors contrary to reg 8 of the 1989 Regulations;

e) Failed to provide adequate information, instruction and training, contrary to reg 11 of the 1989 Regulations.

Particulars of Negligence

f) Failed to provide a safe place and system of work:

   i)   causing or permitting the Exposure;

   ii) failing to minimise the extent of the Exposure (by, for example: the use of hearing protection; job rotation; repairing or adapting the machinery; introducing sound absorbing material, or other measures of the Defendant's choosing);

g) Failed to warn the Claimant of: the dangers to his health caused by the Exposure; the precautions to be taken by him and steps that he should take should he become aware of symptoms;

h) Failed to detect the onset of the Claimant's symptoms by regular testing.

(8) By reason of the above the Claimant suffered pain, injury loss and damage. Please see the attached schedule of details of the claim for past and future expenses and losses.

Particulars of Injury

The Claimant (dob 27/2/40) developed binaural noise induced hearing loss (assessed at 25dB) and tinnitus. The Claimant relies on the report of [*expert*] dated [*date*].

(9) The Claimant's date of knowledge (within the meaning of s 14 of the Limitation Act 1980) was 17/5/06, when he attended at his own doctors and was diagnosed for the first time as suffering from noise induced hearing loss.

(10)   Interest is claimed on damages pursuant to s 69 of the County Courts Act
        1984.

[NAME OF COUNSEL]

(11)   I believe that the facts stated in these Particulars of Claim are true.

        Signed …………………………..

        (Print name) ……………………

        Dated……………………………

        Claimant's address for service:

        [Claimant's address for service]

P25

INDUSTRIAL DEAFNESS – REPLY

IN THE [   ] COUNTY COURT   No [   ]

BETWEEN:

[   ]

Claimant

-and-

[   ]

Defendant

REPLY

---

(1) In the light of the Defendant's [*denial/failure to admit*] that it knew or ought to have known that the Exposure gave rise to a risk of injury to the Deceased, in addition to the particulars set out at paragraph 6 a) – h) of the Particulars of Claim the Claimant relies on the following further particulars of negligence.

Particulars of Negligence

i)   Failed to identify that the Exposure gave rise to a risk of injury, whether by:

      i)   undertaking an assessment of the Deceased's work;

      ii)   Consulting the published warning of the risks of exposure to noise including 'Noise and the Worker' (1963, Safety, Health and Welfare Booklet No 25) (full particulars will be provided if so requested and/or upon disclosure of expert evidence;[23]

      iii)   Obtaining expert advice.

[NAME OF COUNSEL]

(2) I believe that the facts stated in this Reply are true.

---

[23]   There are numerous reports and other publications warning of the dangers of noise exposure. If details are required, refer to specialist materials in this field. If there is any dispute raised, expert evidence may be required.

Signed …………………………..

(Print name) ……………………

Dated……………………………..

P26

WRULD – PARTICULARS OF CLAIM

IN THE [   ] COUNTY COURT   No [   ]

BETWEEN:

[   ]

Claimant

-and-

[   ]

Defendant

PARTICULARS OF CLAIM

---

(1) The Claimant was employed by the Defendant as a production operative at the Defendant's premises at Princess Street, Oxford between January 2000 and March 2003.

(2) The Claimant's work was assembling circuit boards by inserting various components ('the Manual Handling Operation'), which involved repetitive pushing, pulling, twisting and gripping movements of his arms and hands as the Claimant turned the board, twisting the components to secure them and then using a small tool for tightening.

(3) The Claimant worked a 8½ hour a day 5 days a week, with two 15 minute breaks and one 30 minute break for lunch.

(4) The Defendant operated a bonus scheme to encourage higher productivity.

(5) The Defendant (by its officers, servants or agents) knew, or ought to have known, that the Manual Handling Operation gave rise to a risk of injury to the Claimant.[24]

(6) The Manual Handling Operations Regulations 1992 applied.

(7) The Manual Handling Operation caused the Claimant to develop a work related upper limb disorder.

(8) The Claimant's condition was caused by the Defendant's breach of statutory duty and the negligence of the Defendant, its servants or agents.

---

[24] If this is not admitted in the Defence, a Reply will be required. See model pleading **P27** at p 93.

Particulars of Negligence and Breach of Statutory Duty

a) Failed to avoid the need for the Claimant to undertake the Manual Handling Operation, contrary to regulation 4(1)(a) of the Manual Handling Regulations;

b) Failed to reduce the risk arising from the Manual Handling Operation to the lowest level, contrary to regulation 4(1)(b)(ii) of the Manual Handling Regulations;

c) Failed to provide a safe system of work:

      i)   exposing the Claimant to the risk of injury from the Manual Handling Operation;

      ii)   failing to minimise the extent of that risk (by, for example: job rotation, breaks, reducing the rate of work or other measures of the Defendant's choosing);

d) Failed to warn the Claimant of: the dangers to his health caused by the Manual Handling Operation; the precautions to be taken by him and steps that he should take should he become aware of symptoms;

e) Failed to identify the onset of the Claimant's symptoms by a system of health surveillance/monitoring.

(9) By reason of the above the Claimant suffered pain, injury loss and damage. Please see the attached schedule of details of the claim for past and future expenses and losses.

Particulars of Injury

The Claimant (dob 6/362) developed bilateral tenosynovitis. He may require operative treatment. The Claimant is at a disadvantage on the open labour market. He relies on the report of [*expert*] dated [*date*].

(10)   Interest is claimed on damages pursuant to s 69 of the County Courts Act 1984.

[NAME OF COUNSEL]

(11)   I believe that the facts stated in these Particulars of Claim are true.

Signed ....

(Print name) ....

Dated...................................

Claimant's address for service:

[Claimant's address for service]

P27

WRULD – REPLY

IN THE [   ] COUNTY COURT   No [   ]

BETWEEN:

[   ]

Claimant

-and-

[   ]

Defendant

REPLY

---

(1) In the light of the Defendant's [*denial/failure to admit*] that it knew or ought to have known that the Exposure gave rise to a risk of injury to the Deceased, in addition to the particulars set out at paragraph 8 a) – e) of the Particulars of Claim the Claimant relies on the following further particulars of negligence.

Particulars of Negligence

f) Failed to identify that the Manual handling Operation gave rise to a risk of injury, whether by:

    i)   undertaking an assessment of the Deceased's work;

    ii)   consulting the published guidance including the Health and Safety Executive Guidance Note MS10 (1977); and the HSE document 'Work Related Upper Limb Disorders – A Guide to Prevention' (1990 reprinted 1994). Full particulars will be provided if so requested and/or upon disclosure of expert evidence;[25]

    iii) obtaining expert advice.

---

[25] There are numerous reports and other publications warning of the dangers of repetitive activities. If details are required, refer to specialist materials in this field. If there is any dispute raised, expert evidence may be required

[NAME OF COUNSEL]

(2) I believe that the facts stated in this Reply are true.

      Signed …………………………..

      (Print name) …………………….

      Dated…………………………….

STRESS – COMMENTARY

(1) Claims for stress will vary enormously and will require substantial care when drafting pleadings.

(2) A book on pleading is not the appropriate place to set out the way in which the courts will approach this type of case. However, it should be noted that this area is fraught with difficulty for a claimant's lawyer. While the ordinary principles of employer's liability apply, the courts have placed fairly strict limits on these claims. The main difficulties lie in establishing that an injury to health (as opposed to 'occupational stress' itself) was foreseeable by an employer and that there has been a subsequent breach of the employer's duty of care. Before pleading any case, reference should be made to reference works in this area. Also to the leading case of *Sutherland v Hatton* [2002] PIQR P21 (and the appeal to the House of Lords in *Barber v Somerset CC* [2004] PIQR P31); and more recent cases such as *Pratley v Surrey CC* [2004] PIQR P17 and *Hartman v South Essex Mental Health & Community Care NHS Trust* [2005] EWCA Civ 6.

(3) Disclosure is likely to be of particular importance with regards to foreseeability of injury (and also as to other issues) and documentation may be required before the pleading is drafted. Careful instructions will need to be taken from the claimant as to the nature of the work, development of difficulties, and issues which should have put the employer on notice.

(4) In the case of *Clark v Chief Constable of Essex* [2006] EWHC 2290, Tugendhat J held that foreseeability of harm was also required in a case of bullying. In such case it will be necessary to establish both that the bullying occurred during the course of such employment and also that foreseeability of psychiatric injury (as opposed to upset) was foreseeable.

(5) If the conduct amounts to harassment within the meaning of the Protection from Harassment Act 1997, the employer may be vicariously liable for the breach of statutory duty by the 'harassing' employee (per House of Lords in *Majrowski v Guys and St Thomas' NHS Trust* [2006] 3 WLR 125) without the need to prove foreseeability (though Lady Hale observed that in 'most cases' such harm would be foreseeable in any event).

(6) If the defendant is an emanation of the state then it may be possible to plead the European directives (see pleading). Alternatively, there may be a claim under the Working Time Regulations 1998 in an appropriate case.

(7) Medical evidence is likely to be of particular importance. The expert should be familiar with the tests to be applied and will need to deal with the development of any psychiatric injury. Issues of causation will need detailed consideration.

P28

STRESS – PARTICULARS OF CLAIM

IN THE [   ] COUNTY COURT   No [   ]

BETWEEN:

[   ]

Claimant

-and-

[   ]

Defendant

PARTICULARS OF CLAIM

---

(1) From September 1990 to September 2006 the Claimant was employed by the Defendant as an English teacher at the Oxbridge Secondary School ('the School').

(2) Until September 2005, the English Department at the School had been staffed by a head of department and five teaching staff. At the end of the school year 2004/2005, one member of the teaching staff left the department and was not replaced. The teaching responsibilities of that individual were shared amongst the remaining members of staff, including the head of department, resulting in increased workloads and longer hours.

(3) The Claimant and his colleagues complained to the head of department to the effect that the new workload was stressful. The head of department made similar complaints to her line manager, the deputy headmaster, Mr Jones.

(4) In February 2006 the head of department resigned her post stating that she was suffering stress due to the increased workload. The Claimant was promoted to the position of acting head of department as a result of which the Claimant's workload further increased: undertaking all the administrative and organisational duties of the head of department in addition to a full-time teaching role.

(5) The Defendant provided no additional training in relation to the Claimant's role as acting head of department. The Claimant worked most nights (often until midnight) and much of the weekend in order to discharge his duties.

(6) Thereafter:

a) The Claimant reported to Mr Jones on a number of occasions that there were too few members of staff to fulfil the duties within the department. He was assured that staff would be brought 'up to complement' as a matter or urgency;

b) In early March 2006 the Claimant reported to Mr Jones that his workload and that of other members of staff was excessive and that all members of staff were experiencing increased levels of stress and worry. Mr Jones indicated that the matter 'was being dealt with';

c) On or about 22/3/06 the Claimant submitted a written report to the school's headmaster, Mr Brown, stating that he was unable to cope with the work required and that he was experiencing anxiety, stress, exhaustion and loss of sleep. The Claimant received no reply to the written report;

d) On return from the Easter holidays there had been no improvement in conditions and no additional staff members were provided;

e) On 12/4/06 April the Claimant attended at his doctors. He was diagnosed as suffering from 'mental exhaustion' due to pressures of work and told that he required at least two weeks off work. His doctor informed him that if he carried on working at the same level then he would suffer a breakdown;

f) The Claimant informed Mr Jones of this advice. He was absent from work for two weeks. His sick note recorded 'mental exhaustion and depression'. Mr Jones visited the Claimant at home and requested that he returned to work stating that additional assistance would be provided with administrative/organisational tasks and that two supply teachers would be brought in to assist;

g) The Claimant returned to work. Two supply teachers were provided. However, the supply teachers left after a short period of time and were not replaced;

h) The Claimant was unable to continue at work and became ill again. He was absent from 24/5/06 and has been unable to return to work.

(7) The Defendant, by its servants or agents, knew or ought to have known that there was a foreseeable risk of the Claimant developing psychiatric harm as a result of his employment.[26]

(8) The Defendant is an emanation of the state, to which the Framework (89/391/EEC) and the Working Time (93/104/EC) Directives are directly applicable.

(9) The Working Time Regulations 1998 applied.

(10) The Claimant's condition was caused by the Defendant's breach of statutory duty and the negligence of the Defendant, its servants or agents.

---

[26] If this is not admitted in the Defence, a Reply should be served.

Particulars of Breach of Statutory Duty

a) Failed to take the measures necessary for the safety and health protection of the Claimant including (but not limited to) the prevention of occupational risks and the provision of the necessary organisation and means, contrary to Arts 5 and 6 of the Framework Directive (89/391);

b) Failed to ensure that the Claimant had sufficient daily and weekly rests contrary to regs 10 and 11 of the Working Time Regulations;

c) Failed to ensure that the Claimant worked an average of no more than 48 hours a week contrary to reg 4 of the Working Time Regulations;

Particulars of Negligence

d) Provided an excessive workload for the Claimant;

e) Failed to provide the Claimant with appropriate training, supervision and support in relation to the role of acting head of department;

f) Failed to adequately monitor the Claimant's health;

g) Failed to provide confidential advice and counselling services.

(11)   By reason of the above the Claimant suffered pain, injury loss and damage. Please see the attached schedule of details of the claim for past and future expenses and losses.

Particulars of Injury

The Claimant (dob 7/6/69) developed depression and an anxiety disorder. He experienced symptoms of low mood, anxiety, irritability, loss of concentration, insomnia, night sweats. He has been unable to continue in his employment.

There is some prospect of improvement but the Claimant is not likely to be able to return to his previous employment or to any position of responsibility. The Claimant is at a disadvantage on the open labour market. There is loss of congenial employment. The Claimant relies on the report of [*expert*] dated [*date*].

(12)   Interest is claimed on damages pursuant to s 69 of the County Courts Act 1984.

[NAME OF COUNSEL]

(13)   I believe that the facts stated in these Particulars of Claim are true.

Signed ....

(Print name) ....

Dated...................................

Claimant's address for service:

[Claimant's address for service]

HAND ARM VIBRATION SYNDROME – COMMENTARY

(1) During the period following the leading cases of *Armstrong v British Coal*[27] and *Allen v British Rail*.[28], some insurers were willing to concede that all employers should have known of the risks arising from vibratory tools from 1975-1976 and many experts appeared reluctant to challenge this assumption. Claimants often recovered damages in relation to exposure to tools during the late 1970s and early 1980s. The recent Court of Appeal judgments in *Doherty v Rugby Joinery*[29] (1991-1992) and *Brookes v SYPTE*[30] (1989) illustrate the true position: that each case must depend on the evidence before the court. In both cases, the court stressed that its finding did not lay down a date for any particular industry. Experience suggests that defendants have learned from their mistakes and that 'date of knowledge' is likely to be a central issue. The approach to the pleadings suggested in this work should identify the extent of the dispute. The early involvement of an engineer (ideally prior to drafting the reply) is likely to be useful.

(2) Claimants have a tendency to overestimate the length of their exposure ('anger time') and careful questioning will be needed at an early stage.

(3) As the workforce becomes more familiar with 'HAVS' it may become more difficult to argue lack of 'knowledge' by the Claimant. As always, the claimant should deal with limitation only if and when it is raised by the defendant.[31]

(4) These claims typically arise from many years of exposure, often with more than one employer. In some cases[32] the medical evidence suggests that if the exposure had stopped before the onset of symptoms, the condition would not have developed. Difficult issues of causation and attributability may arise.

(5) The Control of Vibration at Work Regulations 2005 came into force on 6/7/05. The provisions mirror those in other regulations in relation to avoiding and minimising risk, assessment, surveillance, training and instruction. The regulation also introduces a strict duty to prevent exposure above a specified level. However the implementation of that provision is postponed, for new tools, until 6/7/07 and for tools provided prior to that date, to 6/7/10

---

[27] 28 November 1996, unreported, CA.

[28] [2001] PIQR Q10.

[29] [2004] ICR 1272.

[30] [2005] EWCA Civ 452.

[31] See p 27 above.

[32] See eg *Brookes* (above).

P29

HAND ARM VIBRATION SYNDROME – PARTICULARS OF CLAIM

IN THE [   ] COUNTY COURT   No [   ]

BETWEEN:

[   ]

Claimant

-and-

[   ]

Defendant

PARTICULARS OF CLAIM

---

(1) The Claimant was employed by the Defendant as a general labourer from March 1980 to 20/1/07.

(2) In the course of his employment, the Claimant was exposed to vibration from vibratory tools and equipment ('the Exposure').

Particulars

The Claimant used various vibrating tools ('the Work Equipment') including jackhammers, jigger picks, whacker plates, Stihl saws and concrete breakers ('the Manual Handling Operation'). He used such equipment for approximately six hours a day five days per week in addition to weekend overtime.

(3) The Defendant (by its officers, servants or agents) knew, or ought to have known, that the Exposure gave rise to a risk of injury to the Claimant.[33]

(4) The following applied:

a) Construction (Working Places) Regulations 1966 and thereafter Construction (Health, Safety and Welfare) Regulations 1996 ('the Constructions Regulations');

b) From 1/1/93:

---

[33]   If this is not admitted in the Defence, a Reply will be required. See model pleading **P30** at p 104.

i) Provision and Use of Work Equipment Regulations 1992 and thereafter Provision and Use of Work Equipment Regulations 1998 ('the Work Equipment Regulations');

ii) Personal Protective Equipment at Work Regulations 1992 ('the PPE Regulations);

iii) Manual Handling Operations Regulations 1992 ('the Manual Handling Regulations');

c) From 6/7/05: the Control of Vibration at Work Regulations 2005 ("the Vibration Regulations").

(5) As a result of the Exposure, the Claimant has developed hand arm vibration syndrome (HAVS).[34]

(6) The Claimant's condition was caused by the Defendant's breach of statutory duty and the negligence of the Defendant, its servants or agents.

Particulars of Breach of Statutory Duty

a) Failed to eliminate the risk from the Exposure, contrary to reg 6(1) of the Vibration Regulations;

b) Failed to reduce the risk from the Exposure to the lowest level, contrary to reg 6 of the Vibration Regulations;

c) Failed to place the Claimant under suitable health surveillance, contrary to reg 7 of the Vibration Regulations;

d) Failed to provide the Claimant and/or his representatives with suitable and/or sufficient information and/or instruction and/or training, contrary to reg 8 of the Vibration Regulations;

e) Failed to make a suitable and/or sufficient assessment contrary to reg 5 of the Vibration Regulations;

f) Failed to avoid the need for the Claimant to undertake the Manual Handling Operation, contrary to reg 4(1)(a) of the Manual Handling Regulations;

g) Failed to reduce the risk arising from the Manual Handling Operation to the lowest level, contrary to reg 4(1)(b)(ii) of the Manual Handling Regulations;

h) Failed to ensure that the Work Equipment was suitable and used only for operations for which and under conditions for which it was suitable, contrary to regs 5 and 4 of the Work Equipment Regulations 1992 and 1998 respectively;

---

[34] The term Hand/Arm Vibration Syndrome is now in more common use than vibration white finger. This is primarily due to the fact that there are often symptoms present other than the 'classic' white finger symptoms. However the latter term remains in common use and medical reports will often refer to either/both.

i) Failed to make and keep safe the Claimant's place of work, contrary to regs 6 and 5 of the Construction Regulations 1966 and 1996 respectively;[35]

j) Failed to ensure that suitable personal protective equipment was provided to the Claimant, contrary to reg 4 of the PPE Regulations.[36]

Particulars of Negligence

k) Failed to provide a safe place and system of work:

  i) causing the Exposure;

  ii) failing to minimise the extent of the Exposure (by, for example, modifying or replacing the work equipment; job rotation or other measures of the Defendant's choosing);

l) Failed to warn the Claimant of: the dangers to his health caused by the Exposure; the precautions to be taken by him, how he should recognise the signs of development of injury and the steps that he should take should he become aware of symptoms;

m) Failed to identify the onset of the Claimant's condition, by means of health surveillance or monitoring.

(7) By reason of the above the Claimant suffered pain, injury loss and damage. Please see the attached schedule of details of the claim for past and future expenses and losses.

Particulars of Injury

The Claimant (dob 25/4/60) has developed Hand Arm Vibration Syndrome, assessed at Stage 3 on the Taylor Pelmear Scale; 3R(3)/3L(3) Stockholm Vascular Scale; 3SN Stockholm Sesorineural Scale. The Claimant's condition is permanent. He is at a disadvantage on the open labour market. The Claimant relies on the report of [*expert*] dated [*date*].

(8) Interest is claimed on damages pursuant to section 69 of the County Courts Act 1984.

[NAME OF COUNSEL]

(9) I believe that the facts stated in these Particulars of Claim are true.

Signed ....

(Print name) ....

Dated................................

---

[35] It is arguable that it is not the Claimant's place of work that is unsafe in the particular example used here. However, extensive use of vibratory tools – particularly in a factory setting – may give rise to an allegation that the place of work was not safe.

[36] There is some dispute as to whether the use of gloves has any causative effect in reducing HAVS.

Claimant's address for service:

[Claimant's address for service]

P30

HAND ARM VIBRATION SYNDROME – REPLY

IN THE [   ] COUNTY COURT   No [   ]

BETWEEN:

[   ]

Claimant

-and-

[   ]

Defendant

REPLY

(1) In the light of the Defendant's [*denial/failure to admit*] that it knew or ought to have known that that the Exposure gave rise to a risk of injury to the Claimant, in addition to the particulars set out at paragraph 6 a) – m) of the Particulars of Claim the Claimant relies on the following further particulars of negligence.

Particulars of Negligence

n)   Failed to identify that the Claimant's work gave rise to a risk of injury, whether by:

    i)   undertaking an assessment of the Claimant's work;

    ii)   Having regard to heed the various publications warning of the risks arising from vibratory equipment, including those from the Chief Inspector of Factories; the Industrial Injuries Advisory Council (1954, 1970, 1975, 1981); the publication VWF in Industry (1975); ABSI publication (1975), BS 6842 1987; HS(G)88.

    iii)   Obtaining expert advice.

[NAME OF COUNSEL]

(2) I believe that the facts stated in this Reply are true.

Signed …………………………..

(Print name) ……………………..

Dated…………………………….

Section 4

ROAD TRAFFIC ACCIDENTS

COMMENTARY

General

Careful Pleading of road traffic accidents is often neglected due to familiarity. The following points should be observed:

a) The appropriate defendant is usually the driver of the vehicle, as opposed to the policy holder, or owner of the vehicle involved.

b) Particular car should be exercised when the client has been made the defendant in the action: if the claimant is the driver, the client can counterclaim; if the claimant is merely the owner, the client must join the driver as Part 20 defendant.

c) In circumstances where the offending vehicle is driven in the course of a person's employment, the appropriate named defendant will be the employer.

d) If the car driven by the claimant was not owned by him, the owner of the vehicle must be joined if a claim for the damage to the vehicle is to be made at trial.

e) Relevant convictions should be pleaded. Convictions are admissible as evidence in civil proceedings (s 11 of the Civil Evidence Act 1968). Although the existence of a conviction based upon those facts giving rise to the claim is not determinative of the issue of guilt, the legal burden of proof shifts to the defendant to disprove those matters, which constitute the offence. Such attempts are extremely rare and in practical terms the existence of a relevant conviction will lead to an admission of negligence. Reliance upon a conviction must be pleaded (Civil Procedure Rules Part 16 PD 8.1(1)).

A succinct account of the circumstances of the accident should be provided, including: street names; direction of travel of each vehicle; identity and type of the vehicles; relevant traffic signs or markings; road layout.

There is temptation to repeat the same allegation of negligence in alternative forms ie 'drove too fast' and 'failed to observe the speed limit'. In road traffic cases, it is important to identify the precisely what element of driving is being complained of.

This will assist the trial judge and aid in the preparation of the case and collation of relevant evidence.

Insurance

At the heart of cases of this type is often the issue of insurance. Frequently drivers are not insured or they cannot be traced. A basic understanding of the Road Traffic Act 1988 ('RTA'), The Motor Insurers' Bureau Agreements ('MIB') and the European Communities (Rights against Insurers) Regulations 2002 ('ECR') is required. Upon receipt of any instructions, the insurance position must be established. There are strict notice requirements in circumstances where involvement of the RTA, MIB or ECR is necessary. An overview is provided below but it is essential that these provisions are studied.

European Communities (Rights against Insurers) Regulations 2002

In circumstances where a vehicle is insured and the negligent driver is the insured person, s 3(2) creates right to issue proceedings against the insurance company. The insurance company will be liable to the claimant to the extent that it would be liable to the insured person. Accordingly, proceedings can be issued against insurer, without recourse to proceeding against the driver.

Road Traffic Act 1988

In circumstances where a policy of insurance exists, whether or not the vehicle is being driven by the insured (unlike the ECR), invariably, the insurer will be required to satisfy any judgment. It is often (mistakenly) believed that because the driver was not insured, immediate recourse to the MIB should be made. While nothing is lost by notifying the MIB, the majority of cases will be dealt with by the insurer of the vehicle and judgment satisfied under s 151 of the Road Traffic Act 1988. It is important to note that an insurers liability is to meet an unsatisfied judgment against the negligent driver.

Motor Insurers' Bureau

The MIB will meet judgments against uninsured or untraced drivers, where recourse cannot made against an insurer of the vehicle. As with all these regimes, strict procedural obligations are a condition precedent to recovery, which require detailed consideration. Regard should also be had to the 'Notes for Guidance of Victims of Road Traffic Accidents', which provide that the MIB should be joined as defendant when deciding to commence legal proceedings.

P31

ROAD TRAFFIC ACCIDENTS – CHILD PEDESTRIAN – PARTICULARS OF CLAIM

IN THE [   ] COUNTY COURT   No [   ]

BETWEEN:

[   ]

Claimant

-and-

[   ]

Defendant

PARTICULARS OF CLAIM

---

(1) At approximately 10.00am on 1/7/06, the Claimant was playing football with a group of boys on an area of wasteland opposite the Co-op supermarket on Headley Street, Headingley, Leeds ('the Street'). The Defendant was driving a Ford Capri, registered number W535 KEV south along the Street.

(2) In the course of the game, the ball was kicked across the Street by one of the boys.

(3) The Claimant ran from the area of wasteland across the Street, to retrieve the ball. As the Claimant crossed the centre of the road into the southbound carriageway, he was struck by the Defendant's vehicle.

(3) The collision was caused by the Defendant's negligence.

Particulars of Negligence

a) Failed to see, in time or at all, or react appropriately to:

    i) the boys playing near to the road;

    ii) the ball being kicked into the road;

    iii) the Claimant running after the ball;

The Defendant should have sounded his horn, undertaken an immediate emergency stop and/or steered to avoid the Claimant;

b) Drove too fast.

(5) As a result of the accident the Claimant suffered pain, injury loss and damage. Please see the attached schedule of details of the claim for past and future expenses and losses.

Particulars of Injury

The Claimant (dob1/1/90) suffered a concussive head injury, with symptoms persisting for 12 months. The Claimant relies on the report of [*expert*] dated [*date*].

(6) Interest is claimed on damages pursuant to s 69 of the County Courts Act 1984.

[NAME OF COUNSEL]

(7) I believe that the facts stated in these Particulars of Claim are true.

Signed ....

(Print name) ....

Dated................................

Claimant's address for service:

[Claimant's address for service]

P32

RTA – COLLISION WITH CYCLIST – PARTICULARS OF CLAIM

IN THE [   ] COUNTY COURT   No [   ]

BETWEEN:

[   ]

Claimant

-and-

[   ]

Defendant

PARTICULARS OF CLAIM

(1) At approximately 10.00am on 1/7/06, the Claimant was cycling south along Headley Street, Headingley, Leeds. The Defendant was travelling in the same direction, driving a White Ford Van, registered number X535 WFE.

(2) As the Defendant approached the junction of Headley Street with Cottage Street, to his left, he overtook, and collided with, the Claimant, causing the Claimant to leave the road and strike a lamppost.

(3) The collision was caused by the negligence of the Defendant.

Particulars of Negligence

a)   failed to see the Claimant, in time or at all;

b)   collided with the Claimant.

(4) As a result of the accident the Claimant suffered pain, injury loss and damage. Please see the attached schedule of details of the claim for past and future expenses and losses.

Particulars of Injury

The Claimant (dob 1/1/70) suffered a Colles fracture to his right wrist, with symptoms persisting for 12 months. The Claimant relies on the report of [*expert*] dated [*date*]

(5) Interest is claimed on damages pursuant to s 69 of the County Courts Act 1984.

(6) I believe that the facts stated in these Particulars of Claim are true.

Signed …………………………..

(Print name) ……………………

Dated…………………………….

Claimant's address for service:

[Claimant's address for service]

P33

RTA – EMERGENCY SERVICES – PARTICULARS OF CLAIM

IN THE [   ] COUNTY COURT   No [   ]

BETWEEN:

[   ]

Claimant

-and-

[   ]

Defendant

PARTICULARS OF CLAIM

---

(1) The Claimant was the driver of a Ford Anglia, registered number X535 WFE. Police Constable Jones was driving a marked Ford Escort police vehicle, registered number, W535 PRT ('the police car'), in the course of his employment with the Defendant.

(2) At approximately 10.00am on 1/7/06 , the Claimant was driving south along Headley Street, Headingley, Leeds, when his vehicle was hit head-on by the police car, travelling north in the south-bound lane.

(3) The collision was caused by the Defendant's negligence

Particulars of Negligence

The Defendant, by his employee Jones:

a) Overtook on a blind bend;

b) Failed to activate the police car's siren or flashing lights;

c) Drove too fast;

d) Drove into collision with the Claimant's vehicle.

(4) The Claimant relies on the circumstances of the accident as evidence of the Defendant's negligence.

(5) As a result of the accident the Claimant suffered pain, injury loss and damage. Please see the attached schedule of details of the claim for past and future expenses and losses.

Particulars of Injury

The Claimant (dob 1/1/70) suffered a whiplash injury, with symptoms persisting for 12 months. The Claimant relies on the report of [*expert*] dated [*date*].

(6) Interest is claimed on damages pursuant to s 69 of the County Courts Act 1984.

[NAME OF COUNSEL]

(7) I believe that the facts stated in these Particulars of Claim are true.

Signed …………………………..

(Print name) …………………….

Dated……………………………

Claimant's address for service:

[Claimant's address for service]

P34

RTA – JUNCTION – PARTICULARS OF CLAIM

IN THE [   ] COUNTY COURT   No [   ]

BETWEEN:

[   ]

Claimant

-and-

[   ]

Defendant

PARTICULARS OF CLAIM

---

(1) The Claimant was the driver of a Ford Anglia, registered number X535 WFE. The Defendant was the driver of Morris Marina, registered number W632 POW.

(2) At approximately 10.00am on 1/7/06, the Claimant was driving south along Headley Street, Headingley, Leeds.

(3) As the Claimant approached the junction of Headley Street with Cottage Street, to his left, the Defendant drove from Cottage Street into the path of, and into collision with, the Claimant.

(4) The entrance of traffic from Cottage Street onto Headley Street was controlled by a 'give way' sign and road markings.

(5) The collision was caused by Defendant's negligence.

Particulars of Negligence

a) Failed to see the Claimant's vehicle, in time or at all;

b) Failed to give way to the Claimant's vehicle;

c) Drove into the path of the Claimant's vehicle.

(6) As a result of the accident the Claimant suffered pain, injury loss and damage. Please see the attached schedule of details of the claim for past and future expenses and losses.

Particulars of Injury

The Claimant (dob 1/1/70) suffered a whiplash injury, with symptoms persisting for 12 months. The Claimant relies on the report of [*expert*] dated [*date*].

(7) Interest is claimed on damages pursuant to s 69 of the County Courts Act 1984.

[NAME OF COUNSEL]

(8) I believe that the facts stated in these Particulars of Claim are true.

Signed …………………………..

(Print name) ……………………….

Dated……………………………….

Claimant's address for service:

[Claimant's address for service]

P35

RTA – PREVIOUS CONVICTIONS – PARTICULARS OF CLAIM

IN THE [   ] COUNTY COURT   No [   ]

BETWEEN:

[   ]

Claimant

-and-

[   ]

Defendant

PARTICULARS OF CLAIM

---

(1) The Claimant was the driver of a Ford Anglia, registered number X535 WFE. The Defendant was the driver of Morris Marina, registered number W632 POW.

(2) At approximately 10.00am on 1/7/06, the Claimant was driving south along Headley Street towards the roundabout at its junction with Cottage Street, and Lounge Street, Headingley, Leeds.

(3) The Claimant entered the roundabout, intending to turn right into Lounge Street. As the Claimant drove around the roundabout, the Defendant pulled out of from Cottage Street into the path of, and into collision with, the Claimant.

(4) The collision was caused by the negligence of the Defendant.

Particulars of Negligence

a) Failed to see the Claimant's vehicle, in time or at all;

b) Failed to give way to the Claimant's vehicle;

c) Failed stop or remain at the give way markings at the junction of Cottage Street with the roundabout;

d) Drove into the path of the Claimant's vehicle.

(5) The Defendant was convicted of having, on 1/7/06, driven without due care and attention at the Headingley Magistrates Court on 10/9/06. The conviction arose out of those matters set out above and relates to the issue of negligence.

(6) As a result of the accident, the Claimant has suffered pain, injury, loss and damage. Please see the attached details of the claim for past and future expense and losses.

Particulars of Injury

The Claimant (dob 1/1/70) suffered a whiplash injury, with symptoms persisting for 12 months. The Claimant relies on the report of [*name of expert*] dated [*date*].

(7) Interest is claimed on damages pursuant to s 69 of the County Courts Act 1984.

[NAME OF COUNSEL]

(8) I believe that the facts stated in these Particulars of Claim are true.

Signed …………………………..

(Print name) ……………………

Dated……………………………

Claimant's address for service:

[Claimant's address for service]

P36

RTA – PASSENGER TRAFFIC LIGHTS – PARTICULARS OF CLAIM

IN THE [   ] COUNTY COURT   No [   ]

BETWEEN:

[   ]

Claimant

-and-

(1) [   ]

(2) [   ]

Defendants

PARTICULARS OF CLAIM

---

(1) The Claimant was a front-seat passenger travelling in a Ford Anglia, registered number X535 WFE ('Claimant's vehicle'), driven by the Second Defendant. The First Defendant was the driver of a Morris Marina, registered number W632 POW.

(2) At approximately 10.00am on 1/7/06, the Claimant was travelling south along Headley Street towards the traffic lights at its junction with Cottage Street.

(3) The Claimant's vehicle entered the junction, intending to turn right into Cottage Street. As the Claimant's vehicle crossed the northbound carriageway of Headley Street, it was hit by the First Defendant's motorcar.

(4) The collision was caused by the negligence of the First and/or Second Defendant.

Particulars of Negligence

THE FIRST DEFENDANT:

a) Drove through a red light;

b) Failed to see the Claimant's vehicle, in time or at all;

c) Failed to give way to the Claimant's vehicle;

d) Failed stop or remain at the give way markings at the junction of Headley Street with Cottage Street;

e) Drove into the path of the Claimant's vehicle.

THE SECOND DEFENDANT:

a) Drove through a red light;

b) Failed to see the First Defendant's vehicle, in time or at all;

c) Turned right across the path of the First Defendant's vehicle.

(5) As a result of the accident, the Claimant has suffered pain, injury, loss and damage. Please see the attached details of the claim for past and future expense and losses.

Particulars of Injury

The Claimant (dob 1/1/70) suffered a whiplash injury, with symptoms persisting for 12 months. The Claimant relies on the report of [*expert*] dated [*date*].

(6) Interest is claimed on damages pursuant to s 69 of the County Courts Act 1984.

[NAME OF COUNSEL]

(7) I believe that the facts stated in these Particulars of Claim are true.

> Signed ……………………………..
>
> (Print name) ……………………….
>
> Dated…………………………….
>
> Claimant's address for service:
>
> [Claimant's address for service]

P37

RTA – REAR END SHUNT – PARTICULARS OF CLAIM

IN THE [   ] COUNTY COURT   No [   ]

BETWEEN:

[   ]

Claimant

-and-

[   ]

Defendant

PARTICULARS OF CLAIM

---

(1) The Claimant was the driver of a Ford Anglia, registered number X535 WFE. The Defendant was the driver of Morris Marina, registered number W632 POW.

(2) At approximately 10.00am on 1/7/06, the Claimant was waiting in a queue of stationary traffic on Headley Street at its junction with Cottage Street, Headingley, Leeds, when his vehicle was struck from behind by the Defendant's motor car.

(3) At the time of the accident, the temperature was below freezing and the road was icy.

(4) The collision was caused by the negligence of the Defendant.

Particulars of Negligence

a)   Drove too fast;

b)   Failed to brake in time;

c)   Braked too hard (causing the wheels to lock);

d)   Collided with the rear of the Claimant's vehicle.

(5) As a result of the accident, the Claimant has suffered pain, injury, loss and damage. Please see the attached details of the claim for past and future expense and losses.

Particulars of Injury

The Claimant (dob 1/1/70) suffered a whiplash injury, with symptoms persisting for 12 months. The Claimant relies on the report of [*expert*] dated [*date*].

(6) Interest is claimed on damages pursuant to s 69 of the County Courts Act 1984.

[NAME OF COUNSEL]

(7) I believe that the facts stated in these Particulars of Claim are true.

Signed …………………………..

(Print name) ……………………

Dated……………………………

Claimant's address for service:

[Claimant's address for service]

P38

RTA – PASSENGER ON BUS – PARTICULARS OF CLAIM

IN THE [   ] COUNTY COURT   No [   ]

BETWEEN:

[   ]

Claimant

-and-

[   ]

Defendant

PARTICULARS OF CLAIM

---

(1) The Claimant was a passenger on a public service bus No 655 ('the bus'), driven by John Brown, in the course of his employment with the Defendant.

(2) At approximately 10am on 1/7/06, the bus was travelling south along Headley Street towards the traffic lights at its junction with Cottage Street, Headingley, Leeds.

(3) As the bus approached standing traffic, John Brown applied the brakes, bringing the bus to a sudden stop, causing the Claimant (who was standing) to fall to the floor.

(4) The accident was caused by the negligence[1] of Defendant by its servant, John Brown.

Particulars of Negligence

a) Drove too fast;

b) Failed see the standing traffic on Headley Street, in time or at all;

---

[1] It is not negligent, per se, for a bus driver to pull away from a stop while passengers are standing (*Fletcher v United Counties Omnibus Co Ltd* [1998] PIQR P154, CA). However, if a bus is brought to a sudden stop or performs an erratic manoeuvre, an explanation is called for, in the absence of which negligence can be inferred (*Parkinson v Liverpool Corpn* [1950] 1 All ER 367). In the pleaded case the facts are known (the bus driver failed to heed the stationary traffic and braked too late). If these facts had not been known to the Claimant, it would have been appropriate to plead res ipsa loquitur.

    c)   Braked too hard and too late.

(5) As a result of the accident, the Claimant has suffered pain, injury, loss and damage. Please see the attached details of the claim for past and future expense and losses.

Particulars of Injury

The Claimant (dob 1/1/70) suffered a Colles fracture, with symptoms persisting for 12 months. The Claimant relies on the report of [*expert*] dated [*date*].

(6) Interest is claimed on damages pursuant to s 69 of the County Courts Act 1984.

[NAME OF COUNSEL]

(7) I believe that the facts stated in these Particulars of Claim are true.

       Signed ……………………………..

       (Print name) ……………………….

       Dated…………………………….

       Claimant's address for service:

       [Claimant's address for service]

P39

RTA – CLAIM AGAINST INSURER (2002 REGULATIONS) – PARTICULARS OF CLAIM

IN THE [   ] COUNTY COURT   No [   ]

BETWEEN:

[   ]

Claimant

-and-

[   ]

Defendant

PARTICULARS OF CLAIM

---

(1) The Claimant was the driver of a Ford Anglia, registered number X535 WFE. John Jones was the driver of a Morris Marina, registered number W632 POW ('the Vehicle').

(2) On 1/7/06, the Claimant was driving south along Headley Street, Headingley, Leeds. As the Claimant approached the junction of Headley Street with Cottage Street, to his left, Jones drove from a parking space into collision with the Claimant's nearside.

(3) The collision was caused by Jones's negligence.

Particulars of Negligence

a) Failed to see the Claimant's vehicle;

b) Failed to give way to the Claimant's vehicle;

c) Pulled away from the parking space when it was unsafe to do so;

d) Drove into collision with the Claimant's vehicle.

(4) The Defendant issued the policy of insurance relating to the use of the Vehicle by Jones on the occasion of the accident.

(5) The Defendant is liable to the Claimant pursuant to the European Communities (Rights Against Insurers) Regulations 2002 ('the Regulations').[2]

(6) As a result of the accident, the Claimant has suffered pain, injury, loss and damage. Please see the attached details of the claim for past and future expense and losses.

Particulars of Injury

The Claimant (dob 1/1/70) suffered a whiplash injury, with symptoms persisting for 12 months. The Claimant relies on the report of [*expert*] dated [*date*].

(7) Interest is claimed on damages pursuant to s 69 of the County Courts Act 1984.

[NAME OF COUNSEL]

(8) I believe that the facts stated in these Particulars of Claim are true.

Signed ……………………………..

(Print name) ……………………….

Dated…………………………………

Claimant's address for service:

[Claimant's address for service]

---

[2]   In force from 19 January 2003. The ABI and DCA suggest that this applies only in respect of accidents after that date. This is not apparent from the regulations and has not yet been tested by the courts.

P40

RTA – UNINSURED DRIVING MIB – PARTICULARS OF CLAIM

IN THE [   ] COUNTY COURT   No [   ]

BETWEEN:

[   ]

Claimant

-and-

(1) [   ]

(2) THE MOTOR INSURERS BUREAU[3]

Defendants

PARTICULARS OF CLAIM

---

(1) The Claimant was the driver of a Ford Anglia, registered number X535 WFE. The First Defendant was the driver of a Morris Marina, registered number W632 POW.

(2) At approximately 10am on 1/7/06, the Claimant was driving south along Headley Street, Headingley, Leeds. As the Claimant approached the junction of Headley Street with Cottage Street, to his left, the First Defendant drove from Cottage Street into the path of the Claimant causing a collision.

(3) The collision was caused by the First Defendant's negligence.

Particulars of Negligence

a) Failed to see the Claimant's vehicle;

b) Failed to give way to the Claimant's vehicle;

c) Failed stop or remain at the give way markings at the junction of Cottage Street with Headley Street;

d) Drove into the path of the Claimant's vehicle.

(4) As a result of the accident, the Claimant has suffered pain, injury, loss and damage. Please see the attached details of the claim for past and future expense and losses.

---

[3] When the Claimant intends to recover from the MIB under the Uninsured Drivers Agreement, the MIB should be joined as a Defendant from the outset.

Particulars of Injury

The Claimant (dob 1/1/70) suffered a whiplash injury, with symptoms persisting for 12 months. The Claimant relies on the report of [*expert*] dated [*date*].

(5) The Second Defendant is a Company limited by guarantee under the Companies Act. Pursuant to an agreement with the Secretary of State for the Environment Transport and the Regions dated 13 August 1999, the Second Defendant provides compensation in certain circumstances to persons suffering injury or damage as a result of the negligence of uninsured motorists.

(6) The Claimant has used all reasonable endeavours to ascertain the liability of an insurer for the First Defendant and at the time of the commencement of these proceedings verily believes that the First Defendant is not insured.

(7) The Claimant accepts that only if a final judgment is obtained against the First Defendant (which judgment is not satisfied in full within seven days from the date upon which the Claimant became entitled to enforce it) can the Second Defendant be required to satisfy the judgment and then only if the terms and conditions set out ion the Agreement are satisfied. Until that time, any liability of the Second Defendant is only contingent.

(8) To avoid the Second Defendant having later to apply to join itself to this action (which the Claimant must consent to in any event, pursuant to Clause 14(b) of the Agreement) the Claimant seeks to include the Second Defendant from the outset recognising fully the Second Defendant's position as reflected in 3 above and the rights of the Second Defendant fully to participate in the action to protect its position as a separate party to the action.

(9) With the above in mind, the Claimant seeks a declaration of the Second Defendant's contingent liability to satisfy the claimant's judgment against the First Defendant[4].

(10)   Interest is claimed on damages pursuant to s 69 of the County Courts Act 1984.

[NAME OF COUNSEL]

(11)   I believe that the facts stated in these Particulars of Claim are true.

Signed ....

(Print name) ....

Dated................................

Claimant's address for service:

[Claimant's address for service]

---

[4]   Paragraphs 5–9 set out the wording requested by the MIB.

P41

RTA – SECTION 151 – PARTICULARS OF CLAIM

IN THE [   ] COUNTY COURT   No [   ]

BETWEEN:

[   ]

Claimant

-and-

[   ]

Defendant

PARTICULARS OF CLAIM

---

(1) On 1/7/06, the Claimant was driving south along Headley Street, Headingley, Leeds, when his vehicle was in collision with a Morris Marina, registered number W632 POW, driven by Wendy Brown.

(2) On 10/12/06, judgment was entered for the Claimant against Wendy Brown in the sum £3,000 with interest of £200 and costs of £2,000; a total of £5,200, for loss and damage suffered in the accident ('the Liability').

(3) The Defendant, is liable to pay the sum of £5,200 to the Claimant pursuant to s 151 of the Road Traffic Act 1988:

    a) Prior to the judgment, the Defendant had delivered, to Wendy Brown, a certificate of insurance;

    b) The Liability was required to be covered by s 145(3) of the Road Traffic Act 1988;

    c) The Liability was covered by the terms of the policy to which the certificate relates.[5]

---

[5] The insurer is also liable if the liability would have been covered by the policy if it applied to all persons (ie if the policy applies to the vehicle but not the particular driver): see s 151(2)(b). If this provision is relied on, this paragraph should read:

'The Liability would be covered by the policy to which the certificate relates if the policy covered the liability of all persons'.

(4) By letter dated 10 January 2005, the Claimant requested payment of £5,200 from the Defendant. The Defendant has failed[6] to pay.

(5) Interest is claimed on the sum of £5,200[7] pursuant to s 69 of the County Courts Act 1984 at the rate of 8%[8] from 10 December 2004 to 10 March 2005[9]: a total of £104 to date and accruing at a daily rate of £1.14.

[NAME OF COUNSEL]

(6) I believe that the facts stated in these Particulars of Claim are true.

Signed ……………………………..

(Print name) ……………………….

Dated……………………………….

Claimant's address for service:

[Claimant's address for service]

---

[6]   Replace with 'refused' if appropriate.

[7]   See CPR 16.4 (2)(b) in relation to claims for interest on specific sums.

[8]   The court has a discretion in relation to the rate. However, with base rates at present levels, the court is unlikely to award more than 8% (the judgement debt rate). Restricting the rate to the judgement debt rate allows the court to award interest if judgment is obtained in default. See CPR 12.6.

[9]   The date of issue: CPR 16.4(2)(b)(iii).

Section 5

HIGHWAYS

COMMENTARY

Identifying the Defendant

The defendant will often be the highway authority. A highway authority's liability normally arises from a failure to 'maintain' the street or the negligent execution of work on the highway, such as inadequate signing during re-surfacing work.

Occasionally, defects or obstructions within the highway are created by the actions of others. Authorised works carried out by utility companies are governed by the New Road and Street Works Act 1991. These utility companies will be liable for negligently performed work, which subsequently deteriorates, as well as dangers created by the work itself.

Occasionally, private individuals (such as builders) may create a hazard within the street. A typical example would be an unlit skip situated within the carriageway.

The Highway Authority[1]

The general duty to take reasonable care, when acting, applies to a highway authority. When a highway authority has acted (for example, by digging a hole in the pavement) and has done so without reasonable care, causing the Claimant's injury, a claim in negligence should be pursued.

However, an important distinction lies between the highway authority that acts carelessly[2] and the one that does not act at all.[3] Despite many pleadings to the contrary, there is no duty at *common law* requiring the highway authority to act: for example by repairing and maintaining the road,[4] installing signs and markings[5]

---

[1]   This is usually the county council or metropolitan district council or (in respect of trunk roads), the Minister. See s 1 of the Highways Act 1980.

[2]   Traditionally referred to as 'misfeasance' in this context.

[3]   Traditionally referred to as 'nonfeasance' in this context.

[4]   *Goodes v East Sussex County Council* [2000] 1 WLR 1356.

[5]   *Gorringe v Calderdale* (HL) [2004] 1 WLR 1057.

removing items from beside the highway that caused visibility problems[6] or gritting (even when it was its usual practice to do so[7]).

The highway authority's duty to act is imposed by s 41 of the Highways Act 1980, which requires it to 'maintain'[8] the highway. 'Maintain' has been recently redefined to include the removal snow and ice.[9] It may also include the removal of some deposits that become so adherent to the surface that they, in effect, become part of it[10]. The duty to maintain the highway includes the duty to maintain the drainage[11]. In a typical 'tripping' claim, where the condition of a road or pavement has simply deteriorated over time, the claimant's cause of action arises only under s 41. The claimant will be required to plead and prove that:

a) The highway was not maintained.

b) The claimant's injury was caused by the failure to maintain.

The Highway authority will often seek to rely on the 'special defence' provided by s 58 of the Highways Act 1980, by which it is a defence to prove that:

> 'the highway authority had taken such care as in all the circumstances was reasonable to secure that part of the highway ... was not dangerous to traffic.'

This is for the defendant to plead and prove and no reference should be made to in the particulars of claim. If the s 58 defence is pleaded in the defence, the claimant should set out, in a reply, any positive case he intends to advance in response.

Statutory Undertakers

Frequently a pedestrian will suffer an injury due to a defect, which has been created following interference to the structure of the pavement or road by a utility company. Such work is governed by the New Roads and Street Works Act 1991 and the Street Works (Reinstatement) Regulations (and Code[12]) 1992. Whilst the Act and regulations imposes obligations in relation to safety measures, reinstatement and maintenance, they are silent on whether a breach is intended to give rise to a cause of action by an individual. This work assumes that no such

---

[6]   *Stovin v Wise* [1996] AC 923.

[7]   *Sandhar v DOT* [2004] EWCA Civ 1440.

[8]   Ie reasonably passable for ordinary traffic without danger caused by its physical condition: Diplock LJ in *Burnside v Emerson* [1968] 1 WLR 1490 at 1496–1497 approved in *Goodes*.

[9]   *Goodes v East Sussex County Council* [2000] 1 WLR 1356; Railways and Transport Safety Act 2003, s 111 inserting s 41A into the Highways Act 1980. In force 31 October 2003:Railways and Transport Safety Act 2003 (Commencement No 1) Order 2003.

[10] *Rich v Pembrokeshire County Council* [2001] EWCA Civ 410.

[11] *Burnside v Emerson* [1968] 1 WLR 1490, *DTER v MacDonald* [2006] EWCA Civ 1089.

[12] The Specifications for the Reinstatement of Openings in Highways.

right arises.[13] However, the Act, regulations and code may provide some guidance at trial as to what might reasonably be expected of the defendant.

---

[13] *Keating v Elvan Reinforced Concrete Co Ltd* [1968] 1 WLR 722 held that a predecessor Act (the Public Utilities and Street Works Act 1950) did not give rise to such a claim. However, the wording is different and there is no authority specifically on the current Act.

P42

HIGHWAYS – FLOODING – PARTICULARS OF CLAIM

IN THE [   ] COUNTY COURT   No [   ]

BETWEEN:

[   ]

Claimant

-and-

[   ]

Defendant

PARTICULARS OF CLAIM

---

(1) The Defendant is the highway authority responsible for the maintenance of Headley Street, Headingley, Leeds ('the Highway') pursuant the Highways Act 1980.

(2) At approximately 7pm on 7/7/06, the Claimant was driving his VW Golf, registered number W535 YOP along the Highway when he lost control of the vehicle on standing water on the carriageway, causing him to veer off the road and into collision with a lamp post.

(3) The presence of the water was caused by a long-standing[14] accumulation of detritus and mud blocking the storm drains[15] situated outside the Co-Op supermarket on Headley Street.

(4) The Claimant's accident was caused by the Defendant's breach of statutory duty

---

[14] Whilst the highway authority is liable to remove long-standing blockages to drains, the position is less clear in relation to 'transient' blockages: see *DTER v MacDonald* [2006] EWCA Civ 1086 and *Goodes v East Sussex County Council* [2000] 1 WLR 1356.

[15] Caution should be adopted with cases of this type. A distinction falls to be made between drains which are not properly maintained causing flooding and a temporary flooding caused by high rainfall an debris being swept into drainage systems which are unable to cope: *Pritchard v Clwyd County Council* [1993] PIQR P21.

Particulars of Breach of Statutory Duty

a)   Failed to maintain the highway contrary to s 41 of the Highways Act 1980.

(5) As a result of the accident, the Claimant has suffered pain, injury, loss and damage. Please see the attached details of the claim for past and future expense and losses.

Particulars of Injury

The Claimant (dob 1/1/70) suffered a Colles fracture, with symptoms persisting for 12 months. The Claimant relies on the report of [*expert*] dated [*date*].

(7) Interest is claimed on damages pursuant to s 69 of the County Courts Act 1984.

[NAME OF COUNSEL]

(8) I believe that the facts stated in these Particulars of Claim are true.

Signed …………………………..

(Print name) …………………….

Dated……………………………..

Claimant's address for service:

[Claimant's address for service]

P43

HIGHWAYS – ICE AND SNOW – PARTICULARS OF CLAIM

IN THE [   ] COUNTY COURT   No [   ]

BETWEEN:

[   ]

Claimant

-and-

[   ]

Defendant

PARTICULARS OF CLAIM

---

(1) The Defendant is the highway authority responsible for the maintenance of Headley Street, Headingley, Leeds ('the Highway') pursuant to the Highways Act 1980.

(2) At approximately 7am on 7/1/06, the Claimant was driving his VW Golf motor car registered number LY04VWX along the Highway when he lost control of the vehicle due to the presence of ice and/or snow on the carriageway, causing him to collide with the shop front of WH Brown estate agents.

(3) The accident was caused by the Defendant's breach of statutory duty.

Particulars of Breach of Statutory Duty

a) Failed to ensure that safe passage along the Highway was not endangered by ice or snow, contrary to s 41(1A) of the Highways Act 1980.[16]

(4) As a result of the accident, the Claimant has suffered pain and injury, loss and damage. Please see the attached schedule of details of the claim for past and future expenses and losses.

---

[16]   Section 41(1A) provides a 'reasonable practicability 'defence'. This is for the Defendant to plead and prove and should not be referred to in the Particulars.

Particulars of Injury

The Claimant (dob 1/1/70) suffered a fractured right radius. The Claimant is at a disadvantage on the open labour market. The Claimant relies on the report of [*expert*] dated [*date*].

(5) Interest is claimed on damages pursuant to s 69 of the County Courts Act 1984.

[NAME OF COUNSEL]

(6) I believe that the facts stated in these Particulars of Claim are true.

Signed …………………………..

(Print name) …………………….

Dated……………………………..

Claimant's address for service:

[Claimant's address for service]

P44

HIGHWAYS – LOOSE CHIPPINGS – PARTICULARS OF CLAIM

IN THE [   ] COUNTY COURT   No [   ]

BETWEEN:

[   ]

Claimant

-and-

[   ]

Defendant

PARTICULARS OF CLAIM

---

(1) The Defendant is the highway authority responsible for the maintenance of Headley Street, Headingley, Leeds ('the Highway') pursuant to the Highways Act 1980.

(2) At approximately 7am on 7/1/06, the Claimant was driving his VW Golf motor car registered number LY04VWX along the Highway when he lost control of the vehicle due to the presence of detritus/loose chippings on the carriageway; causing him to collide with the shop front of W H Brown estate agents.

(3) The detritus/loose chippings were present as a result of resurfacing works carried out by the Defendant between 1 and –5/7/06.

(4) The accident was caused by the negligence of the Defendant, its servants or agents.

Particulars of Negligence

a) caused or permitted detritus/loose chippings to be left upon the surface of the carriageway;

b) failed to implement and/or enforce an adequate system of sweeping/removal of detritus/loose chippings;

c) failed to implement and/or enforce any adequate system of inspection;

d) failed to erect adequate signs, which:

      i)   warned the Claimant of the presence of loose chippings/detritus;

      ii)   reduced the speed limit to 20 mph;

e) failed to close the street to vehicular traffic when it was in an unsafe state;

f) failed to have adequate regard to published guidance, in particular the Road Surface Dressing Association – Surface Dressing – Code of Practice.[17]

(5) As a result of the accident, the Claimant has suffered pain and injury, loss and damage. Please see the attached schedule of details of the claim for past and future expenses and losses.

Particulars of Injury

The Claimant (dob 1/1/70) suffered a fractured right radius. The Claimant is at a disadvantage on the open labour market. The Claimant relies on the report of [*expert*] dated [*date*].

[NAME OF COUNSEL]

(6) I believe that the facts stated in these Particulars of Claim are true.

      Signed …………………………..

      (Print name) ……………………….

      Dated……………………………..

      Claimant's address for service:

      [Claimant's address for service]

---

[17]   The code of practice, unlike the Safety at Street Works and Road Works Code of Practice (issued by the Secretary of State for Transport, Local Government and the Regions under ss 65 and 124 of the New Roads and Street Works Act 1991) is a document published by the Road Surface Dressing Association . It sets in detail precautions to be taken when undertaking surface dressing. Although failure to comply with these guidelines does not give rise to a cause of action, they provide a useful baseline against which to assess negligence.

P45

HIGHWAYS – OBSTRUCTION – PARTICULARS OF CLAIM

IN THE [   ] COUNTY COURT   No [   ]

BETWEEN:

[   ]

Claimant

-and-

[   ]

Defendant

PARTICULARS OF CLAIM

---

(1) The Defendant was engaged in building works at the Co-op supermarket on Headley Street, Headingley, Leeds ('the Highway').

(2) At approximately 7pm on 7/2/06, the Claimant was cycling south along the Highway when he collided with a skip and a pile of sand ('the Obstruction'), which had been left in carriageway by the Defendant, without the consent of the Highway authority.

(3) The accident was caused by the negligence of the Defendant, its servants or agents.

Particulars of negligence

a) Obstructing the Highway;

b) Failing to alert the Claimant to the presence of the Obstruction by, for example, lighting, signs, bollards or barriers.

Alternatively, if the Obstruction was placed in the highway with the consent of the highway authority, the accident was caused by the Defendant's breach of statutory duty and the Claimant relies on the following further particulars.

Particulars of Breach of Statutory Duty

c) Failed to ensure that the skip was properly lighted during the hours of darkness contrary to s 139 of the Highways Act 1980;

b) Failed to properly fence and light the sand, contrary to s 171 of the Highways Act.

(4) The Defendant caused a nuisance on the highway.

(5) As a result of the accident, the Claimant has suffered pain, injury, loss and damage. Please see the attached details of the claim for past and future expense and losses.

Particulars of Injury

The Claimant (dob 1/1/70) suffered a concussive head injury, with symptoms persisting for 12 months. The Claimant relies on the report of [*expert*] dated [*date*].

(6) Interest is claimed on damages pursuant to s 69 of the County Courts Act 1984.

[NAME OF COUNSEL]

(7) I believe that the facts stated in these Particulars of Claim are true.

Signed …………………………..

(Print name) ……………………….

Dated……………………………….

Claimant's address for service:

[Claimant's address for service]

P46

HIGHWAYS – FAILED REINSTATEMENT – PARTICULARS OF CLAIM

IN THE [   ] COUNTY COURT   No [   ]

BETWEEN:

[   ]

Claimant

-and-

(1) [   ]
(2) [   ]

Defendants

PARTICULARS OF CLAIM

---

(1) The First Defendant is the highway authority responsible for the maintenance of Headley Street, Headingley, Leeds ('the Highway') pursuant to the Highways Act 1980.

(2) At approximately 7pm on 7/7/06, the Claimant was walking along the street when he tripped over a defect situated within the pavement outside the Co-op supermarket.

(3) The defect was created by subsidence following work undertaken by the Second Defendant between 7/5/06 and 10/5/06 ('the Work') pursuant to the provisions of the New Roads and Street Works Act 1991.

(4) The Defect is illustrated in the attached photograph.

(5) On 10/6/06, Mrs Wood, of 59 Headley Street, Headingley, complained to the First Defendant that the Defect was present.[18]

(6) The accident was caused by the First Defendants' breach of statutory duty and the negligence of the Defendants, their servants or agents.

---

[18] Arguably the complaint of Mrs Wood, putting the Highway Authority on notice of the defect, need only be raised in response to a section 58 Defence. However, the existence of a complaint is evidence of the public's view of the state of highway and therefore the complaint goes towards the overall assessment of whether the highway could be considered 'dangerous' in the normal course of human affairs *Littler v Liverpool Corpn* [1968] 2 All ER 343 .

Particulars of Breach of Statutory Duty

FIRST DEFENDANT:

a) Failed to maintain the Highway contrary to s 41 of the Highways Act 1980;

Particulars of Negligence

SECOND DEFENDANT:

b) Undertook the Works in such a way that the Defect was created, contrary to the Street Works (Reinstatement) Regulations (and Code[19]) 1992;

c) Failed to repair the Defect;

d) Failed to prevent the Claimant coming into contact with the Defect (by way of signs, barriers, or other, effective, means of the Second Defendant's choosing).

(7) The First and Second Defendants created or permitted the existence of a nuisance on the Highway.

(8) As a result of the accident, the Claimant has suffered pain and injury, loss and damage. Please see the attached schedule of details of the claim for past and future expenses and losses.

Particulars of Injury

The Claimant (dob 1/1/70) suffered a Colles fracture, with symptoms persisting for 12 months. The Claimant relies on the report of [*expert*] dated [*date*].

(9) Interest is claimed on damages pursuant to section 69 of the County Courts Act 1984.

[NAME OF COUNSEL]

(10) I believe that the facts stated in these Particulars of Claim are true.

Signed ....

(Print name) ....

Dated..................................

Claimant's address for service:

[Claimant's address for service]

---

[19] The Specifications for the Reinstatement of Openings in Highways.

P47

HIGHWAYS – RAISED STOPCOCK – PARTICULARS OF CLAIM

IN THE [   ] COUNTY COURT   No [   ]

BETWEEN:

[   ]

Claimant

-and-

(1) [   ]

(2) [   ]

Defendants

PARTICULARS OF CLAIM

---

(1) The First Defendant is the highway authority responsible for the maintenance of Headley Street, Headingley, Leeds ('the Highway) pursuant to the Highways Act 1980.

(2) The Second Defendant is a company engaged in the business of providing water utilities/services.

(3) At approximately 7pm on 7/7/06, the Claimant was walking along the Highway when he tripped over a stopcock box ('the Box') that was proud of the surrounding pavement ("the Defect"), outside the Co-op Supermarket.

(4) The Defect is illustrated in the attached photograph.

(5) On 10/6/06, Mrs Wood, of 59 Headley Street, Headingley, complained to the First Defendant that the Defect was present.[20]

---

[20]   Arguably the complaint of Mrs Wood, putting the Highway on notice of the defect, need only be raised in response to a section 58 Defence. However, the existence of a complaint is evidence of the public's view of the state of highway and therefore the complaint goes towards the overall assessment of whether the highway could be considered 'dangerous' in the normal course of human affairs *Littler v Liverpool Corpn* [1968] 2 All ER 343.

(6) The Box was street furniture owned by the Second Defendant and situated within the Highway pursuant to the provisions of the New Roads and Street Works Act 1991.

(7) The accident was caused by the First Defendant's breach of statutory duty and the negligence of the Second Defendant, its servants or agents.

Particulars of Breach of Statutory Duty

FIRST DEFENDANT:

a)   Failed to maintain the Highway contrary to s 41 of the Highways Act 1980.

Particulars of Negligence

SECOND DEFENDANT:

b)   Installed the Box in such a way that the Defect arose;

c)   Failed to repair the Defect;

d)   Failed to prevent the Claimant coming into contact with the Defect (by way of signs, barriers, or other means of the Second Defendant's choosing).

(8) The First and Second Defendants created or permitted the existence of a nuisance on the Highway.

(9) As a result of the accident, the Claimant has suffered pain and injury, loss and damage. Please see the attached schedule of details of the claim for past and future expenses and losses.

Particulars of Injury

The Claimant (dob 1/1/70) suffered a Colles fracture, with symptoms persisting for 12 months. The Claimant relies on the report of [*expert*] dated [*date*].

(10)   Interest is claimed on damages pursuant to s 69 of the County Courts Act 1984.

[NAME OF COUNSEL]

(11)   I believe that the facts stated in these Particulars of Claim are true.

Signed ……………………………..

(Print name) ……………………….

Dated……………………………….

Claimant's address for service:

[Claimant's address for service]

P48

HIGHWAYS – UNGUARDED EXCAVATION– PARTICULARS OF CLAIM

IN THE [   ] COUNTY COURT   No [   ]

BETWEEN:

[   ]

Claimant

-and-

[   ]

Defendant

PARTICULARS OF CLAIM

---

(1) The Defendant is a company engaged in the business of laying telecommunications cables.

(2) At approximately 7pm on 7/7/06, the Claimant was walking along Headley Street, Headingley, Leeds ('the Highway'), when he fell into an unguarded excavation situated within the pavement outside the Co-op supermarket.

(3) The excavation had been created during works undertaken by the Defendant between 1/7/06 and 14/7/06, pursuant to the New Roads and Street Works Act 1991.

(4) The accident was caused by the negligence of the Defendant, its servants or agents.

Particulars of Negligence

a) Failed to ensure that the excavation was adequately guarded or lit and contrary to s 65 of the New Roads and Street Works Act 1991

b) Failed to have sufficient regard to the Safety at Street Works and Road Works Code of Practice, created under the New Roads and Street Works Act 1991.[21]

---

[21] The code of practice, which came into force on 1 February 2002, was issued by the Secretary of State for Transport, Local Government and the Regions under ss 65 and 124 of the New Roads and Street Works Act

(5) The Defendant created or permitted the existence of a nuisance on the highway.

(6) As a result of the accident, the Claimant has suffered pain, injury, loss and damage. Please see the attached details of the claim for past and future expense and losses.

Particulars of Injury

The Claimant (dob 1/1/70) suffered a concussive head injury, with symptoms persisting for 12 months. The Claimant relies on the report of [*expert*] dated [*date*].

(7) Interest is claimed on damages pursuant to section 69 of the County Courts Act 1984.

[NAME OF COUNSEL]

(8) I believe that the facts stated in these Particulars of Claim are true.

Signed …………………………..

(Print name) …………………….

Dated……………………………..

Claimant's address for service:

[Claimant's address for service]

1991. It sets in detail precautions to be taken when interfering with the Highway. Although failure to comply with these guidelines does not give rise to a cause of action, they provide a useful baseline against which to assess negligence.

Section 6

OCCUPIERS' LIABILITY

COMMENTARY

The Occupiers' Liability Acts[1] replace the:

> 'rules of the common law, to regulate the duty which an occupier of premises owes to his visitors in respect of dangers due to the state of the premises or to things done or omitted to be done on them'[2]

and

> 'to determine:
>
> (a)   whether any duty is owed by a person as occupier of premises to persons other than his visitors in respect of any risk of their suffering injury on the premises by reason of any danger due to the state of the premises or to things done or omitted to be done on them; and
>
> (b)   if so, what that duty is'.[3]

Where the Act creates a particular duty, it excludes the like duty in negligence, which should not normally be pleaded. If the defendant's status as occupier is in doubt, the duty should be pleaded both in negligence and pursuant to statute. A defendant may owe a duty both as occupier and in some other capacity. In such cases, both duties should be pleaded[4].

---

[1]   1957 and 1984.

[2]   Occupiers' Liability Act 1957, s 1.

[3]   Occupiers' Liability Act 1984, s 1.

[4]   Eg a claim by child against a school. See model pleading **P49** at p 150.

P49

SCHOOL – PARTICULARS OF CLAIM

IN THE [   ] COUNTY COURT   No [   ]

BETWEEN:

[   ]

Claimant

-and-

[   ]

Defendant

PARTICULARS OF CLAIM

---

(1) The Defendant was the occupier and the Claimant a visitor to Manor Way Infant School, Crewe, within the meaning of the Occupiers' Liability Act 1957.

(2) The Claimant was three years old at the time of the accident and attended the school as a pupil. The Defendant stood in loco parentis.

(3) At approximately 1.30pm on 1/4/06, the Claimant was playing, together with fellow pupils, in the school playground in the normal course of her school day. The play was conducted under the Defendant's supervision through its teacher Miss Jones, in full view of whom the play took place. The Claimant attempted to run through the plate-glass 'patio' door (which she believed to be open) connecting the classroom to the playground in order to use the toilet. As she did so, she collided with the glass (the door, in fact, being closed).

(4) The art-work which normally covered the glass had been removed.

(5) The glass measured approximately 0.77 x 1.87m. The door (as covered with art-work) is illustrated in the attached photographs.

(6) The accident was caused by the Defendant's negligence and/or breach of statutory duty and negligence.

Particulars of Breach of Statutory Duty

a) Removed the artwork but failed to mark the glass in an alternative fashion so as to make it readily apparent that the door was closed contrary to s 2 of the Occupiers' Liability Act 1957.

Particulars of Negligence

b) Allowing the Claimant to attempt to gain unsupervised access to the classroom from the playground.

(7) As a result of the accident, the Claimant has suffered pain and injury, loss and damage. Please see the attached schedule of details of the claim for past and future expenses and losses.

Particulars of Injury

The Claimant (dob 1/3/01) suffered a broken nose. The Claimant relies on the report of [*expert*] dated [*date*].

(8) Interest is claimed on damages pursuant to s 69 of the County Courts Act 1984.

[NAME OF COUNSEL]

(9) I believe that the facts stated in these Particulars of Claim are true.

Signed ……………………………..

(Print name) …………………….

Dated…………………………….

Claimant's address for service:

[Claimant's address for service]

P50

SLIP – PARTICULARS OF CLAIM

IN THE [   ] COUNTY COURT   No [   ]

BETWEEN:

[   ]

Claimant

-and-

[   ]

Defendant

PARTICULARS OF CLAIM

---

(1) The Defendant was the occupier of, and the Claimant a visitor to, the Defendant's supermarket at Bromsgrove, Worcestershire, within the meaning of the Occupiers' Liability Act 1957.

(2) At approximately 10.45am on the 1/4/06, the Claimant slipped on a piece of cucumber on the floor of the 'dairy aisle', causing her to fall.

(3) The accident was caused by the Defendant's breach of statutory duty.

Particulars of Breach of Statutory Duty

a) Allowed the Claimant to step on the cucumber contrary to s 2 of the Occupiers' Liability Act 1957. The Defendant was free to prevent the accident in a manner of its choosing. By way of example: the Defendant could have: operated a system of inspection, cleaning or the use of mats; or prevented access to the cucumber with barriers or cones[5].

(4) As a result of the accident, the Claimant has suffered pain and injury, loss and damage. Please see the attached schedule of details of the claim for past and future expenses and losses.

---

[5]   If an accident happens because the floor of a shop is covered with spillage, some explanation should be forthcoming from defendant to show that it did not arise through want of care on their part: *Ward v Tesco Stores Ltd* [1976] 1 WLR 810, CA.

Particulars of Injury

The Claimant (dob 1/3/35) suffered a fractured femur. The Claimant relies on the report of [*expert*] dated [*date*].

(5) Interest is claimed on damages pursuant to s 69 of the County Courts Act 1984.

[NAME OF COUNSEL]

(6) I believe that the facts stated in these Particulars of Claim are true.

Signed …………………………..

(Print name) ……………………….

Dated…………………………….

Claimant's address for service:

[Claimant's address for service]

P51

TRIP – PARTICULARS OF CLAIM

IN THE [   ] COUNTY COURT   No [   ]

BETWEEN:

[   ]

Claimant

-and-

[   ]

Defendant

PARTICULARS OF CLAIM

---

(1) The Defendant was the occupier and the Claimant a visitor to the footpath[6] ('the Footpath') adjacent to Kendrick Place, Scholes, Wigan, within the meaning of the Occupiers' Liability Act 1957.

(2) The Footpath was discontinuous, uneven and thereby defective around an inspection cover as illustrated in the attached photographs marked '1' and '2' ('the Defect').

(3) At approximately 6pm on 1/4/06, the Claimant was mounting the steps in the Footpath when her foot came into contact with the Defect causing her to lose her balance and fall.

(4) The Defect was poorly lit: the lighting column (H129), to the Claimant's rear, was not illuminated.

(5) The accident was caused by the Defendant's breach of statutory duty and the negligence of the Defendant, its servants or gents.

Particulars of Breach of Statutory Duty

Contrary to s 2 of the Occupiers' Liability Act:

   a)   Constructed the Footpath in such a way that the Defect was present at the time of construction and/or liable to develop over time;

---

6   The footpath in the example is occupied by the local authority, but is not part of a highway.

b) Failed to devise and implement any or any adequate system of inspection which would have identified the defect;

c) Failed to repair the Defect until after the accident;

d) Failed to ensure that the Defect was apparent to the Claimant. The Claimant does not contend for any one method over another: the Defendant was free to chose whatever method it wished, provided that it was effective. By way of example, the Defendant might have provided adequate lighting, barriers, cones, signs or markings on the footpath.

Particulars of Negligence

e) Constructed the Footpath in such a way that the Defect was present at the time of construction and/or liable to develop over time

(6) As a result of the accident, the Claimant has suffered pain and injury, loss and damage. Please see the attached schedule of details of the claim for past and future expenses and losses.

Particulars of Injury

The Claimant (dob 1/3/35) suffered a fractured femur. The Claimant relies on the report of [*expert*] dated [*date*].

(7) Interest is claimed on damages pursuant to s 69 of the County Courts Act 1984.

[NAME OF COUNSEL]

(8) I believe that the facts stated in these Particulars of Claim are true.

Signed …………………………..

(Print name) ……………………

Dated……………………………..

Claimant's address for service:

[Claimant's address for service]

Section 7

DEFECTIVE PREMISES

COMMENTARY

A landlord whose premises have defects that he is required to repair under the provisions of the lease is not liable for resulting injuries under the Occupiers Liability Acts, or at common law. They should not be pleaded. The duty is owed under s 4 of the Defective Premises Act 1972 in respect of such defects of which he knew or ought to have known.

P52

DEFECTIVE PREMISES – PARTICULARS OF CLAIM

IN THE [   ] COUNTY COURT   No [   ]

BETWEEN:

[   ]

Claimant

-and-

[   ]

Defendant

PARTICULARS OF CLAIM

---

(1) The Claimant's father was the tenant ('the Tenant') and the Defendant the landlord of premises at 160 Victoria Road, Alton, pursuant to a written agreement dated 1/4/03 ('the Agreement').

(2) Clause 4 of the Agreement imposed on the Defendant an obligation to the Tenant to repair and maintain the premises.

(3) On the 1/10/05, the Tenant reported to the Defendant that the stair carpet had come away from its fixings.

(4) On 1/4/06, the Claimant was visiting her father when she slipped on the stair carpet and fell.

(5) The accident was caused by the Defendant's breach of statutory duty.

Particulars of Breach of Statutory Duty

   a)   Failed to ensure that the Claimant was reasonably safe from personal injury contrary to s 4 of the Defective Premises Act 1972.[1]

(6) As a result of the accident, the Claimant has suffered pain and injury, loss and damage. Please see the attached schedule of details of the claim for past and future expenses and losses.

---

[1]   The landlord is not an occupier for the purposes of the Occupiers' Liability Act 1957 nor does he owe a duty at common law.

Particulars of Injury

The Claimant (dob 1/1/70) suffered a Colles fractured left femur. The Claimant is at a disadvantage on the open labour market. The Claimant relies on the report of [*expert*] dated [*date*].

(7) Interest is claimed on damages pursuant to s 69 of the County Courts Act 1984.

[NAME OF COUNSEL]

(8) I believe that the facts stated in these Particulars of Claim are true.

Signed …………………………..

(Print name) ……………………….

Dated……………………………….

Claimant's address for service:

[Claimant's address for service]

Section 8

CONSUMER PROTECTION AND PRODUCT LIABILITY

COMMENTARY

(1) The claimant may have a number of causes of action in relation to injury caused by defective products. If the claimant has entered into a contract to purchase/hire goods then there may be a claim for breach of express/implied term (see, for example the Sale of Goods Act 1979 and the Supply of Goods and Services Act 1982). There may be a claim for negligence. In any event, if the case falls within the Consumer Protection Act 1987 then this will provide an alternative cause of action.

(2) The Consumer Protection Act 1987 imposes strict liability on 'producers' of products which are defective regardless of any negligence/breach of statutory duty. 'Product' is construed very widely in this context. The product contains a defect where its safety is not such as persons generally are entitled to expect (Consumer Protection Act 1987 s 3). Section 2 of the Act sets out the wide range of potential defendants.

(3) As with all other cases, it will be necessary to prove causation (ie that the defect caused the injury in question).

P53

MANUFACTURER – PARTICULARS OF CLAIM

IN THE [   ] COUNTY COURT   No [   ]

BETWEEN:

[   ]

Claimant

-and-

[   ]

Defendant

PARTICULARS OF CLAIM

---

(1) On 7/6/06 the Claimant was riding a Jones 'C' bicycle, manufactured by the Defendant, when the front forks of the bicycle fractured, causing the Claimant to fall to ground.

(2) The Defendant was the producer of the bicycle within the meaning of the Consumer Protection Act 1987.

(3) This accident was caused by a defect in the bicycle within the meaning of s 3 of the Consumer Protection Act 1987, for which the Defendant is liable under s 2 of that Act.

Particulars of breach of statutory duty

The bicycle was defective contrary to s 3 of the Consumer Protection Act 1987 in that the front forks were liable to fracture after only a short period of use.

(4) The accident was caused by the negligence of the Defendant, its servants or agents.

Particulars of Negligence

a) Failed to exercise reasonable care in the design, manufacture, examination and testing of the bicycle (the front forks were liable to fracture after only a short period of use);

   i)   in light of previous similar failures;

      ii)   at all.

  b) Failed to warn the Claimant of the previous similar failures.

(5) As a result of the accident, the Claimant suffered pain, injury loss and damage. Please see the attached schedule of details of the claim for past and future expenses and losses.

Particulars of Injury

The Claimant (dob 7/1/82) sustained a fracture to the right wrist and soft tissue injuries. The Claimant relies on the report of [*expert*] dated [*date*].

(6) Interest is claimed on damages pursuant to s 69 of the County Courts Act 1984.

[NAME OF COUNSEL]

(7) I believe that the facts stated in these Particulars of Claim are true.

    Signed …………………………..

    (Print name) ……………………….

    Dated……………………………..

    Claimant's address for service:

    [Claimant's address for service]

P54

RETAILER – PARTICULARS OF CLAIM

IN THE [   ] COUNTY COURT   No [   ]

BETWEEN:

[   ]

Claimant

-and-

[   ]

Defendant

PARTICULARS OF CLAIM

---

(1) The Defendant was a retailer of garden equipment.

(2) On 7/6/06 the Claimant visited the Defendant's store at Winchester and purchased garden furniture, including a table and four chairs ('the Chairs').

(3) There were implied terms of the sale agreement between the Claimant and the Defendant that:

   i)   the chairs would be of satisfactory quality;

   ii) the chairs would be fit for the purpose for which they were intended and provided.

(4) On 8/6/06 the Claimant sat down upon one of the Chairs. As she did so, the chair collapsed (as a result of a defect in the Chair leg) causing the Claimant to fall to the floor.

(5) The accident was caused by the Defendant's breach of contract in that the Chair was not of satisfactory quality, nor was it fit for its purpose.

(6) As a result of the accident, the Claimant suffered pain, injury loss and damage. Please see the attached schedule of details of the claim for past and future expenses and losses.

Particulars of Injury

The Claimant (dob 24/1/72) sustained a soft tissue injury to the lower back. The Claimant relies on the report of [*expert*] dated [*date*].

(7) Interest is claimed on damages pursuant to s 69 of the County Courts Act 1984.

[NAME OF COUNSEL]

(8) I believe that the facts stated in these Particulars of Claim are true.

Signed …………………………..

(Print name) …………………….

Dated…………………………….

Claimant's address for service:

[Claimant's address for service]

P55

FAILURE TO IDENTIFY MANUFACTURER – PARTICULARS OF CLAIM

IN THE [   ] COUNTY COURT   No [   ]

BETWEEN:

[   ]

Claimant

-and-

[   ]

Defendant

PARTICULARS OF CLAIM

---

(1) The Defendant was a retail supplier of kitchen equipment, trading from premises at Diamond Street, Swansea.

(2) On 7/6/06 the Claimant's father purchased a fruit squeezer ('the Product') from the Defendant.

(3) On 9/6/06 the Claimant was using the Product when its handle broke and the Claimant sustained injury.

(4) The accident was caused by a defect in the Product within the meaning of s 3 of the Consumer Protection Act 1987.

Particulars

The Product was defective in that it was liable to break under normal use.

(5) The Defendant is liable for the injury sustained by the Claimant by reason of s 2(3) of the Consumer Protection Act 1987:

    a)   The Defendant was the supplier of the product;

    b)   On 7/7/06 the Claimant requested the Defendant to identify one or more of the persons to whom s 2(2) of the 1987 Act applied;

c) That request was made within a reasonable after the Claimant sustaining damage and at a time when it was not reasonably practicable for the Claimant to identify those persons;

d) The Defendant failed within a reasonable period after receiving the request to comply with it or to identify the person who supplied the product to him.

(6) As a result of the accident, the Claimant suffered pain, injury loss and damage. Please see the attached schedule of details of the claim for past and future expenses and losses.

Particulars of Injury

The Claimant (dob 7/1/88) sustained a laceration to her left arm, leaving permanent scarring. The Claimant relies on the report of [*expert*] dated [*date*].

(7) Interest is claimed on damages pursuant to s 69 of the County Courts Act 1984.

[NAME OF COUNSEL]

(8) I believe that the facts stated in these Particulars of Claim are true.

Signed …………………………..

(Print name) ……………………….

Dated……………………………….

Claimant's address for service:

[Claimant's address for service]

Section 9

FATAL ACCIDENTS

COMMENTARY

Claims involving a person's death can be broken down as follows.

The Deceased's Claim

Most causes of action[1] that the claimant could have pursued before death can be pursued by the estate after death. Where the death occurs at the time of the accident, the claimant will suffer no recoverable loss.[2] However, if the claimant dies later, there may be a claim for pain, suffering and loss of amenity prior to death and financial losses such as care, cost of treatment or lost earnings.

Funeral Expenses[3]

Funeral expense can be recovered if incurred by

    a)   The estate;[4]

    b)   The dependents.[5]

Claims by the Estate

These can be pursued by:

    a)   The personal representative;[6]

---

[1] Section 1 of the Law Reform (Miscellaneous Provisions) Act 1934. The section provides some exceptions that do not survive such as claims for bereavement or exemplary damages.

[2] Other than funeral expenses, any loss to the estate, which result from the death, cannot be recovered (eg loss of expected earnings after the date of death): Section 1(2)(c) of the Law Reform (Miscellaneous Provisions) Act 1934.

[3] This claim is a creation of statute: whilst the accident may have brought forward the funeral expenses, they would have been incurred in any event.

[4] Section 1(2)(c) of the Law Reform (Miscellaneous Provisions) Act 1934.

[5] Section 3(5) of the Fatal Accidents Act 1976.

b) If there is a claim under the Fatal Accidents Act (see below), by the claimant in that claim;[7]

c) If there is no personal representative, the court can appoint a representative or order the claim to proceed without one.[8]

The Deceased's Dependants

The dependants[9] can bring a claim[10] for loss of financial support or gratuitous services referred to as 'dependency'. All the dependants must be included: only one action can be brought.[11] The claim is pursued by:[12]

a) The personal representatives; or

b) If there is no personal representative, or no claim is brought by the personal representatives within six months of the death: by any or all of the dependants.

Bereavement[13]

The award is currently set at £10,000.[14] It is payable to:

a) The deceased's spouse; or

b) If the deceased was a minor who never marries, his parents (if he was 'legitimate') or his mother (if he was 'illegitimate').[15] Where the award is made to both parents, it is divided equally between them.[16]

Matters which must be Pleaded

a) That the claim is brought under the Fatal Accidents Act;[17]

---

[6] The executor/executrix of deceased's will or the administrator/administratrix following letters of administration in the event that the deceased died intestate.

[7] CPR 16 PD 5.3.

[8] CPR 19.8. This provision appears to exclude any claim by the estate for funeral expenses.

[9] As defined by s 3 of the Fatal Accidents Act 1976, as substituted by the Administration of Justice Act 1982.

[10] Section 1 of the Fatal Accidents Act 1976.

[11] Section 2(3) of the Fatal Accidents Act 1976.

[12] Section 2(1), (2) of the Fatal Accidents Act 1976.

[13] Section 1A of the Fatal Accidents Act 1976.

[14] Fatal Accident Act 1976, as amended by the Administration of Justice Act 1982, further amended by SI 2002/644.

[15] Section 1A(2)(b)(ii) of the Fatal Accidents Act 1976.

[16] Section 1A(4) of the Fatal Accidents Act 1976.

b)   The dependants on whose behalf the claim is made;[18]

c)   The date of birth of each dependent;[19]

d)   Details of the nature of the dependency claim.[20]

---

[17]   16PD5.1.

[18]   Ibid.

[19]   Ibid.

[20]   Ibid. The practice direction does not specify the extent of the detail required. Section 2(4) of the Fatal Accidents Act 1976 requires 'full particulars' to be delivered.

P56

ADULT MALE – PARTICULARS OF CLAIM

IN THE [   ] COUNTY COURT   No [   ]

BETWEEN:

[   ]

(Widow[21] and administratrix[22] of the estate
JOHN SMITH deceased)

Claimant

-and-

[   ]

Defendant

PARTICULARS OF CLAIM

---

(1) The Claimant is the widow and administratrix of the estate of John Smith ('the Deceased')

(2) At approximately 10am on 1/7/06, the Deceased was walking south along Headley Street, Headingley, Leeds. The Defendant was driving a Ford Capri, registered

(3) At a point outside the Co-Op supermarket, the Deceased turned across the carriageway, towards the Flying Horse Public House.

---

[21] Claims involving death normally have constituent parts: the claim of the estate (see below) and the claim brought by the dependants under the Fatal Accidents Act 1976. In this example the Claimant is the widow of the deceased and a dependant as well the administratrix (or representative) of the estate. Usually the claim is brought in the name of the executor or administrator of the estate (as in this case) but if there is no personal representative or a claim is not brought within six months of the death, then the claim may be brought on behalf of all or any of the Dependants.

[22] Claims brought on behalf of a deceased's estate are normally pursued by the appropriate representative, appointed by grant of probate – executor – (if a will exists) or Letters of Administration – administrator – (if intestate). Alternatively an application may be made for person to represent the estate of the deceased or for the claim to proceed in the absence of such a person (CPR 19.8).

(4) As the Deceased stepped from the central reservation into the northbound carriageway, he was hit from his left by the Defendant's vehicle.

(5) The collision was caused by the negligence of the Defendant.

Particulars of Negligence

a) failed to see the Deceased, in time or at all;

b) drove too fast;

c) failed to slow down or brake;

d) collided with the Deceased;

e) failed to sound his horn.

(6) As a result of the accident, the Deceased suffered pain, injury, loss and damage. Please see the attached details of the claim for past expense and losses.[23]

Particulars of Injury

The Deceased (dob 1/1/60) suffered multiple internal injuries. He remained conscious and in distress until his death on 2 July 2006.[24] The Claimant relies on the report of [*expert*] dated [*date*].

(7) The Claim is brought under the Fatal Accidents Act 1976 and the Law Reform (Miscellaneous Provisions) Act 1934.

(8)

a) The Deceased's dependants are:[25]

Joanne Smith (widow) dob 1/2/60

Jeremy Smith (son) dob 1/1/94

Jane Smith (daughter) dob 1/2/95.

b) The Deceased was 44 years of age at the date of his death. He was employed as bus driver and in good health. He would have continued to support his wife throughout his life and his children would remain financially dependent through further education and until they had secured stable employment.

---

[23] These are the details of any costs incurred by the deceased during the two days prior to death. These may include medical expenses, lost income, loss or damage to personal items, care and attention etc.

[24] In this example, the deceased was not killed instantly. Prior to death, he suffered pain and injury for a period of two days. His claim for general damages survives his death for the benefit of his estate (Law Reform (Miscellaneous Provisions) Act 1934) and therefore should be included.

[25] A list of the dependants and their dates of birth must be specifically pleaded (CPR Part 16 PD 5.1). Only one action may be brought on their behalf and they must all be included in the single action.

    c) The Deceased had a normal life expectancy and would have retired at age 65 with a pension. The Claimant was in receipt of a state pension.

(9) Damages are claimed for bereavement.

(10)   Interest is claimed on damages pursuant to s 69 of the County Courts Act 1984.

[NAME OF COUNSEL]

(11)   I believe that the facts stated in these Particulars of Claim are true.

    Signed …………………………..

    (Print name) …………………….

    Dated……………………………..

    Claimant's address for service:

    [Claimant's address for service]

P57

CHILD – PARTICULARS OF CLAIM

IN THE [   ] COUNTY COURT   No [   ]

BETWEEN:

[   ]

(Mother and administratrix of the estate of
JEREMY SMITH deceased)

Claimant

-and-

[   ]

Defendant

PARTICULARS OF CLAIM

---

(1) The Claimant is the mother and administratrix of the estate of Jeremy Smith ("the Deceased")

(2) At approximately 10.00am on 1/7/06, 'the Deceased was walking south with a group of friends, along Headley Street, Headingley, Leeds. The Defendant was driving a Ford Capri, registered number W535 KEV.

(3) At a point outside the Co-Op supermarket, three of the Deceased's friends ran across the road towards the Flying Horse Public House.

(4) The Deceased followed his friends as far as the central reservation, where he paused for a few seconds before running into the northbound carriageway. As he did so, he was struck by the Defendant's vehicle from his left.

(5) The collision was caused by the negligence of the Defendant.

Particulars of Negligence

a) Failed to see the Deceased's friends running across the road, in time or at all;

b) Failed to see the Deceased at the central reservation, in time or at all;

c) Drove too fast;

d) Failed to slow down or brake;

e) Collided with the Deceased;

f) Failed to sound his horn.

(6) As a result of the accident, the Deceased suffered pain, injury, loss and damage. Please see the attached details of the claim for past expense and losses.[26]

Particulars of Injury

The Deceased (dob 1/1/89) suffered multiple internal injuries. He remained conscious and in distress until his death two days later.[27] The Claimant relies on the report of [*expert*] dated [*date*].

(7) The Claim is brought under the Fatal Accidents Act 1976 and the Law Reform (Miscellaneous Provisions) Act 1934.

(8)

a) The Deceased's dependant is:[28]

  Joanne Smith (mother) dob 1/2/49;

b) The Deceased was 17 years of age at the date of his death. He was part way through his A-level studies and had secured a place at Hull University on the accountancy course;

c) The Claimant is 55 years of age. She (and her husband – deceased) made significant sacrifices for the Deceased's education. The Claimant, who is currently employed as ticket inspector with British Rail, will retire at 60 years of age, at which date the Deceased would have commenced employment as an accountant, from which he would have derived a significant income in the future;

d) In recognition of the sacrifices made by the Claimant, financial support would have been provided by the Deceased following his mother's retirement.

(9) Damages are claimed for bereavement.[29]

(10)   Interest is claimed on damages pursuant to section 69 of the County Courts Act 1984.

---

[26]   These are the costs incurred by the deceased during the two days prior to death. These may include medical expenses, lost income, loss or damage to personal items, care and attention etc.

[27]   In this claim the deceased was not killed instantly. Prior to death, he suffered pain and injury for a period of two days. His claim for general damages survives his death for the benefit of his estate (Law Reform (Miscellaneous Provisions) Act 1934 and therefore should be included.

[28]   A list of the dependants and their dates of birth must be specifically pleaded (CPR Part 16 PD 5.1). This is because only one action may be brought on their behalf and they must all be included in the single action.

[29]   A mother and father (if legitimate) will have a claim for bereavement only when the child is a minor.

[NAME OF COUNSEL]

(11)   I believe that the facts stated in these Particulars of Claim are true.

Signed …………………………..

(Print name) ……………………

Dated……………………………

Claimant's address for service:

[Claimant's address for service]

P58

MOTHER'S SERVICES – PARTICULARS OF CLAIM

IN THE [   ] COUNTY COURT   No [   ]

BETWEEN:

[   ]

(Widower[30] and administrator[31] of the estate
JOANNE SMITH deceased)

Claimant

-and-

[   ]

Defendant

PARTICULARS OF CLAIM

---

(1) The Claimant is the widower and administrator of the estate of Joanne Smith ('the Deceased').

(2) The Deceased was the driver of a Ford Anglia, registered number X535 WFE. The Defendant was the driver of a Ford Granada, registered number, W535 PRT.

---

[30] Claims involving death normally have constituent parts: the claim of the estate (see below) and the claim brought by the dependants under the Fatal Accidents Act 1976. In this case Joanne Brown, as the widow of the deceased, is one of his dependants as well the administratrix (or representative) of the estate. Usually the claim is brought in the name of the executor or administrator of the estate (as in this case) but if there is no personal representative or a claim is not brought within six months of the death, then the claim may be brought on behalf of all or any of the Dependants.

[31] Claims brought on behalf of a deceased's estate are normally pursued by the appropriate representative, appointed by grant of probate – executor – (if a will exists) or Letters of Administration – administrator – (if intestate). Alternatively an application may be made for person to represent the estate of the deceased or for the claim to proceed in the absence of such a person (CPR 19.8).

(3) At approximately 10am on 1/7/06, the Deceased was driving south along Headley Street, Headingley, Leeds, when her vehicle was hit head-on by the Defendant's vehicle.

(4) The collision was caused by the negligence of the Defendant.

Particulars of Negligence

a) overtook on a 'blind' bend;

b) drove too fast;

c) drove into collision with the Deceased's vehicle.

(5) The Defendant was convicted of causing death by dangerous driving at the Leeds Crown Court on 10/9/06. The conviction arose out of those matters set out above and is relevant to the Defendant's negligence.[32]

(6) Further, the Claimant will rely upon the circumstances of this accident as evidence of the Defendant's negligence. In particular, the Defendant is required to prove that the presence of his vehicle in the southbound carriageway of Headley Street was not caused by his negligence.

(7) As a result of the accident, the Deceased suffered pain, injury, loss and damage. Please see the attached details of the claim for past expense and losses.[33]

Particulars of Injury

The Deceased (dob 1/1/60) suffered a multiple internal injuries. She remained conscious and in distress until her death two days later. The Claimant relies on the report of [*expert*] dated [*date*].

(8) The Claim is brought under the Fatal Accidents Act 1976 and the Law Reform (Miscellaneous Provisions) Act 1934.

(9)

a) The Deceased's dependants are:[34]

John Smith (widower) dob 1/2/60

Jeremy Smith (son) dob 1/1/94

---

[32] Convictions are admissible as evidence in civil proceedings (see Civil Evidence Act 1968 s 11). Although the existence of a conviction based upon those facts giving rise to the claim is not determinative of the issue of guilt, the legal burden of proof shifts to the Defendant to disprove those matters which constitute the offence. Such attempts are extremely rare and in practical terms the existence of a relevant conviction will lead to an admission of negligence. Reliance upon or denial of a conviction must be pleaded (Civil Procedure Rules Part 16 PD 8.1(1)).

[33] What is envisaged is the any costs incurred by the deceased during the two days prior to death. These may include medical expenses, lost income, loss or damage to personal items, care and attention etc

[34] A list of the dependants and their dates of birth must be specifically pleaded (CPR Part 16 PD 5.1). Only one action may be brought on their behalf and they must all be included in the single action.

        Jane Smith (daughter) dob 1/2/95.

b) The deceased was 44 years of age at the date of her death. She was a full-time mother. At the date of her death, Jeremy and Jane were 10 and 9 years of age respectively.

c) The dependants have lost the deceased services as a wife and mother, who was dedicated to the management of the home.

d) The Deceased had a normal life expectancy and would have received a state pension in retirement.

(10)   Damages are claimed for bereavement.

(11)   Interest is claimed on damages pursuant to s 69 of the County Courts Act 1984.

[NAME OF COUNSEL]

(12)   I believe that the facts stated in these Particulars of Claim are true.

        Signed ……………………………..

        (Print name) ……………………….

        Dated…………………………….

        Claimant's address for service:

        [Claimant's address for service]

Section 10

MISCELLANEOUS

P59

PART 18 REQUEST

Below is a typical Defence that might be received in response to the Manual Handling Particulars of Claim (see model pleading **P1** at p 27) followed by a model Part 18 Request.

IN THE [   ] COUNTY COURT   No [   ]

BETWEEN:

[   ]

Claimant

-and-

[   ]

Defendant

DEFENCE

---

(1) The Claimant was employed by the Defendant company on the pleaded date. The circumstances and happening of the accident are not admitted. The accident was first notified in the letter of claim of 1/6/06.

(2) It is denied that the Defendant was negligent or in breach of statutory duty as alleged or at all.

(3) The Defendant could not reasonably have avoided the Manual Handling Operation.

(4) The accident was caused by the Defendant's own negligence.

Particulars of Negligence and Breach of Statutory Duty

a) Doing that which he now complains of as dangerous;

b) Failing to heed his training and instruction;

c) Failing to take reasonable care for his own safety.

(5) The Defendant neither agrees nor disputes but has no knowledge of the matters contained in the Claimant's medical report or schedule.

(6) The Defendant believes that the facts stated in this Defence are true.

Signed ....

Andrew Brown, partner in the firm of Endeavour & Co.

Dated 1/10/04

IN THE [   ] COUNTY COURT   No [   ]

BETWEEN:

[   ]

Claimant

-and-

[   ]

Defendant

CLAIMANT'S PART 18 REQUEST TO THE DEFENDANT

Please look at paragraph 2 of the Particulars of Claim

(1)

    a) Does the Defendant admit, deny or not admit that the Manual Handling Regulations Applied?

    b) If denied, please set out all facts and matter relied on in support of that denial.

Please look at paragraph 2 of the Defence and paragraph 3(a) of the Particulars of Claim[1].

(2) Please set out all facts and matters relied on in support of the denial.

Please look at paragraph 3 of the Defence.

(3)

    a) What is said to be the relevance of this allegation?

    b) Does the Defendant intent to allege that it was not reasonably practicable to avoid the need for the Claimant to undertake the manual Handling Operation?

    c) If so, please set out all facts and matter relied on in support of that denial.

---

[1]   See model pleading **P1** at p 27.

Please look at paragraph 2 of the Defence and paragraph 3(b) of the Particulars of Claim.

(4)

    a) Does the Defendant intend to advance any positive case in relation to reg 4(1)(ii)(b)?

    b) If so, please provide full particulars of that case, including all facts and matters relied on in support.

Please look at paragraph 2 of the Defence and paragraph 3(c) of the Particulars of Claim.

(5)

    a) Does the Defendant admit, deny or not admit that the Manual Handling Operation was liable to cause injury?

    b) If denied, please set out all facts and matters relied on in support of that denial.

Please look at paragraph 4(a) of the Defence.

(6)

    a) Is it the Defendant's case that the Claimant:

        i)   knew;

        ii)   ought to have known;

        that the Manual Handling Operation was liable to cause injury?

    b) If the answer to 6(a)(ii) is in the affirmative, please set out al facts and matters in support.

Please look at paragraph 4(b) of the Defence.

(7)

    a) In respect of each item of training and instructing relied on, please state:

        i)   the date, time and place at which it was delivered;

        ii)   by whom it was delivered;

        iii)   the gist of the words used;
        and disclose any relevant documents.

    b) What is it said the Claimant did, that he ought not to have done or did not do that he ought to have done, so as to have 'heeded' his training and instruction.

Please look at paragraph 4(c) of the Defence;

(8)

    a)   Is this allegation intended to add, materially, to the allegations at paragraphs 4 a) and b) of the Defence?

    b)   If so, what is it said the Claimant did, that he ought not to have done or did not do that he ought to have done, so as to have 'taken reasonable care for his own safety'.

The Claimant expects a response by [*date*][2]

---

[2]   The court is likely to consider around three weeks as a reasonable period for responding to a straightforward request such as this.

P60

ANIMALS – PARTICULARS OF CLAIM

IN THE [   ] COUNTY COURT   No [   ]

BETWEEN:

[   ]

Claimant

-and-

[   ]

Defendant

PARTICULARS OF CLAIM

---

(1) The Defendant is the landlady of the White Horse Public House, Old Chester Road, Holmes Chapel ('the Pub').

(2) On 1/4/06, the Claimant was walking along the footpath adjacent to the car park of the Pub, when the Defendant released her German Shepherd dog into the car park. The dog attacked the Claimant: biting him to the buttocks and the arms.

(3) The Defendant is liable for the damage pursuant to the Animals Act 1971 on the grounds that:

    a) The damage was of a kind which the animal, unless restrained was likely to cause or, which, if caused, was likely to be severe;

    b) The likelihood of the damage, or of it being severe was due to characteristics of the animal which are not normally found in dogs or are not normally found except at particular times or in particular circumstances;

    c) Those characteristics were known to the Defendant.

(4) Alternatively, the incident was caused by the Defendant's negligence.

Particulars of Negligence

    a) Released the dog into the car park, unaccompanied and unrestrained, when the Claimant was in the vicinity.

Dogs are, inherently, territorial animals that present an inevitable risk of injury by biting. The magnitude of the risk increases (as in this instance):

i)   when a stranger is present on the dog's territory;

ii)   when the dog is not accompanied by its mistress (because the mistress cannot intervene and because the dog is more likely to take responsibility, itself, for protecting the territory);

iii)   with the size of the dog (there being less chance of taking avoiding action and any bite is liable to be larger and more forceful);

iv)   when the dog is of a breed, such as a German Shepherd, which has been bred to retain its inherent territorialism.

(5) As a result of the accident, the Claimant has suffered pain and injury, loss and damage. Please see the attached schedule of details of the claim for past and future expenses and losses.

Particulars of Injury

The Claimant (dob 1/1/70) suffered bites to his arms and buttocks. The Claimant relies on the report of [*expert*] dated [*date*].

(6) Interest is claimed on damages pursuant to s 69 of the County Courts Act 1984.

[NAME OF COUNSEL]

(7) I believe that the facts stated in these Particulars of Claim are true.

Signed …………………………..

(Print name) …………………….

Dated……………………………

Claimant's address for service:

[Claimant's address for service]

P61

LIABILITY ADMITTED PRE-ACTION – PARTICULARS OF CLAIM

IN THE [   ] COUNTY COURT   No [   ]

BETWEEN:

[   ].

Claimant

-and-

[   ].

Defendant

PARTICULARS OF CLAIM

---

(1) On 1/4/06, in the course of his employment with the Defendant, the Claimant's hand was trapped in a printing press.

(2) The Defendant has conceded liability.[3]

(3) As a result of the accident, the Claimant has suffered pain and injury, loss and damage. Please see the attached schedule of details of the claim for past and future expenses and losses.

---

[3]   Replace with 'primary liability', 'liability subject to causation' etc as appropriate.

   Where the Defendant has admitted liability either in full, or subject to contributory negligence, the Claimant should:

a)   rely on that admission in his particulars;

b)   plead the circumstances in sufficient detail to allow the incident to be identified and the reader to create a simple mental picture of the incident;

c)   not plead any particulars of negligence of breach of statutory duty.

   Pleading detailed circumstances or particulars of breach allows the Defendant to rely on the Claimant's own case when contending for contributory negligence or seeking permission to resile for its admission.

   Where the admission is subject to causation, also set out those details of the mechanism of the accident that may be relevant to causation.

Particulars of Injury

The Claimant (dob 1/1/70) suffered fractures to the 1st, 2nd and 3rd fingers of the dominant right hand. The Claimant is at a disadvantage on the open labour market. The Claimant relies on the report of [*expert*] dated [*date*].

(4) Interest is claimed on damages pursuant to s 69 of the County Courts Act 1984.

[NAME OF COUNSEL]

(5) I believe that the facts stated in these Particulars of Claim are true.

Signed …………………………..

(Print name) ………………………

Dated…………………………….

P62

LIABILITY ADMITTED PRE-ACTION – REPLY

Below is a defence that might typically be received where primary liability is admitted

IN THE [   ] COUNTY COURT   No [   ]

BETWEEN:

[   ]

Claimant

-and-

[   ]

Defendant

DEFENCE

---

(1) Paragraph 1 of the Particulars of claim is admitted.

(2) For the purposes of this claim, it is admitted that the accident was caused by the Defendant's breach.

(3) Approximately 1 week prior to the accident, the Claimant had reported that the power supply switch had ceased to operate. The Defendant disconnected the switch and replaced it with a new switch, located at the rear of the work equipment.

(4) The accident was contributed to by the Claimant's own negligence.

Particulars of negligence

a) Placed his hands into the work equipment, without having first turned off the power supply.

[NAME OF COUNSEL]

(5) I believe that the facts stated in this Defence are true.

Signed …………………………..

(Print name) ……………………….

(Position held)…………………..

Dated…………………………….

IN THE [   ] COUNTY COURT   No [   ]

BETWEEN:

[   ]

Claimant

-and-

[   ]

Defendant

REPLY

---

(1) A sheet of paper became stuck to the lower plate on press number 5 ('the Work Equipment'). The Claimant turned the power supply switch ('the Switch') to the 'off position', causing the press to come to a stop. The Claimant reached into the Work Equipment to remove the paper. As he did so, the Work Equipment began to operate causing the plates to close, trapping the Claimant's hand.

(2) It is denied that:[4]

    a)   The Claimant was aware that:

        i)   the Switch had ceased to operate;

        ii)   the Defendant had installed a replacement power supply switch ('the New Switch'), which was located at the rear of the Work Equipment.

    b)   The Claimant was negligent as alleged or at all.

(3) The Provision and Use of Work Equipment Regulations 1998 ('the Work Equipment Regulations') applied.

---

[4]   The Defendant is required to prove matters raised in the Defence but not dealt with the Reply: CPR 16.7(2) However, the Claimant should plead those matters on which he intends to advance a positive case.

(4) The accident was caused by the Defendant's breach of statutory duty and the negligence of the Defendant, its servants or agents.

Particulars of Breach of Statutory Duty

a) Failed to maintain the Work Equipment in an efficient state, in efficient working order and in good repair, contrary to reg 5 of the Work Equipment Regulations;

b) The Work Equipment was not suitable, contrary to reg 4 of the Work Equipment Regulations;

c) Failed to prevent access to the plates or stop the movement of the plates before the Claimant entered the danger zone, contrary to reg 11(1) of the Work Equipment Regulations;

d) The Claimant did not have available to him any or any adequate information or written instructions or training to the effect that the Switch had ceased to operate, had been replaced with the the New Switch and that the New Switch must be turned to 'off' before reaching in to the Work Equipment, contrary to regs 8 and 9 of the Work Equipment Regulations;

Particulars of Negligence

e) Negligently: failed to provide the Claimant with safe equipment and a safe place and system of work. The Work Equipment was liable to cause trapping injuries.

[NAME OF COUNSEL]

(5) I believe that the facts stated in this Reply are true.

Signed …………………………..

(Print name) …………………….

Dated……………………………..

Part II

APPLICATIONS

A1

THE INSOLVENT CORPORATE DEFENDANT

COMMENTARY

Discovering, when you come to issue proceedings for damages for personal injuries, that the Defendant company is dissolved and there are three weeks left until limitation, is one of the worst nightmares that can befall a Claimant personal injury lawyer. That is exactly what happened in *Re: Workvale Limited (No 2).*[1] Proceedings were issued 24 days before the end of the limitation period but the Claimants had not noticed that the company had been dissolved some 7 weeks earlier. An application to strike out the claim inevitably succeeded as the Defendant company had no legal status at the time the proceedings were issued.

Should you find that proceedings you have issued are a nullity, whether because the company was dissolved, in compulsory liquidation or in Administration at the time that they were issued, then the best course would be to discontinue these and make the appropriate application to remedy the problems caused by the Defendant's status. Then you should issue a second set of proceedings seeking Section 33 Limitation Act discretion should that second set of proceedings happen to be 'out of time'. You may rely heavily on the arguments advanced in *Clay v Chamberlain*[2] to show that the second set of proceedings are not an abuse of process.

It is far better, however, to regularise the position before issuing the first set of proceedings. Any pre-action application, eg pre-action disclosure, would be proceedings for this purpose.

The mere mention of the Insolvency Act 1986 or the Companies Act 1985 can make the most experienced personal injury lawyer glaze over. However, while the rules and the applications differ markedly between the different 'states' that a company can get into, the rules are capable of being stated clearly.

---

[1]   [1992] 2 All ER 627, [1992] 1 WLR 416.

[2]   [2002] EWHC 2529.

Liquidation

A company can go into three different types of liquidation

(1) Compulsory liquidation under Order of the Court.

(2) Members' voluntary liquidation.

(3) Creditors' voluntary liquidation.

If a company is in compulsory liquidation then you will need permission to sue it, or to continue proceedings against it, because of the automatic stay imposed by Section 130 Insolvency Act. If your proceedings against the company are already started and it then goes into compulsory liquidation you will need permission for the proceedings to continue. If you do not get permission (to issue or to continue as appropriate) then the proceedings are a nullity.[3] Note that you cannot apply for permission retrospectively.[4] There should be no problem getting permission provided that the Defendant company was insured but note that the limitation period still runs.

If the company is in voluntary liquidation, either a Creditors' or Members' voluntary liquidation, then no permission to sue is required but both the Liquidator and the Registered Office (if different) should be served.

Be sure, however, to maintain a close watch on the company's future status.

Administrative Receivership

If a company is in Administrative Receivership this means that the Administrative Receiver will usually have been appointed by a Bank, or other holder of floating charge, under that charge. There is no stay so proceedings can be issued, served and continued without difficulty. Both the Administrative Receiver and the Registered Office (if different) should be served.

Maintain a close watch on the company's future status.

Administration

It used to be that if the company was in Administration, then this Administration was under Order of the Court. Accordingly, from the date that the petition for Administration was presented the automatic stay of proceedings against the company took effect. You therefore needed the permission of the Court to sue.

---

[3] *Tandberg v Strand Wood Co* (unreported) April 1905.

[4] See *Re National Employers Mutual General Insurance Association Ltd (in liquidation)* [1995] 1 BCLC 233, [1995] BCC 632.

The whole system of Administration was changed on 16 September 2003 by the Enterprise Act 2002. A new section 8[5] and Schedule B1[6] were introduced to the Insolvency Act, to which the reader is directed for full details of the new system.

It is sufficient for our purposes, however, to note that an Administrator may now be appointed by Order of the Court, by the holder of a floating charge or even by the company itself. The Administrator is still an officer of the court, however, no matter who appoints him. Thus, the automatic stay preventing issue or continuance of proceedings against a company in Administration remains.[7]

Accordingly permission is still needed to issue or to continue proceedings against a company in Administration.

Now, however, the Administrator can provide that permission (by simple letter upon your request outlining the position fully) or if that is not forthcoming, or if the Administrator refuses, an application to the Court should be made for permission to sue (paragraph 43(6) Schedule B1 Insolvency Act 1986). If proceedings were validly issued before the Administration, then either the permission of the Administrator or of the Court is required to continue the action.

Note that in all the scenarios so far the company itself continues to exist, ie has not been dissolved or struck off.

Dissolution or Striking Off

The effect of a dissolution or striking off is that the company ceases to exist and may not therefore be sued.[8]

There is a difference between dissolution and striking off.

Dissolution can occur in two ways.

(1) Following a compulsory liquidation the company is automatically dissolved three months after the liquidator has filed his final returns with the Registrar of Companies.

(2) Following a voluntary liquidation (either Creditors' or Members') when the liquidator subsequently files his returns, the company is dissolved three months after those returns.

Striking off, on the other hand, is used by the Registrar of Companies to deal with defunct companies. There is no liquidation as such. The company ceases trading,

---

[5]   Enterprise Act 2002, s248(1).

[6]   Ibid, Sch 16.

[7]   Insolvency Act 1986, Sch B1, para 43(6) (as amended).

[8]   See, for example, *Re: Workvale Ltd* (above).

ceases filing returns and is struck off by the Registrar under s 652 of the Companies Act 1985 (normal diarying process) or upon the company's application under s 652A of the Companies Act. Such striking off of defunct companies does not follow liquidation.

The application you should make differs between these three situations. There are two sections of the Companies Act which are relevant, namely s 651 and s 653.

(1) Company dissolved following compulsory liquidation – s 651applies.

(2) Company dissolved following voluntary liquidation – s 651 applies.

(3) Company struck off (no liquidation involved) – s 653 applies.

The Section 651 Jurisdiction

An application under s 651 is for an Order declaring the dissolution of the company void. The effect of the Order is to void the dissolution *ab initio*. One effect of this is that the limitation period for the personal injury action is not suspended, unless the Court declares otherwise under s 651(6).[9]

Note that, by s 651(5), if the purpose of the application is to bring a claim for personal injuries or fatality against the company then the application may be made at any time but will not be granted if the Court concludes that the personal injury action is statute barred. The Part 8 Claim Form and supporting evidence should be served on the Treasury Solicitor, Bona Vacantia Division, Queen Anne's Chambers, 28 Broadway, London SW1H 9JS and upon the Registrar of Companies at Registration Office, Crown Way, Maindy, Cardiff CF4 3UZ and on the company itself. The company itself should be named as Defendants.

Whilst a Section 651 application to declare the dissolution of a company void may, as a matter of practice, be accompanied by a Section 653 application to restore the company to the register, if a company has been dissolved following winding up (whether compulsory or voluntary) there is, strictly, no jurisdiction to order restoration of the company to the register under s 653, as opposed to declaring the dissolution void under s 651 as was the case in *Re: M Belmont & Co Ltd*.[10]

As will be seen, the Section 653 jurisdiction can only work if less than 20 years has elapsed since striking off, so that if more than that time has elapsed, the Claimant's only chance to try to pursue the matter is to take his chances that *Re: M Belmont &*

---

[9]   A practice had developed of obtaining a Direction under s 651(6) that the period between the dissolution and the making of the voiding Order should be excluded in calculating the limitation period. Since this effectively decides s33 Limitation Act 1980 issues in the absence of the Defendant, such Directions will normally not now be made: see *Smith v White Knight Laundry Ltd* [2001] EWCA Civ 660, [2002] 1 WLR 616.

[10]   [1952] Ch 10, [1951] 2 All ER 898.

Co. Ltd is overlooked by Insurers and their personal injury solicitors, and apply under s 651 anyway.

The Section 653 Jurisdiction

If the company has been struck off (as opposed to dissolved) then the appropriate application is to restore the name of the company to the register under s 653 of the Companies Act.

This Order cannot be made if a company has been dissolved following winding up.[11] The effect of an Order restoring the name of a company is to put all parties concerned in the same position as if the company had never been struck off.[12] Accordingly the limitation period for the personal injury claim always continues to run.[13]

Despite the 'company law phrasing' of s 653 your injured victim as a contingent or prospective creditor has sufficient standing to make the Section 653 application. Contingent or prospective creditors may do so.[14]

Any application under s 653 must be made within 20 years of the publication in the London Gazette of the notice by the Registrar of Companies of his intention to strike off the company. If more than 20 years has elapsed therefore the s 651 route (voiding the dissolution) is all that can be tried, with debateable effectiveness, instead of the s 653 route (restoring to the Register).

A Part 8 Claim Form under s 653 should name the company as Defendant and again must be served on the Registrar of Companies and the Treasury Solicitor.

In both cases the Treasury Solicitor will want his costs paying and there may well be a further charge made by him for the 'bona vacantia' letter.[15] With the Court fee to pay as well it can be seen that these are expensive processes. An Order should therefore be sought that the costs of the Part 8 application be costs in the pending personal injury action. Depending upon the nominal capital of the insolvent company the County Court may have jurisdiction to make these Orders but the safest course is to apply to the District Judge in the Chancery Division of the High

---

[11] Ibid.

[12] Section 653(3).

[13] A similar practice had developed to exclude for limitation purposes the period during which the company was struck off by seeking a Direction under s653(3). It is likely however that this will no longer work bearing in mind the *White Knight Laundry*(supra) and *Re: Advance Insulation Ltd* (1989) 5 BCC 557.

[14] *Re: Harvest Lane Motor Bodies Ltd* [1969] 1 Ch 457, [1968] 3 WLR 220.

[15] A letter in standard terms confirming that the Crown has no call upon the assets of the company and that the Crown has no objection to making of the Order.

Court (or if in London to the Companies Court) by way of Part 8 Claim Form supported by appropriate evidence and a draft Order.

The Court will require evidence of service upon the Treasury Solicitor (Form N215) to which the 'bona vacantia' letter should be attached. You will be obliged to undertake to inform the Registrar of Companies of the title and action number of your personal injury proceedings, when issued, and to undertake to inform the Registrar immediately of the conclusion of those proceedings.

A sealed copy of any Order under s 651 or s 653 must be sent to the Registrar of Companies.

Other Possible Consequences

If you are taking proceedings against a company in liquidation (whether voluntary or, with permission, compulsory liquidation) you should notify the Registrar of Companies and seek to postpone the dissolution process. This should be done by outlining to the Secretary of State for Trade & Industry the personal injury victim's interest in the matter and ask that pursuant to s 205(3) of the Insolvency Act the Secretary of State give a direction deferring the date on which the dissolution of the company (or striking off) is to take effect. On receipt of that direction a copy must be sent by you to the Registrar of Companies. If necessary there is an appeal to the Court from the Secretary of State's decision (to be brought within 28 days) but that is outside the terms of this book.

It is not possible to circumvent any of the rules outlined above by agreement with insurers or their solicitors because, in the light of these rules, those persons have no locus standi to act.

Note also that if later you wish to bring action against insurers under the Third Party (Rights Against Insurers) Act 1930, the amount of your clients judgment (damages and costs) must first have been crystallised so it is necessary to keep a company 'alive' until that stage has been reached.[16]

The following table is an attempt to summarise the position, but the reader should also refer to CPR 49.2(f) 'Specialist Proceedings' and the accompanying Practice Direction 49B 'Applications under the Companies Act 1985'.[17]

Hopefully the need to repeat company searches regularly throughout the lifetime of a case is now clear.

---

[16]   See *Woolwich Building Society v Taylor* [1995] 1 BCLC 132; and *Bradley v Eagle Star* [1989] 1 AC 957, [1989] 2 WLR 568.

[17]   For a detailed commentary see *Civil Court Service 2005* 'The Brown Book' (Jordan Publishing), at p1140 et seq.

PROBLEM	DISCUSSION	APPLICATION TO COURT
Voluntary Liquidation (Members' or Creditors')	No special requirements to sue but serve Liquidator and registered office if different. Seek to delay impending dissolution by contacting Secretary of State, with s 205(3) Insolvency Act request.	 Appeal to Court if needs be.
Administrative Receivership	No special requirements to sue but serve Administrative Receiver and registered office if different. Beware company's future status.	
Compulsory Liquidation	s 130 Insolvency Act stay. Permission of Court required. Seek to delay dissolution by contacting Registrar of Companies with s 205(3) Insolvency Act request.	Permission to sue – see **A2.**
Administration	Schedule B1 Insolvency Act stay. Permission of Administrator, or Court, to sue is required. Beware company's future status.	Permission to sue – see **A3.**
Struck off as defunct (s652) or on company's own application (s652A). No prior liquidation	Company has ceased to exist. Restore under s653 if less than 20 years ago, or if more than 20 years elapsed, try, if possible, to void the dissolution under s651, or both.	To restore to the Register – see **A4** - and/or (if it may work) to void the dissolution.
Dissolved after Compulsory Liquidation	Company has ceased to exist. Need to void the dissolution under s 651 but company still in compulsory liquidation so need permission to sue.	Both to void the dissolution and for permission to sue. **A2** and **A5** may conveniently be combined.

PROBLEM	DISCUSSION	APPLICATION TO COURT
Dissolved after Voluntary Liquidation (whether Members' or Creditors')	Company has ceased to exist. Need to void the dissolution under s 651.	To void the dissolution – see **A5**.

A2

PERMISSION TO SUE A COMPANY IN COMPULSORY LIQUIDATION

A2.1

COMMENTARY

Where a winding up Order has been made, it is necessary to apply to the Court for permission to commence proceedings or, if those proceedings have been commenced, for permission to continue those proceedings.

If no such permission is obtained then proceedings against a company in compulsory liquidation are a nullity.[1]

The application is made by Part 8, with witness evidence in support. It must be served on the liquidator and (if different) the Registered Office address of the company. The liquidator should be asked whether he has any objection to the application and his reply (if any) must be available at the hearing. In any event, a Certificate of Service in Form N215 should be filed with the Court.

The application is heard (if in London) by the Companies Court or (if outside London) by the District Judge of the Chancery Division and should be made to the Court which made the winding up Order. After the hearing, the Court should draw the Order and serve the parties but you should, to be on the safe side, serve the liquidator with the Order yourself.

The true purpose of s 130 of the Insolvency Act 1986, and the stay that it imposes, is to prevent creditors of the company jockeying for position. The stay ensures that the company's assets are distributed properly and in accordance with insolvency law. Your evidence, in the application for permission to sue, should therefore confirm that your client does not seek to make any claim upon the assets of the company itself. Rather, your evidence should make plain that the company was insured and that it is those insurers who will satisfy the claim, not the assets of the company.

---

[1] See *Roberts Petroleum Ltd v Bernard Kenny Ltd* [1983] 2 AC 192, [1983] 1 All ER 564; and *Tandberg v Strand Wood Co* (unreported) April 1905, supra.

The Court, once satisfied that the real purpose of s 130 of the Insolvency Act will not be undermined, should grant permission.

Once obtained, you may now issue or proceed against the Defendant in liquidation. You still need to keep a close eye on its future status, as you may need to seek to defer dissolution of the company.

A2.2

CLAIM FORM

Claim Form (CPR Part 8)	**In the High Court of Justice** **Chancery Division** **Anytown District Registry**
	Claim No.

Claimant

Mr A Goodchap
13 The Street
Anytown
Any Place

SEAL

Defendant(s)

Dodgy Corporateveil Limited (in Liquidation)
R/O Smart Clever & Rich
Chartered Accountants & Insolvency Practitioners
Technical Quicksand House
Windfall Defence Town XX1 1ZZ

Does, or will, your claim include any issues under the Human Rights Act 1998?   ☐ Yes   ☒ No

Details of claim *(see also overleaf)*

The Claimant applies for an order that he be at liberty to [commence or continue] an action against Dodgy Corporateveil Limited (in Liquidation) in the [Anytwon County Court] [Action No:...] notwithstanding the Order to wind up the said company dated [...] and that the costs of this application be costs in the pending identified action.

		£
Defendant's name and address	Dodgy Corporateveil Limited (in Liquidation) R/O Smart Clever & Rich Chartered Accountants & Insolvency Practitioners Technical Quicksand House Windfall Defence Town XX1 1ZZ	

Court fee	
Solicitor's costs	
Issue date	

The court office at

is open between 10 am and 4 pm Monday to Friday. When corresponding with the court, please address forms or letters to the Court Manager and quote the claim number.

Claim No.	

Details of claim *(continued)*
See witness statement attached.

Statement of Truth
*(I believe)(The Claimant believes) that the facts stated in these particulars of claim are true.
* I am duly authorised by the claimant to sign this statement.

Full name _____

Name of claimant's solicitor's firm [STATE NAME OF FIRM]

signed _____ position or office held [PARTNER]
*(Claimant)(Litigation friend)(Claimant's solicitor) (if signing on behalf of a firm or company)
*delete as appropriate

[STATE NAME AND ADDRESS OF FIRM AND REFERENCE]

Claimant's or claimant's solicitor's address to which documents should be sent if different from overleaf. If you are prepared to accept service by DX, fax or e-mail, please add details.

A2.3

STATEMENT OF TRUTH

1. ON BEHALF OF THE CLAIMANT:
2. INITIALS AND SURNAME OF WITNESS:
3. NO. OF STATEMENT:
4. INITIALS AND NUMBERS OF EACH EXHIBIT:
5. DATE:

IN THE ANYTOWN COUNTY COURT   CLAIM NO

BETWEEN:

MR A GOODCHAP

Claimant

-and-

DODGY CORPORATEVEIL LIMITED (IN LIQUIDATION)

Defendant

STATEMENT OF [state name of solicitor]

I, **[STATE NAME OF SOLICITOR]** of [STATE ADDRESS OF FIRM OR EMPLOYER], [STATE POSITION HELD] will say as follows:-

1. I have the care and conduct of this case on behalf of the Claimant. I am duly authorised by him to make this statement in support of his application.

2. The Claimant was employed by the Defendant when he suffered injuries [*state date of accident and brief details of injuries or dates of employment and brief details of disease*] during the course of his employment with them. The Claimant now wishes to [*commence/continue*] an action against the Defendant in the [*state name of Court*] [*if action commenced state action number*] in respect of those injuries.

3. On or about the [*date*] a winding up Order was made by this Court in respect of the Defendant and [*name of liquidator*] of [*address of liquidator*] is the liquidator.

By reason of the winding up Order

EITHER

[*s 130 of the Insolvency Act 1986 prevents the issue of proceedings against the Defendant*]

OR

[*the automatic stay operated by s 130 of the Insolvency Act prevents the Claimant continuing with the action already commenced*]

4. I believe that the purpose of s 130 of the Insolvency Act 1986 is to ensure the fair distribution of the Defendant company's assets, in accordance with Insolvency Law. By granting permission to this Claimant for his action [*to issue or to continue*] this Court would not be interfering in that process since the Claimant himself will not make any call upon the assets of the company itself. This is because the Defendant company was, at all material times, insured in respect of their liability to the Claimant with [*state name of insurer*].

5. The permission sought will therefore merely allow the Claimant to [*issue or continue*] his action for damages for personal injuries which if successful will be met by those insurers, not the assets of the Defendant company itself. Should the personal injury action proceed to Judgment and, for any unknown reason such Judgment is not satisfied by the identified insurers, this would in turn allow the Claimant to proceed against the insurers under the provisions of the Third Parties (Rights Against Insurers) Act 1930.

STATEMENT OF TRUTH

I believe that the facts stated in this statement are true.

SIGNED...

DATED..

[*Claimant's Solicitors signature*]

Ref:

PERMISSION TO SUE A COMPANY IN ADMINISTRATION

A3.1

COMMENTARY

The correct approach is to contact the Administrator to seek his permission to issue or to continue (as appropriate) the proceedings against the company in administration. Although most Administrators will be well aware of the legal background, some may not. It is therefore thought best to outline the legal position fully, quoting the stay imposed by paragraph 43 of Schedule B1 to the Insolvency Act 1986 and specifically confirming that the Administrator may himself grant the necessary permission. It is best to go further and point out that there will be no claim upon the assets of the company since the company is insured against the Claimant's claim and that giving permission for your action to continue will not adversely affect the administration, or the company, in any way. The insurer should be identified with their name, address, reference and telephone number and, if in doubt, the Administrator should be asked to contact the insurers for advice and/or confirmation of the insurance cover.

Should the Administrator fail to respond or if the Administrator declines to grant permission, then an application to the Court for that permission becomes necessary.

If you think that the Administrator has unreasonably withheld his permission and/or that the insurer has advised or instructed the Administrator to do so, then the possibility arises of an Order for costs being obtained on that basis. If an Order for costs is to be sought do not forget to file and serve a Statement of Costs in Form N260.

The application is made by Part 8, with witness evidence in support. It must be served on the Administrator and (if different) the Registered Office address of the company. A Certificate of Service should be filed.

The application is heard (if in London) by the Companies Court or (if outside London) by the District Judge of the Chancery Division. After the hearing the Court should draw the Order and serve the parties but you should, to be on the safe side, serve the Order yourself.

The true purpose of the stay imposed by Schedule B1 of the Insolvency Act 1986 is to protect the assets of the company so as to allow the Administrator to perform their important function of seeking to rescue the business of the company or allowing for its orderly closure. Your evidence, in the application for permission to sue, should therefore confirm that your client does not seek to make any claim upon the assets of the company itself. Rather, your evidence should make plain that the company was insured and it is those insurers who will satisfy the claim, not the assets of the company.

The Court, once satisfied that the real purpose of the Schedule B1 of the Insolvency Act stay will not be undermined, should grant permission.

Once obtained, you may now issue or proceed against the Defendant in Administration. You will still need to keep a close eye on its future status as it may well proceed into liquidation.

A3.2

CLAIM FORM

Claim Form (CPR Part 8)	**In the High Court of Justice** **Chancery Division** **Anytown District Registry**
	Claim No.

Claimant
Mr A Goodchap
13 The Street
Anytown
Any Place

SEAL

Defendant(s)
Dodgy Corporateveil Limited (in Administration)
R/O Smart Clever & Rich
Chartered Accountants & Insolvency Practitioners
Technical Quicksand House
Windfall Defence Town XX1 1ZZ

Does, or will, your claim include any issues under the Human Rights Act 1998? ☐ Yes ☒ No

Details of claim *(see also overleaf)*

IN THE MATTER OF DODGY CORPORATEVEIL LIMITED.

IN THE MATTER OF THE INSOLVENCY ACT 1986.

The claimant applies for an order that he be at liberty to [commence or continue] an action against Dodgy Corporateveil limited in the [Anytown County Court][Action N:...] notwithstanding the administration of the said company by the appointment of [state name and address of Administration] as Administrator of the company on [date].

AND for an Order that costs of these proceedings be paid by the Administrator or be otherwise provided for.

Defendant's name and address	Dodgy Corporateveil Limited (in Administration) R/O Smart Clever & Rich Chartered Accountants & Insolvency Practitioners Technical Quicksand House Windfall Defence Town XX1 1ZZ	

	£
Court fee	
Solicitor's costs	
Issue date	

The court office at

is open between 10 am and 4 pm Monday to Friday. When corresponding with the court, please address forms or letters to the Court Manager and quote the claim number.

Claim No.	

Details of claim *(continued)*
See witness statement attached.

Statement of Truth
*~~(I believe)~~(The Claimant believes) that the facts stated in these particulars of claim are true.
*~~I am duly authorised by the claimant to sign this statement.~~

Full name _____

Name of claimant's solicitor's firm [STATE NAME OF FIRM]_____

signed _____ position or office held [PARTNER]
*~~(Claimant)(Litigation friend)~~(Claimant's solicitor) (if signing on behalf of a firm or company)
*delete as appropriate

[STATE NAME AND ADDRESS OF FIRM AND
REFERENCE]

Claimant's or claimant's solicitor's address to
which documents should be sent if different from
overleaf. If you are prepared to accept service by
DX, fax or e-mail, please add details.

A3.3

STATEMENT OF TRUTH

1. ON BEHALF OF THE CLAIMANT:

2. INITIALS AND SURNAME OF WITNESS:

3. NO. OF STATEMENT:

4. INITIALS AND NUMBERS OF EACH EXHIBIT:

5. DATE:

IN THE ANYTOWN COUNTY COURT   CLAIM NO

BETWEEN:

MR A GOODCHAP

Claimant

-and-

DODGY CORPORATEVEIL LIMITED (IN ADMINISTRATION)

Defendant

STATEMENT OF [State name of solicitor]

I, **[STATE NAME OF SOLICITOR]** of [STATE ADDRESS OF FIRM OR EMPLOYER], [STATE POSITION HELD] will say as follows:-

1. I have the care and conduct of this case on behalf of the Claimant. I am duly authorised by him to make this statement in support of his application.

2. The Claimant was employed by the Defendant when he suffered injuries [*state date of accident and brief details of injuries or dates of employment and brief details of disease*] during the course of his employment with them. The Claimant now wishes to [*commence/continue*] an action against the Defendant in the [*state name of Court*] [*if action commenced state action number*] in respect of those injuries.

3. On or about the [*date*] the Defendant company went into administration with the appointment of [*name of Administrator*] of [*address of Administrator*] as Administrator.

4. By reason of the appointment of the Administrator

EITHER

[paragraph 43 of Schedule B1 to the Insolvency Act 1986 prevents the
issue of proceedings against the Defendant]

OR

> [*the automatic stay imposed by paragraph 43 of Schedule B1 to the Insolvency Act 1986 prevents the Claimant continuing with the action already commenced*].

5. I believe that the purpose of Schedule B1 of the Insolvency Act 1986 is to ensure the preservation of the Defendant company's assets, either to allow 'rescue' of the Defendants business or its orderly closure in accordance with Insolvency Law. By granting permission to this Claimant for his action [*to issue or to continue*] this Court would not be interfering in that process since the Claimant himself will not make any call upon the assets of the company itself. This is because the Defendant company was, at all material times, insured in respect of their liability to the Claimant with [*state name of insurer*].

6. The permission sought will therefore merely allow the Claimant to [*issue or continue*] his action for damages for personal injuries which if successful will be met by those insurers, not the assets of the Defendant company itself. Should the personal injury action proceed to Judgment and, for any unknown reason such Judgment is not satisfied by the identified insurers, this would in turn allow the Claimant to proceed against the insurers under the provisions of the Third Parties (Rights Against Insurers) Act 1930.

7. The Insolvency Act allows the Administrator himself to grant permission. Prior to making this application to the Court I contacted the Administrator and there is now produced to me and marked [*state initials and number of exhibit*] copies of all my correspondence with the Administrator [*and of any file notes of telephone conversations*] from which it will be seen that the Administrator has failed to give that permission, notwithstanding the full explanation given. I submit that, in the circumstances, it was unreasonable of the Administrator to fail to grant permission and further submit that this application to the Court has only become necessary because of that unreasonable failure. [*if you can show that the insurers had a hand in this tactic, outline details here*]

8. Accordingly an Order for costs against the Defendant and/or the Administrator is sought.

STATEMENT OF TRUTH

I believe that the facts stated in this statement are true.

SIGNED...

DATED.....................................

[*Claimant's Solicitors signature*]

Ref:

APPLICATION TO RESTORE THE NAME OF A COMPANY TO THE REGISTER UNDER SECTION 653 OF THE COMPANIES ACT 1985

A4.1

COMMENTARY

If a company has been struck off as defunct (s 652) or had its name removed from the register on its own application (s 652A) then you will need to resurrect the company in order to sue it. The correct course of action is to apply under s 653 of the Companies Act 1985 for an Order that the name of the company be restored to the Register of Companies. The effect of the Order is to put all parties in the same position as if the company had never been struck off. Accordingly the limitation period for the personal injury claim always continues to run.

The rules require you to show how the Claimant is a prospective creditor of the company ie to detail his personal injury action and go on to show that should that action succeed he will become a creditor of the company. A full company search should be exhibited to the witness statement showing date of Incorporation of the Company, the Registered Office, the Companies Objects, its Share Capital and an explanation as to the circumstances surrounding the striking off of the company.

It should also state the date on which the company was struck off and the date of publication of notice of that in the London Gazette.

The Part 8 Claim Form and supporting evidence must be served on the Registrar of Companies and on the Treasury Solicitor as bona vacantia agent of the Crown. Evidence of service [Form N215] will be required and the bona vacantia letter should be exhibited to that.

Note that the time limit for an application to restore a company is twenty years after the publication in the London Gazette of notice of its striking off.

It is good practice to provide copies of all documents to the insurers and invite them to apply as interveners should they have any objection.[1]

The Claimant should, in the Order, undertake to inform the Registrar of Companies of the title and Court reference number of the litigation referred to and also to undertake to inform the Registrar of Companies immediately upon the conclusion of that litigation. There should be a further Order that the Registrar of Companies advertise notice of the Order in his official name in the London Gazette. There will inevitably be an Order that the Claimant do pay the Registrar of Companies his costs of the application. You are obliged to provide the Registrar of Companies with a sealed copy of the Order.

Once done, the effect is as if the company had never been struck off. Accordingly the personal injury action may now be issued against it.

---

[1]   See *Re Regent Insulation Ltd* (1981) *The Times*, November 5.

A4.2

CLAIM FORM

A4.2

**Claim Form
(CPR Part 8)**

In the High Court of Justice **Chancery Division** **Anytown District Registry**
Claim No.

Claimant
Mr A Goodchap
13 The Street
Anytown
Any Place

SEAL

Defendant(s)

Dodgy Corporateveil Limited
R/O Smart Clever & Rich
Chartered Accountants & Insolvency Practitioners
Technical Quicksand House
Windfall Defence Town XX1 1ZZ

Does, or will, your claim include any issues under the Human Rights Act 1998? ☐ Yes ☒ No

Details of claim *(see also overleaf)*

IN THE MATTER OF DODGY CORPORATEVEIL LIMITED.

IN THE MATTER OF THE INSOLVENCY ACT 1986.

The claimant who is a propsective creditor of the above named Defendant company applies for an Order that the name of the Defendant company be restored to the Register of , a draft of which is attached.

AND for an Order that costs of these proceedings be costs in the identified pending personal injury action.

		£

Defendant's name and address	Registrar of Companies Registration Office Crown Way Maindy Cardiff CF4 3UZ and also The Treasury Solicitor Bona Vacantia Division Queen Anne's Chambers Broadway London WS1H 9JS		

Court fee	
Solicitor's costs	
Issue date	

The court office at

is open between 10 am and 4 pm Monday to Friday. When corresponding with the court, please address forms or letters to the Court Manager and quote the claim number.

N208 Claim Form (CPR Part 8) 10/00   © Crown Copyright. Produced by infolaw 11/04

<table>
<tr><td>Claim No.</td><td></td></tr>
</table>

Details of claim *(continued)*
Please see attached statement.

Statement of Truth
~~(I believe)~~(The Claimant believes) that the facts stated in these particulars of claim are true.
* ~~I am duly authorised by the claimant to sign this statement.~~

Full name _____

Name of claimant's solicitor's firm [STATE NAME OF FIRM]_____

signed _____ position or office held [PARTNER]
*~~(Claimant)(Litigation friend)~~(Claimant's solicitor) (if signing on behalf of a firm or company)
delete as appropriate

STATE NAME AND ADDRESS OF FIRM AND
REFERENCE

Claimant's or claimant's solicitor's address to
which documents should be sent if different from
overleaf. If you are prepared to accept service by
DX, fax or e-mail, please add details.

A4.3

STATEMENT OF TRUTH

1. ON BEHALF OF THE CLAIMANT:

2. INITIALS AND SURNAME OF WITNESS:

3. NO. OF STATEMENT:

4. INITIALS AND NUMBERS OF EACH EXHIBIT:

5. DATE:

IN THE ANYTOWN COUNTY COURT   CLAIM NO.

BETWEEN:

MR A GOODCHAP

Claimant

-and-

DODGY CORPORATEVEIL LIMITED

Defendant

STATEMENT OF [State name of solicitor]

I, **[STATE NAME OF SOLICITOR]** of [STATE ADDRESS OF FIRM OR EMPLOYER], [STATE POSITION HELD] will say as follows:-

1. I have the care and conduct of this case on behalf of the Claimant. I am duly authorised by him to make this statement in support of his application.

2. The Claimant is a prospective creditor of the Defendant company.

3. The Claimant was employed by the Defendant when he suffered injuries [*state date of accident and brief details of injuries or dates of employment and brief details of disease*] during the course of his employment with them. The Claimant now wishes to commence an action against the Defendant in the [*state name of Court*] in respect of those injuries.

4. There is now produced to me and marked [*state initials and number of exhibit*] a company search from which the date of the incorporation of the company, the registered office, the company's objects, its share capital and the circumstances surrounding the striking off of the company can be seen.

5. The company was struck off on the [*date*] following publication of a notice thereof in the London Gazette on [*date*]. Since the restoration of the name of the company to the Register of Companies is for the purposes of bringing a claim for damages for personal injuries against it I confirm that this date of publication in the London Gazette is less than twenty years ago.

6. The Defendant company had the benefit of employers liability insurance at the time that the Claimants cause of action accrued.

7. In those circumstances the Claimant claims that it would be just and equitable for this Court to restore the name of Dodgy Corporateveil Limited to the Register of Companies.

STATEMENT OF TRUTH

I believe that the facts stated in this statement are true.

SIGNED...

DATED...

[Claimant's Solicitors signature]

Ref:

A4.4

DRAFT ORDER

IN THE HIGH COURT OF JUSTICE   CLAIM NO

CHANCERY DIVISION

ANYTOWN DISTRICT REGISTRY

BETWEEN:

MR A GOODCHAP

Claimant

-and-

DODGY CORPORATEVEIL LIMITED

Defendant

IN THE MATTER OF SECTION 653 OF THE
COMPANIES ACT 1985
Draft Order

Upon the application of Mr A Goodchap of [*address*], a creditor of Dodgy Corporateveil Limited on [*date of application*]

And Upon hearing the solicitor for the Claimant and the Registrar of Companies consenting

And Upon Reading the Evidence

And there being no opposition on behalf of Her Majesty to the relief sought by the said application as appears from the evidence of service and exhibit thereto

And the Claimant by his solicitors undertaking to:-

Inform the Registrar of Companies of the title and Court reference number of the proposed litigation referred to in the witness statement of [*name of solicitor*] immediately after issue and

Inform the Registrar of Companies immediately on the conclusion of the said litigation or any appeal therefrom.

THIS COURT DOTH ORDER that the name of Dodgy Corporateveil Limited be restored to the Register of Companies

AND IT IS ORDERED THAT the Registrar of Companies do advertise notice of this Order in his official name in the 'London Gazette'.

AND IT IS ORDERED that the Claimant do within 21 days hereof deliver an office copy of this Order to the Registrar of Companies.

AND IT IS ORDERED that the Claimant do pay the Registrar of Companies costs of this application in the agreed sum of [*insert amount*]

AND IT IS FURTHER ORDERED that the Claimant's costs of this application be costs in the discretion of the Court hearing the personal injury action.

Dated this   day of   200

APPLICATION TO VOID THE DISSOLUTION OF A COMPANY UNDER SECTION 651 OF THE COMPANIES ACT 1985

A5.1

COMMENTARY

If a company has been dissolved following compulsory or voluntary liquidation and you wish to resurrect the company in order to sue it, the correct course of action is to apply under s 651 of the Companies Act 1985 for an Order declaring the dissolution of the company void. The effect of the Order is to void the dissolution ab initio, thus allowing proceedings to issue against the company.

Beware, however, since if the dissolution was preceded by compulsory liquidation then permission to sue will still be required (see **A2** above) and further beware that limitation continues to run.

Historical records from Companies House can be unclear as to whether the company was dissolved or struck off. In such a situation, it may well be appropriate to combine this application under s 651 with an application under s 653 to restore the name of the company to the register (ie combine **A4** and **A5**).

The application is made by Part 8, with witness evidence in support. Exhibiting as full a company search as may be available is important since the rules require the evidence in support of the application to contain particulars of the interest of the Claimant (ie his personal injury claim), the date of incorporation of the company, the registered office, the company's objects, its share capital and an explanation as to the circumstances surrounding the dissolution of the company. It should also state the date on which the company was dissolved. Rather than repeating all of this in a witness statement, it seems simpler to exhibit a full company search.

The Part 8 Claim Form and supporting evidence must be served on the Registrar of Companies and on the Treasury Solicitor as bona vacantia Agent of the Crown.

Evidence of service (Form N215) will be required and the 'bona vacantia' letter should be exhibited to that.

Note that the general time limit for an application to declare the dissolution void is two years from the dissolution of the company but that if the reason for declaring the dissolution void is to bring a claim for damages for personal injuries against it then no time limit applies.

Since an Order declaring the dissolution void will not be made if it appears to the Court that the personal injury action itself is statute barred it is good practice to provide copies of all documents to the insurers and, if they consider that to be the case, to invite them to apply as interveners, on these grounds, should they wish to do so. This is because the Court may allow an interested third party to appear and to be joined as a Defendant.[1]

Since the Order has been sought with a view to commencing proceedings in the personal injury action it is best to ask the Court to order that the costs of the dissolution proceedings be in the discretion of the Court hearing the proposed claim.

The Claimant should, in the Order, undertake to inform the Registrar of Companies of the title and Court reference number of the litigation referred to and also undertake to inform the Registrar of Companies immediately upon the conclusion of that litigation. There should be a further Order that the Registrar of Companies advertise notice of the Order in his official name in the London Gazette. There will inevitably be an Order that the Claimant pay the Registrar of Companies his costs of the application.

Once done, the effect is that the dissolution has never taken place and (if appropriate permission to sue a company in compulsory liquidation has also been obtained) proceedings can then be commenced.

---

[1]   See *Re: Workvale Ltd (No 2)* [1992] 2 All ER 627, [1992] 1 WLR 416; *Re Forte's (Manufacturing) Ltd* [1994] BCC 84; and *Smith v White Knight Laundry* [2001] EWCA Civ 660, [2002] 1 WLR 616.

A5.2

CLAIM FORM

**Claim Form
(CPR Part 8)**

In the High Court of Justice Chancery Division Anytown District Registry	
Claim No.	

Claimant
Mr A Goodchap
13 The Street
Anytown
Any Place

SEAL

Defendant(s)
Dodgy Corporateveil Limited
R/O Smart Clever & Rich
Chartered Accountants & Insolvency Practitioners
Technical Quicksand House
Windfall Defence Town XX1 1ZZ

Does, or will, your claim include any issues under the Human Rights Act 1998? ☐ Yes ☒ No

Details of claim *(see also overleaf)*

IN THE MATTER OF DODGY CORPORATEVEIL LIMITED.

IN THE MATTER OF THE INSOLVENCY ACT 1986.

The claimant who is a propsective creditor of the above named Defendant company applies for an Order that the name of the dissolution of the Defendant company be declared void, a draft of which is attached.

AND for an Order that costs of these proceedings be costs in the identified pending personal injury action.

	£
Defendant's name and address
Registrar of Companies
Registration Office
Crown Way
Maindy
Cardiff CF4 3UZ and also
The Treasury Solicitor
Bona Vacantia Division
Queen Anne's Chambers
Broadway
London WS1H 9JS

Court fee	
Solicitor's costs	
Issue date	

The court office at

is open between 10 am and 4 pm Monday to Friday. When corresponding with the court, please address forms or letters to the Court Manager and quote the claim number.

N208 Claim Form (CPR Part 8) 10/00   © Crown Copyright. Produced by infolaw 11/04

Claim No.	

Details of claim *(continued)*
Please see attached statement.

Statement of Truth
~~(I believe)~~ (The Claimant believes) that the facts stated in these particulars of claim are true.
~~* I am duly authorised by the claimant to sign this statement.~~

Full name _____

Name of claimant's solicitor's firm [STATE NAME OF FIRM]_____

signed _____ position or office held [PARTNER]
*~~(Claimant)(Litigation friend)~~(Claimant's solicitor) (if signing on behalf of a firm or company)
delete as appropriate

[STATE NAME AND ADDRESS OF FIRM AND
REFERENCE]

Claimant's or claimant's solicitor's address to
which documents should be sent if different from
overleaf. If you are prepared to accept service by
DX, fax or e-mail, please add details.

A5.3

STATEMENT OF TRUTH

1. ON BEHALF OF THE CLAIMANT:

2. INITIALS AND SURNAME OF WITNESS:

3. NO. OF STATEMENT:

4. INITIALS AND NUMBERS OF EACH EXHIBIT:

5. DATE:

IN THE HIGH COURT OF JUSTICE   CLAIM NO

CHANCERY DIVISION

ANYTOWN DISTRICT REGISTRY

BETWEEN:

MR A GOODCHAP

Claimant

-and-

DODGY CORPORATEVEIL LIMITED

Defendant

_____

STATEMENT OF [State name of solicitor]

_____

I, **[STATE NAME OF SOLICITOR]** of [STATE ADDRESS OF FIRM OR EMPLOYER], [STATE POSITION HELD] will say as follows:-

1. I have the care and conduct of this case on behalf of the Claimant. I am duly authorised by him to make this statement in support of his application.

2. The Claimant is a prospective creditor of the Defendant company.

3. The Claimant was employed by the Defendant when he suffered injuries [*state date of accident and brief details of injuries or dates of employment and brief details of disease*] during the course of his employment with them. The Claimant now wishes to commence an action against the Defendant in the [*state name of Court*] in respect of those injuries.

4. There is now produced to me and marked [*state initials and number of exhibit*] a company search from which the date of the incorporation of the company, the

registered office, the company's objects, its share capital and the circumstances surrounding the dissolution of the company can be seen.

5. The company was dissolved on [*date*]. Since the declaration of the dissolution to be void is for the purposes of bringing a claim for damages for personal injuries against the company I confirm that this declaration may be made at any time.

6. The Claimant's proposed action for damages for personal injuries against the Defendant is not statute barred [*set out reasons why*].

7. The Defendant company had the benefit of employers liability insurance at the time that the Claimants cause of action accrued.

8. In those circumstances the Claimant claims that it would be just and equitable for this Court to declare that the dissolution of Dodgy Corporateveil Limited be void.

STATEMENT OF TRUTH

I believe that the facts stated in this statement are true.

SIGNED...

DATED...

[Claimant's Solicitors signature]

Ref:

A5.4

DRAFT ORDER

IN THE HIGH COURT OF JUSTICE   CLAIM NO:

CHANCERY DIVISION

ANYTOWN DISTRICT REGISTRY

BETWEEN:-

MR A GOODCHAP

Claimant

-and-

DODGY CORPORATEVEIL LIMITED

Defendant

IN THE MATTER OF SECTION 651 OF THE
COMPANIES ACT 1985
Draft Order

Upon the application of Mr A Goodchap of [*address*], a creditor of Dodgy Corporateveil Limited on [*date of application*]

And Upon hearing the solicitor for the Claimant and the Registrar of Companies consenting

And Upon Reading the Evidence

And there being no opposition on behalf of Her Majesty to the relief sought by the said application as appears from the evidence of service and exhibit thereto

And the Claimant by his solicitors undertaking to:-

(a) Inform the Registrar of Companies of the title and Court reference number of the proposed litigation referred to in the witness statement of [*name of solicitor*] immediately after issue and

(b) Inform the Registrar of Companies immediately on the conclusion of the said litigation or any appeal therefrom

THIS COURT DOTH DECLARE the dissolution of the above named company void.

AND IT IS ORDERED THAT an Office Copy of this Order be delivered to the Registrar of Companies.

AND pursuant to the above mentioned Act the said Dodgy Corporateveil Limited is thereupon deemed to have continued in existence as if its name had not been struck off.

AND IT IS ORDERED that the Registrar of Companies do advertise notice of this Order in his official name in the 'London Gazette'.

AND IT IS ORDERED that the Claimant do pay the Registrar of Companies costs of this application in the agreed sum of [*insert amount*].

AND IT IS FURTHER ORDERED that the Claimants costs of this application be costs in the discretion of the Court hearing the personal injury action.

Dated this   day of   200

PRE-ACTION DISCLOSURE

A6.1

COMMENTARY

Pre-action disclosure is still probably the most under utilised procedural weapon for Claimants in CPR. For any solicitor acting on a CFA basis full information about the case, as early as possible, is important. If the potential Defendants have not complied with their disclosure obligations under the pre-action protocol then the appropriate route for the Claimant is to make an Application for pre-action disclosure under CPR 31.16. The Application is made on an ordinary Application Notice (Form N244) and not by Part 8. An action number will be assigned by the Court, which number will stay the same should you then issue proceedings in the main action.

A Statement of Costs in form N260, and a Witness Statement or other evidence should accompany the Application Notice. If a draft Order accompanies the Application then the chances of the District Judge dealing with the Application without a Hearing are increased.

Some Courts seem more willing to make these Orders than others. It is wise to restrict your request to the documents that you can truly show are relevant to the matter, specifying those as clearly as you possibly can.

However the protocol and its provisions for pre-action disclosure received judicial approval at the highest level. In *Carlson v Townsend*[1] Brooke LJ observed that '(The protocols) are guides to good litigation and pre-litigation practice, drafted and agreed by those who know all about the difference between good and bad practice'[2] and *Bermuda International Securities Ltd v KPMG*[3] is authority for the proposition that pre-action disclosure should now be seen as part of the usual pre-action exchange of information so that, in default, costs penalties against the Defendant are likely to follow. The decision in *Bermuda International Securities* has been widely followed including in *Moresfield Ltd v Banners 2003*.[4]

---

[1]   [2001] EWCA Civ 511, [2001] 1 WLR 2415.

[2]   Ibid at para 31.

[3]   [2001] EWCA Civ 269.

[4]   [2003] EWHC 1602 (Ch).

A6.2

APPLICATION NOTICE

Application Notice

	In the
You should provide this information for listing the application	
1. How do you wish to have your application dealt with	**Claim no.**
a) at a hearing? ☐ } *complete all questions below*	**Warrant no.** (if applicable)
b) at a telephone conference? ☐	
c) without a hearing? ☐ *complete Qs 5 and 6 below*	**Claimant** (including ref.)
2. Give a time estimate for the hearing/conference	
_____ (hours) _____ (mins)	**Defendant(s)** (including ref.)
3. Is this agreed by all parties? ☐ Yes ☐ No	
4. Give dates of any trial period or fixed trial date	**Date**
5. Level of judge	
6. Parties to be served	

Note You must complete Parts A **and** B, **and** Part C if applicable. Send any relevant fee and the completed application to the court with any draft order, witness statement or other evidence; and sufficient copies for service on each respondent

Part A

1. Enter your full name, or name of solicitor — I(We) [1] [STATE NAME OF FIRM] on behalf of the claimant/defendant

2. State clearly what order you are seeking and if possible attach a draft — intend to apply for an order (a draft of which is attached) that [2]

because[3]

3. Briefly set out why you are seeking the order. Include the material facts on which you rely, identifying any rule or statutory provision

Part B

I(We) wish to rely on: *tick one box*

4. If you are not already a party to the proceedings, you must provide an address for service of documents

the attached (witness statement)(affidavit) ☒   my statement of case ☐

evidence in Part C in support of my application ☐

Signed		**Position or office held**	[PARTNER]
	(Applicant)('s Solicitor)('s litigation friend)	(if signing on behalf of a firm or company)	

Address to which documents about this claim should be sent (including reference if appropriate)[4]

		if applicable
	fax no.	
	DX no.	
Tel. no. Postcode	e-mail	

The court office at ANYTOWN COUNTY COURT, ANY STREET, ANY PLACE, ANYTOWN.

is open from 10am to 4pm Monday to Friday. When corresponding with the court please address forms or letters to the Court Manager and quote the claim number.

N244 Application notice 04/00   © Crown copyright. Produced by infolaw 11/04

Part C   Claim No. ⎡   ⎤

I̶ (We) wish to rely on the following evidence in support of this application:
PLEASE SEE THE ATTACHED WITNESS STATEMENT.

Statement of Truth

* (I̶ b̶e̶l̶i̶e̶v̶e̶)(The Applicant believes) that the facts stated in Part C are true

delete as appropriate

Signed		**Position or office held**	[PARTNER]
	(Applicant)(̶ 's Solicitor)(̶ 's litigation friend)̶	(if signing on behalf of firm or company)	
		Date	

A6.3

STATEMENT OF TRUTH

1. ON BEHALF OF THE CLAIMANT:

2. INITIALS AND SURNAME OF WITNESS:

3. NO. OF STATEMENT:

4. INITIALS AND NUMBERS OF EACH EXHIBIT:

5. DATE:

IN THE ANYTOWN COUNTY COURT   CLAIM NO

BETWEEN:

MR A GOODCHAP

Claimant

-and-

EMPLOYER PLC

Defendant

STATEMENT OF [State name of solicitor]

I, **[STATE NAME OF SOLICITOR]** of [STATE ADDRESS OF FIRM OR EMPLOYER], [STATE POSITION HELD], state as follows:-

1. I have the care and conduct of this case on behalf of the Claimant. I am authorised by him to make this statement in support of his application for Pre-action Disclosure.

2. There is attached to this statement an indexed bundle of correspondence marked [*state initials and number of exhibit*] to which I ask the Court to refer where appropriate.

3. The Claimant alleges [*set out brief details of accident circumstances*]. A full protocol Letter of Claim was sent to the Defendant company on [*date*] which included a request for Pre-action Disclosure in accordance with the Personal Injury Pre-action Protocol. I particularly required the Defendants to produce [*state documents – identifying as closely as possible*].

4. [State here what, if any, documents have been provided, what, if any, efforts the Defendants have made to provide disclosure or state the contrary if not].

5. The requested documents are necessary so as to allow me to properly advise the Claimant on the question of further pursuit of the claim, and the issue of any main proceedings against the Defendant.

6. The Defendants are in breach of the Pre-action Protocol [*state how*].

7. The purposes of the protocol include the pre-action exchange of considerable information, thereby preventing considerable litigation. The importance of the protocol has been emphasised at the highest judicial level. In *Carlson v Townsend* ([2001] EWCA Civ 511) **Brooke LJ** observed that '(The protocols) are guides to good litigation and pre-litigation practice, drafted **and agreed** by those who know all about the difference between good and bad practice' (at para 31). As the learned Lord Justice observed representatives of Defendants agreed to these procedures, which procedures demonstrate good practice.

8. I further submit that pre-action disclosure should now be seen as part of the usual pre-action exchange of information so that, in default, costs sanctions should follow – see *Bermuda International Securities Limited v KPMG* [2001] EWCA Civ 269.

9. The Claimant and Defendant are likely to be party to subsequent proceedings for damages for personal injury and consequential loss and if the proceedings had started the Defendants duty by way of Standard Disclosure would extend to the documents and classes of documents of which the Claimant now seeks disclosure.

10. Further disclosure before proceedings is desirable in that it will dispose fairly of the anticipated proceedings and may well even assist in the dispute being resolved without the need for proceedings. The Claimant anticipates that the requested disclosure will show that the accident was caused by [*state brief details of negligence alleged that the documents will or may support*].

11. Should this disclosure resolve the claim without the need for proceedings considerable costs will be saved.

STATEMENT OF TRUTH

The Claimant believes that the facts stated in this statement are true.

SIGNED...

DATED......................................

[Claimant's Solicitors signature]

Ref:

A6.4

DRAFT ORDER

IN THE ANYTOWN COUNTY COURT   CASE NO:

BETWEEN :

MR A GOODCHAP

Claimant

-AND-

EMPLOYER PLC

Defendant

DRAFT ORDER

Upon Reading the Application Notice and the Statement of [*state name of solicitor*] it is Ordered as follows:-

1. The Defendant do within 14 days disclose to the Claimant's solicitors

    (a) [state documents sought specifying their identity as closely as possible]

    (b) [state other documents sought specifying their identity as closely as possible]

2. Should the Defendant no longer have these documents within its control it must state what has happened to such documents by identifying those documents which are no longer within its control identifying any documents in respect of which the Defendant claims a right or duty to withhold inspection.

3. The Defendant do pay the Claimant's costs of this Application to be assessed [*state whether standard or indemnity*] basis in accordance with the form N260 filed and served herewith.

Dated this   day of   200

ENFORCEMENT OF PRE-ACTION DISCLOSURE

A7.1

COMMENTARY

The Civil Procedure Rules merely provide, at CPR 31.21, that a party may not rely on any document which he fails to disclose. Given that a defendant in default may not wish that document to see light of day in any event, this is hardly a severe penalty.

A practice has grown up in some County Courts whereby Orders are made debarring a Defendant from defending liability in the main action which follows. Whilst undoubtedly helpful for Claimants, the jurisdiction of the Court to make such an Order seems at best unclear and at worst non-existent.[1] The risk of following such a route is that a properly advised Defendant would successfully challenge an Order, with negative costs consequences.

However, not all of the County Court rules were revoked by CPR and the relevant CCR is Order 29 – Committal for Breach of Order or Undertaking. This provides that where a person required by an Order to do an act refuses or neglects to do it within the time fixed by that Order or any subsequent Order then that Order may be enforced, by Order of the Judge, by a Committal Order against that person or if that person is a body corporate, against any Director or officer of the body. The procedure is set out in CCR Order 29 and unless dispensed with by the Court under the relevant rule, a copy of the Order should have been served personally on the person (or officer of the company) required to do the act. The safest and most convenient course for the enforcement of a pre-action disclosure Order therefore seems to be to apply by ordinary Application Notice with the same action number (Form N244) for time for compliance with the Order to be extended, for a penal

---

[1] An argument of wonderful ingenuity has been advanced that CPR 25.1 (b) allows the Court to grant a declaration, which by CPR 25.2 may be before the issue of proceedings and that by CPR 25.4 might be made even if there were to be no subsequent related claim. However ingenious, it is not an argument that this writer finds attractive. To introduce the concept of interim declarations (and by its very name an interim declaration could of course be set aside) into personal injury litigation seems inappropriate. Further, all declaratory relief is of course in the discretion of the Court. As all practitioners know, District Judges (even in the same Court) exercise their discretion differently.

notice (in standard Court Form N77) to be attached and because of the Defendant's continuing default, for costs.

Personal service of the Order, with a penal notice attached, usually proves sufficient to force even the most reluctant Defendant to comply.

A7.2

APPLICATION NOTICE

Application Notice

You should provide this information for listing the application

1. How do you wish to have your application dealt with

    a) at a hearing? ☐ ⎫
    b) at a telephone conference? ☐ ⎬ *complete all questions below*
    c) without a hearing? ☒ *complete Qs 5 and 6 below*

2. Give a time estimate for the hearing/conference
    _____ (hours) _____ (mins)

3. Is this agreed by all parties? ☐ Yes ☐ No

4. Give dates of any trial period or fixed trial date

5. Level of judge   District Judge

6. Parties to be served

In the ANYTOWN COUNTY COURT	
Claim no.	
Warrant no. (if applicable)	
Claimant (including ref.)	MR A GOODCHAP
Defendant(s) (including ref.)	EMPLOYER PLC
Date	

Note You must complete Parts A **and** B, **and** Part C if applicable. Send any relevant fee and the completed application to the court with any draft order, witness statement or other evidence; and sufficient copies for service on each respondent

Part A

1. Enter your full name, or name of solicitor

I We[1] [STATE NAME OF FIRM] on behalf of the claimant/~~defendant~~

2. State clearly what order you are seeking and if possible attach a draft

intend to apply for an order (a draft of which is attached) that [2] (1) The time for compliance with the Oredr dated [insert date of pre-action disclosure Order] be extended until 14 days from the date of this Order. (2) A penal notice in Form N77 be attached to the Order.

3. Briefly set out why you are seeking the order. Include the material facts on which you rely, identifying any rule or statutory provision

because[3] (3) The Defendant do pay the Claimant's costs of the Application to be summarily assessed because the Defendant is in breach of the Order dated [insert date of pre-action disclosure Order].

Part B

I We wish to rely on: *tick one box*

4. If you are not already a party to the proceedings, you must provide an address for service of documents

the attached (witness statement)~~(affidavit)~~ ☒   my statement of case ☐

evidence in Part C in support of my application ☐

Signed _____   **Position or office held** [PARTNER]

(Applicant)('s Solicitor)(~~'s litigation friend~~) (if signing on behalf of a firm or company)

Address to which documents about this claim should be sent (including reference if appropriate)[4]

		if applicable	
	fax no.		
	DX no.		
Tel. no. Postcode	e-mail		

The court office at ANYTOWN COUNTY COURT, ANY STREET, ANY PLACE, ANYTOWN.

is open from 10am to 4pm Monday to Friday. When corresponding with the court please address forms or letters to the Court Manager and quote the claim number.

N244 Application notice 04/00   © Crown copyright. Produced by infolaw 11/04

Part C   Claim No. [   ]

~~I~~-We wish to rely on the following evidence in support of this application:
Please see attached witness statement.

Statement of Truth

* ~~(I believe)~~(The Applicant believes) that the facts stated in Part C are true
delete as appropriate

Signed [   ]   Position or office held   [PARTNER]

(Applicant)('s Solicitor)~~('s litigation friend)~~   (if signing on behalf of firm or company)

                                          Date [   ]

A7.3

STATEMENT OF TRUTH

1. ON BEHALF OF THE CLAIMANT:

2. INITIALS AND SURNAME OF WITNESS:

3. NO. OF STATEMENT:

4. INITIALS AND NUMBERS OF EACH EXHIBIT:

5. DATE:

IN THE ANYTOWN COUNTY COURT   CLAIM NO.

BETWEEN:

MR A GOODCHAP

Claimant

-and-

EMPLOYER PLC

Defendant

STATEMENT OF [State name of solicitor]

I, [STATE NAME OF SOLICITOR] of [STATE ADDRESS OF FIRM OR EMPLOYER], [STATE POSITION HELD], state as follows:-

1. I have the care and conduct of this case on behalf of the Claimant. I am authorised by him to make this statement in support of this application.

2. There is attached to this statement an indexed bundle of correspondence marked [*state initial and number of exhibit*] to which I ask the Court to refer where appropriate.

3. On the [*state date of pre-action disclosure Order*] this Court ordered the Defendant to provide pre-action disclosure in accordance with CPR 31.16. That Order was served [*state how, whether by Court or by Claimant's solicitor*] on or about [*state date*]. It required the Defendant to comply with the terms of the Order by [*state date*].

4. The Defendant has not complied with the Order [*state details of non-compliance or partial compliance*] and is thus I submit in contempt of this Court.

5. Pursuant to County Court Rule Order 29 the Claimant now wishes to take steps to enforce the earlier Order. To allow this to be done, in accordance with that County Court Rule, the Order will require to be served personally on the [*state if Defendant or Officers of Defendant company*] and a penal notice in standard format (Form N77) should be attached.

6. Should the Defendant continue in contempt of Court following the extended period for compliance of the Order, then it will be the Claimant's intention to apply for the committal to prison of [*state whether Defendant or Officer of the Defendant company*].

7. Since this application has only been necessary due to the Defendants continuing default the Claimant requests that the Court Orders the Defendant to meet the costs of this application, to be summarily assessed in accordance with the Schedule of Costs attached (Form N260).

STATEMENT OF TRUTH

The Claimant believes that the facts stated in this statement are true.

SIGNED..

DATED.....................................

[*Claimant's Solicitors signature*]

Ref:

A7.4

DRAFT ORDER

IN THE ANYTOWN COUNTY COURT   CASE NO:

BETWEEN:

MR A GOODCHAP

Claimant

-AND-

EMPLOYER PLC

Defendant

DRAFT ORDER

Upon Reading the Application Notice and the Statement of [*state name of solicitor*] it is Ordered as follows:-

1. The time for compliance with the Order dated [*insert date of pre-action disclosure Order*] be extended until 4pm on   the [*insert date*].

2. A Penal notice in Form N77 be attached to the Order.

3. The Defendant do pay the Claimant's costs of this application to be assessed [*state whether on standard or indemnity*] basis in accordance with the Form N260 filed and served herewith.

Dated this   day of   200

APPLICATION TO COMMIT TO PRISON

A8.1

COMMENTARY

Should the Defendants still not have complied with the pre-action disclosure Order the next course for the determined Claimant is to apply, pursuant to CCR Order 29.1(1) for the committal of the Defendant or Officer of the Defendant company, to prison for contempt of Court. The power of District Judges to commit is limited to specified circumstances so that this application, made again by ordinary application notice (Form N244) should be made to the Circuit Judge. It is difficult to envisage a case where the Defendant would remain tardy to the extent of risking imprisonment but, if after service of the time extended Order endorsed with penal notice, the Defendant still fails to comply it seems difficult to criticise a Claimant for following the procedure set out in the County Court Rules.

Note that as well as your application to commit to prison, all relevant evidence, including your statement supporting the application, should be served personally.

EXTENSION OF TIME
FOR SERVING CLAIM FORM

A9.1

COMMENTARY

After a Claim Form has been issued it must be served on the Defendant within four months of the date of issue.[1] Service of proceedings is the one main area where the CPR, and decisions made under it, are a real minefield for the Claimant's solicitor. The best tactics are to serve promptly and, if in doubt as to who should be served, both the Defendant and any solicitors who may be involved should be served. In this regard it is perfectly possible to issue as many Claim Forms as one likes, so long as any additional Claim Forms are clearly marked Concurrent Proceedings.

Hopefully such simple tactic will avoid the need for the extremely perilous application for an extension of time for serving a Claim Form. The court's general discretionary power in CPR 3.1(2)(a) to extend the time for compliance with a rule or order does not apply to extending time for service of a Claim Form.[2] Furthermore CPR 6.9 which allows the court to dispense with service cannot be invoked when that would effectively do what CPR 7.6(3) forbids.[3]

If however you must make the application then it is without notice by ordinary application notice (form N244) supported by evidence (whether statement or affidavit). Precedents follow but it is submitted most strongly that it would be more appropriate to serve the Claim Form promptly in all cases and where necessary apply subsequently for a stay and/or Directions.

It is difficult to see how an extension of time for service can ever be preferable to service by an alternative method, CPR 6.8 or service on last-known address.[4] In

---

[1]   CPR 7.5.

[2]   See *Vinos v Marks & Spencer plc* [2001] 3 All ER 784.

[3]   See *Godwin v Swindon Borough Council* [2001] EWCA Civ 1478, [2002] 1 WLR 997.

[4]   CPR 6.5(6).

addition, in an RTA case, the insurers can of course be sued directly under the European Communities (Rights against Insurers) Regulations 2002.[5]

The 'last-known address' solution is very wide[6] but beware that you have taken reasonable steps to find out the address.[7] Note however that if a solicitor is acting for a party, but has not confirmed authority to accept service on behalf of that party, then the last-known address provision does not apply and the party must be served personally or by substituted service.[8]

An extension of time for service may be obtained where, for example, between issue and service of proceedings, a corporate defendant has gone into compulsory liquidation or administration. In this situation an application may be made to extend time until an application for permission to continue can be heard (see **A9.2** et seq).

Alternatively, in a wholly unusual situation, an application may be appropriate. The only situation that one can think of at this time is where a rogue sole trader employer is evading service, where for some reason no usual or last-known residence or place of business address is known (see **A9.1** et seq.).

---

5   SI 2002/3061.

6   See *Smith v Hughes* [2003] EWCA Civ 656.

7   See *Mersey Docks Property Holding v Kilgour* [2004] All ER (D) 303.

8   See *Marshall v Maggs* [2005] All ER (D) 172 (Jan).

A9.2

APPLICATION NOTICE

Application Notice

You should provide this information for listing the application

1. How do you wish to have your application dealt with

   a) at a hearing? ☐ } *complete all questions below*
   b) at a telephone conference? ☐
   c) without a hearing? ☐ *complete Qs 5 and 6 below*

2. Give a time estimate for the hearing/conference
   _____ (hours) _____ (mins)

3. Is this agreed by all parties? ☐ Yes ☐ No

4. Give dates of any trial period or fixed trial date

5. Level of judge

6. Parties to be served

In the	
Claim no.	
Warrant no. (if applicable)	
Claimant (including ref.)	
Defendant(s) (including ref.)	
Date	

Note You must complete Parts A **and** B, **and** Part C if applicable. Send any relevant fee and the completed application to the court with any draft order, witness statement or other evidence; and sufficient copies for service on each respondent

1. Enter your full name, or name of solicitor

Part A

I̶(We)[1] [STATE NAME OF FIRM] on behalf of claimant/~~defendant~~

2. State clearly what order you are seeking and if possible attach a draft

intend to apply for an order (a draft of which is attached) that [2] pursuant to CPR 7.6 the time for service of the claim form and all supporting documentation be extended for 14 days over the hearing by the Court of the attached draft application for permission for these proceedings to continue.
because[3] the Defendant has gone into administration between issue and service .

3. Briefly set out why you are seeking the order. Include the material facts on which you rely, identifying any rule or statutory provision

AND for an Order that the costs of this application be the Claimants in any event.

Part B

I̶(We) wish to rely on: *tick one box*

4. If you are not already a party to the proceedings, you must provide an address for service of documents

the attached (witness statement)~~(affidavit)~~ ☒   my statement of case ☐

evidence in Part C in support of my application ☐

Signed		**Position or office held** *(if signing on behalf of a firm or company)*	[PARTNER]
	(Applicant)('s Solicitor)~~(a litigation friend)~~		

Address to which documents about this claim should be sent (including reference if appropriate)[4]

	if applicable	
	fax no.	
	DX no.	
Tel. no. Postcode	e-mail	

The court office at ANYTOWN COUNTY COURT, ANYSTREET, ANYPLACE, ANYTOWN
is open from 10am to 4pm Monday to Friday. When corresponding with the court please address forms or letters to the Court Manager and quote the claim number.

Part C   Claim No. [   ]

~~I~~ (We) wish to rely on the following evidence in support of this application:
PLEASE SEE ATTACHED WITNESS STATEMENT.

Statement of Truth

* ~~(I believe)~~ (The Applicant believes) that the facts stated in Part C are true
**delete as appropriate*

Signed		Position or office held	[PARTNER]
	(Applicant)('s Solicitor)(~~'s litigation Friend~~)	(if signing on behalf of firm or company)	
		Date	

A9.3

STATEMENT OF TRUTH

1. ON BEHALF OF THE CLAIMANT:

2. INITIALS AND SURNAME OF WITNESS:

3. NO. OF STATEMENT:

4. INITIALS AND NUMBERS OF EACH EXHIBIT:

5. DATE:

IN THE ANYTOWN COUNTY COURT   CLAIM NO

BETWEEN:

MR A GOODCHAP

Claimant

-and-

DODGY CORPORATEVEIL LIMITED (IN ADMINISTRATION)

Defendant

STATEMENT [State name of solicitor]

I, **[*STATE NAME OF SOLICITOR*]** of [STATE ADDRESS OF FIRM OR EMPLOYER], [STATE POSITION HELD] will say as follows:-

1. I have the care and conduct of this case on behalf of the Claimant. I am duly authorised by him to make this statement in support of his application.

2. The Claimant was employed by the Defendant when he suffered injuries [*state date of accident and brief details of injuries, or dates of employment and brief details of disease*] during the course of his employment with them. The Claimant commenced this action against the Defendant in respect of those injuries by the issue of proceedings herein on the [*date*]. On that date there was no bar or hindrance to issuing or to continuing proceedings against the Defendant company.

3. The Defendant is insured in respect of the Claimant's claim.

4. However, on or about the *[date]* the Defendant company went into administration with the appointment of *[name of administrator]* of *[address of administrator]* as administrator.

5. Thus the administrator was appointed **after** the issue of these proceedings but **before** I have been able to serve the Defendant company.

6. Accordingly, by reason of paragraph 43 of Schedule B1 of the Insolvency Act 1986 the permission of the administrator or the Court is now required for this action to be able to continue. It is therefore not possible to validly serve the claim form and supporting documentation in this case without either the permission of the administrator or the permission of the Court.

7. There is now produced to me and marked *[state initials and number of exhibit]* from where it will be seen that the administrator is not able to give his consent to these proceedings continuing. I suspect this to be tactical on behalf of the Defendants insurers in seeking to obtain a 'windfall' from the stay contained in the Insolvency Act.

8. I believe that the stay imposed by the Insolvency Act is to ensure the preservation of the Defendant company's assets either to allow 'rescue' of the Defendants business or its orderly closure in accordance with insolvency law. I do not believe that it is to provide windfall defences for employers liability insurers.

9. Accordingly, to regularise the position, the permission of the Court for these proceedings to continue must be obtained before service can be effected.

10. I therefore submit that it is just, fair and equitable for the validity of the claim form and supporting documentation in this instance for service to be extended for the time requested.

11. This application was made promptly (ie as soon as the administration of the Defendant company came to my attention) and I note in passing that none of the service methods provided for by CPR will create valid service because of the automatic stay imposed by the Insolvency Act.

12. There is now produced to me and marked *[state initials and number of exhibit]* my draft application for permission to continue proceedings against a company in administration, with witness statement and draft Order in support of that application.

STATEMENT OF TRUTH

I believe that the facts stated in this statement are true.

SIGNED...

DATED..

[Claimant's Solicitors signature]

Ref:

A9.4

DRAFT ORDER

IN THE ANYTOWN COUNTY COURT   CLAIM NO:

BETWEEN:

MR A GOODCHAP

Claimant

-and-

DODGY CORPORATEVEIL LIMITED (IN ADMINISTRATION)

Defendant

_____

DRAFT ORDER

_____

Upon reading the application notice dated [*state date*] and upon reading the statement of [*state name of deponent to witness statement*] dated [*insert date*] IT IS HEREBY ORDERED:-

1. Pursuant to CPR 7.6 the time for service of the claim form and all supporting documentation be extended for 14 days over the hearing by the Court of the attached draft application for permission for these proceedings to continue, and

2. The costs of this application be the Defendants in any event.

DATED this   day of   200

A10

APPLICATION TO AMEND
THE STATEMENT OF CASE UNDER CPR 17.3

A10.1

COMMENTARY

Amendments to the Particulars of Claim can be made at any time before service. Where service is effected any amendment requires either the consent of the other party or parties, or the permission of the court (CPR 17.1(2)(b)).

If the amendment involves the addition, substitution or removal of a party, permission is required regardless of the other parties' consent (CPR 17.1(3)). In this regard see also CPR 19.5 (addition and substitution of parties). Where the amendment is made after the expiry of a relevant limitation period see CPR 17.4.

Where the amendment has the effect of adding or substituting a new cause of action, correcting a mistake as to the name of the party, or to alter the capacity of a party see CPR 17.4(2)(3) and (4).

This draft application envisages the most common or straightforward amendments made within the primary limitation period and where no new cause of action is raised but the amendment is necessary to respond to issues raised in the defence, a response to a Part 18 request or to matters raised in the opponent's witness evidence or disclosure documents.

The general principles that the court should apply in considering whether to grant an amendment are not given anywhere in CPR 17 but reliance should be placed upon the overriding objective of the CPR to deal with cases justly. Amendments in general ought to be allowed in order that the real dispute between the parties can be decided. Any prejudice to either party can be compensated for in costs. In *Cobbold v Greenwich LBC*[1] Peter Gibson LJ stated:

> 'The overriding objective is that the Courts should deal with cases justly... Amendments in general ought to be allowed so that the real dispute between the parties can be adjudicated upon provided that any prejudice to the other party caused by the amendment can be compensated for in costs...'.

---

[1]   [1999] EWCA Civ 2074.

In *Peter Gabriel v Colin Hayward*[2] the Claimant made prolix amendments to the original statement of claim. It was held that the interest of justice required that the amendments be allowed even though the Defendants might not be adequately compensated in costs in respect of answering such lengthy amendments. In so far as the amended pleadings merely provided further detail or confirmation of matters which had been implicit in the original pleadings, they would be allowed. On balance, and although it was not possible to fully compensate the respondent by way of a costs order, such disadvantage did not outweigh the considerations of justice to the applicant.

As to prejudice to one or other of the parties, the proximity of the trial date will be an important factor. Any amendment should be sought at the earliest opportunity and it is advisable to give an explanation as to when the factors or evidence which necessitate the amendment became known.

The order requested that allows the amendment may also require provision for further directions dependent upon the nature of the amendment sought.

The court may also give directions as to amendments to be made to any other statement of case, and as to service of any amended statement of case (CPR 17.3).

Where the primary limitation period has expired CPR 17.4 gives the court power to allow such amendments in three specified classes of case defined in CPR 17.4(2), (3) and (4). The Limitation Act 1980 s 35(3) allows amendments to be made after the expiry of the primary limitation period in personal injury cases but the court must make a direction under s 33 to the effect that the usual limitation period does not apply (Limitation Act 1980 s 35(3)).

Where the amendment introduces a new cause of action that arises out of the same facts or substantially the same facts as are already in issue such amendments will usually be allowed subject to considerations of prejudice to the other party, the court's exercise of discretion under the Limitation Act 1980 s 33 and even Art 6 of the European Convention on Human Rights (right to a fair trial) (see *Goode v Hugh Martin* [2001] 3 All ER 562).

Essentially if the amendment introduces a new allegation which goes beyond merely pleading an additional fact, or further particularising a breach of statutory duty, then it will in general amount to a new cause of action.

Where the court's permission is required, the amended Statement of Case and the court copy should be endorsed as follows:

'Amended (Particulars of Claim *or as may be*) by Order of [MASTER   ] [DISTRICT JUDGE   ] (*or as may be*) dated [DATE]'.

See Practice Direction – amendments to Statements of Case CPR Part 17.

---

[2]   *Peter Gabriel v Colin Hayward* (unreported) 22 October 2004, QBD.

A10.2

APPLICATION NOTICE WITH PART 'C' STATEMENT OF TRUTH

Application Notice

	In the ANY TOWN COUNTY COURT

You should provide this information for listing the application

1. How do you wish to have your application dealt with

   a) at a hearing? ☐ }complete all questions below

   b) at a telephone conference? ☐

   c) without a hearing? ☐ *complete Qs 5 and 6 below*

2. Give a time estimate for the hearing/conference
_____ (hours) _____ (mins)

3. Is this agreed by all parties? ☐ Yes ☐ No

4. Give dates of any trial period or fixed trial date

5. Level of judge

6. Parties to be served

Claim no.	
Warrant no. (if applicable)	
Claimant (including ref.)	MR A GOODCHAP
Defendant(s) (including ref.)	ASBESTOS SHIPPING LIMITED
Date	

Note You must complete Parts A **and** B, **and** Part C if applicable. Send any relevant fee and the completed application to the court with any draft order, witness statement or other evidence; and sufficient copies for service on each respondent

1. Enter your full name, or name of solicitor

Part A

I (We) [1] [STATE NAME OF FIRM] on behalf of the claimant/defendant

2. State clearly what order you are seeking and if possible attach a draft

intend to apply for an order (a draft of which is attached) that [2] (1) Leave is granted to the claimant to amend the Statement of Case pursuant to CPR r 17.3. (2) the costs of and incidental to this application shall be paid by the claimant.

3. Briefly set out why you are seeking the order. Include the material facts on which you rely, identifying any rule or statutory provision

because[3] The Statement of Case has been served on [Date]. Proceedings were issued on [Date]. The claimant requires amendments to be made to the State of case as set out in the anexed draft amendment. The defendants do not consent to the amendments and as such the permission of the Court is required under CPR r 17.3

Part B

I (We) wish to rely on: *tick one box*

4. If you are not already a party to the proceedings, you must provide an address for service of documents

the attached (witness statement)(affidavit) ☐   my statement of case ☐

evidence in Part C in support of my application ☒

Signed		**Position or office held** (if signing on behalf of a firm or company)	[PARTNER]
	(Applicant)('s Solicitor)('s litigation friend)		

Address to which documents about this claim should be sent (including reference if appropriate)[4]

		if applicable	
	fax no.		
	DX no.		
Tel. no. Postcode	e-mail		

The court office at
is open from 10am to 4pm Monday to Friday. When corresponding with the court please address forms or letters to the Court Manager and quote the claim number.

N244 Application notice 04/00   © Crown copyright. Produced by infolaw 11/04

Part C   Claim No. [   ]

I (We) wish to rely on the following evidence in support of this application:

The claimant's claim is for damages for injuries sustained in an accident at work on [Date]. Proceedings were served on [Date] which was within the primary limitation period under the Limitation Act 1980. the relevant period of limitation will not expire until [Date].

A copy of the Statement of Casee with the proposed amendments is attached hereto and exhibited as "AB1". [SEE PRACTICE DIRECTION SUPPLEMENTAL Part 17 FOR CORRECT FORM AND ENDORSEMENT TO BE ADDED.]

The amendments consist of [BRIEF EXPLANATION AS TO THE NATURE OF THE AMENDMENT AND THE REASON FOR THE AMENDMENT, eg THE AMENDMENT CONSISTS OF A RESPONSE TO THE DEFENDANTS' VERSION OF EVENTS].

It is submitted that the amendments do not alter significantly the substance of the Statement of Case, nor do the amendments amount to a new cause of action.

The Court is referred to the Court of Appeal Judgment in Cobbold v Greenwich LBC [1999] EWCA Civ 2074 in which Peter Cobson LJ stated "The overriding objective in that the Court should deal with cases justly...Amendments in general ought to be allowed so that the real dispute between the parties can be adjudicated upon provided that any prejudice to the other party caused by the amendment can be compensated for in costs..."

The effect of the proposed amendments will not cause the defendant to suffer any or any substantial prejudice of its case.

I respectfully request that the order is made in the terms sought.

Statement of Truth

* (I believe) (the Applicant believes) that the facts stated in Part C are true

delete as appropriate

Signed [   ]   **Position or office held** [PARTNER]

(Applicant)('s Solicitor)('s litigation friend)   (if signing on behalf of firm or company)

Date [   ]

A10.3

DRAFT ORDER

IN THE ANYTOWN COUNTY COURT   CLAIM NO   12345

BETWEEN:

MR A GOODCHAP

Claimant

AND

ASBESTOS SHIPPING LTD

Defendant

DRAFT ORDER

We intend to apply for an Order that:

1. Permission is granted to the Claimant to make such amendments to the Statement of Case as are set out and delineated in the draft attached hereto.

2. The Claimant shall within 14 days of the date of this Order file with the Court the amended Statement of Case.

3. Within 14 days of this Order the Claimant shall serve a copy of this Order together with the amended Statement of Case upon the Defendant.

4. The costs of and incidental to this Application be the Defendants in any event/shall be costs in the case [*delete as appropriate*].

Dated this   day of   2006

Signed.................................... Signed.....................................

Solicitors for the Claimant   Solicitors for the Defendant

Ref: Ref:

ADMISSION BY NOTICE IN WRITING –
APPLICATION FOR JUDGMENT PURSUANT TO
CPR 14.3

A11.1

COMMENTARY

Where the defendants admit liability the claimant may apply to the court for such judgment that he is entitled to without waiting for any further issues to be decided. CPR 14.3 enables the court to give judgment for the claimant in the same way as judgment can be given under CPR 24 (summary judgment). In a case where the defendant admits liability CPR 14.3 should be used. Note that the admission must involve not only an admission of negligence but also an admission that the claimant has suffered damage. An admission of negligence only is not sufficient to allow the court to enter judgment under CPR 14.3.

If the defendant admits negligence only without an admission of damage the claimant can turn to CPR 24 to obtain summary judgment (see *Dummer v Brown* (1953)).

PRE-ACTION ADMISSIONS

In *Sowerby v Charlton* [2006] 1 WLR 568 the court held that CPR 14.1(5), which provides that the court may allow a party to amend or withdraw an admission, only applies to admissions which are made in the course of proceedings and not to pre-action admissions.

The correct approach to be adopted where a pre-action admission is withdrawn is for the claimant to apply to strike out the defence, or part of it, under CPR 3.4(2)(b) on the basis that the withdrawal of an admission amounts to an abuse of the court's process (see A16*).

In *Stoke-on-Trent City Council v Walley* [2006] EWCA Civ 1137 an admission of liability which was made prior to proceedings was withdrawn. The claimant issued proceedings. The defendants filed a defence denying liability and alleging contributory negligence. The claimant then applied under CPR 3.4(2)(b) to strike out the defence as an abuse of process. The defendants cross-applied for permission to withdraw the earlier admission of liability under CPR 14.1(5).

It was held that in order for the claimant to show that the withdrawal of an admission prior to proceedings amounted to an abuse of process it would be necessary to show that the defendants had acted in bad faith. There was no evidence to support that contention in this case.

It should be noted that with effect from 6 April 2007 a new rule will be inserted into the CPR covering admissions made before the commencement of proceedings. This will be rule 14.1(A), however, the new rules do not provide any guidance as to the factors which the court should take into account in considering an application to withdraw an admission. In addition, no distinction is made between pre-action admissions made in fast track cases and multi track cases. In *Sowerby* this distinction was made clear ie the court is less likely to allow a withdrawal of an admission made pre-action in a fast track case than it would in a multi track case.

A11.2

APPLICATION NOTICE WITH PART 'C' STATEMENT OF TRUTH

Application Notice	In the ANY TOWN COUNTY COURT	

You should provide this information for listing the application	
1. How do you wish to have your application dealt with	**Claim no.**	

a) at a hearing? ☐ } complete all questions below
b) at a telephone conference? ☐
c) without a hearing? ☐ complete Qs 5 and 6 below

Warrant no. (if applicable)	

2. Give a time estimate for the hearing/conference
_____ (hours) _____ (mins)

Claimant (including ref.)	MR A GOODCHAP

3. Is this agreed by all parties? ☐ Yes ☐ No
4. Give dates of any trial period or fixed trial date

Defendant(s) (including ref.)	DODGY CORPORATEVEIL LIMITED

5. Level of judge
6. Parties to be served

Date	

Note You must complete Parts A **and** B, and Part C if applicable. Send any relevant fee and the completed application to the court with any draft order, witness statement or other evidence; and sufficient copies for service on each respondent

1. Enter your full name, or name of solicitor

Part A
I (We) [1]   on behalf of the claimant/defendant

2. State clearly what order you are seeking and if possible attach a draft

intend to apply for an order (a draft of which is attached) that [2] (1) pursuant to CPR 14.3 judgment be entered for the claimant with damages to be assessed and costs. (2) The costs of and incidental to this application be the claimant's in any event.

3. Briefly set out why you are seeking the order. Include the material facts on which you rely, identifying any rule or statutory provision

because [3] the defendant's have admitted liability in writing to pay damages to the claimant.

Part B
I (We) wish to rely on: *tick one box*

the attached (witness statement)(affidavit) ☐   my statement of case ☐

4. If you are not already a party to the proceedings, you must provide an address for service of documents

evidence in Part C in support of my application ☒

Signed		Position or office held	[PARTNER]

(Applicant)('s Solicitor)('s litigation friend)   (if signing on behalf of a firm or company)

Address to which documents about this claim should be sent (including reference if appropriate) [4]

	if applicable	
	fax no.	
	DX no.	
Tel. no. Postcode	e-mail	

The court office at
is open from 10am to 4pm Monday to Friday. When corresponding with the court please address forms or letters to the Court Manager and quote the claim number.
N244 Application notice 04/00   © Crown copyright. Produced by infolaw 11/04

Part C   Claim No. [   ]

I (We) wish to rely on the following evidence in support of this application:

The claimant makes this application for judgment to be entered against the claimant pursuant to CPR 14.3 for damages to be assessed and costs in relation to a claim for damages arising out of injuries sustained by the claimant as a result of [ACCIDENT AT WORK][DEVELOPMENT OF WORK RELATED DISEASE/CONDITION] during the course of his employment with the defendants at their premises [STATE DEFENDANTS NAME AND ADDRESS].

Proceedings were issued against the defendants on [DATE]. By their defence dated [DATE] the defendants denied liability and/or alleged contributory negligence on the part of the claimant.

By letter dated [DATE] the defendants have admitted liability to pay the claimant's claim where it is stated:

"Liability is conceded" [OR STATE PRECISE WORDING OF THE WRITTEN ADMISSION].

In reliance on the full and open admission of liability previously made, the claimant has taken no further steps to investigate the issue if liability in this claim and the claimant invites the Court to enter judgment in his favour on the issue of liability with damages to be assessed and costs.

Statement of Truth

*(I believe)(The Applicant believes) that the facts stated in Part C are true

delete as appropriate

Signed		Position or office held	[PARTNER]
	(Applicant)('s Solicitor)('s litigation friend)	(if signing on behalf of firm or company)	
		Date	

A11.3

DRAFT ORDER

IN THE ANY TOWN COUNTY COURT   CLAIM NO AT12345

BETWEEN:

MR A GOODCHAP

Claimant

-and-

DODGY CORPORATEVEIL LIMITED

Defendant

DRAFT ORDER

IT IS ORDERED THAT

1. Judgment be entered for the Claimant with damages to be assessed and costs.

2. The costs of and incidental to this application be paid by the Defendants in any event.

3. [*State further directions sought for disposal of the case.*]

APPLICATION FOR FURTHER AND BETTER PARTICULARS UNDER CPR 18

A12.1

COMMENTARY

Part 18 replaces the former RSC in relation to requests for further and better particulars on the particulars of claim or defence. Since the introduction of the CPR the term 'pleadings' is replaced by 'Statements of Case'. This includes the particulars of claim, defence, Part 20 claim, or a reply to a defence. It also includes any information given by one party voluntarily or by an order for further information under CPR 18.1.

CPR 18.1 gives the court power to order one party to clarify or to give additional information in relation to any matter which is in dispute. It is not confined to matters set out in the statement of case and can include any matters or issues which arise from the proceedings generally. The Practice Direction which supplements Part 18 sets out the procedure which should be considered prior to making a request for an order under CPR 18.1. Before an application is made the party seeking clarification or information should serve a request for information in writing and should state the date by which a response to the request should be served. A reasonable time should be given for the response. (See PD 18.1.)

Requests should be concise and strictly confined to matters which are reasonably necessary and proportionate to enable the first party to prepare his own case or to understand the case he has to meet.

If the party to whom the request is made objects to answering the request then those objections must be set out in writing and must state the reasons for the objection.

In cases which are allocated to the fast track it is good practice to make the request for further information at the time of filing the allocation questionnaire. The court may then give directions as to request for further information upon allocation or at case management conference stage. (See Practice Direction supplement to CPR

Part 28 PD2.8.) The same power is contained in respect of multi track cases: see Practice Direction supplement to CPR 29.3.8.

If the defendants do not respond to a request for further information, the claimant is entitled to apply to the court for an order requiring the defendant to reply within a particular time. Under the Practice Direction supplement to Part 18 (PD 28.5.5) where the defendant has made no response to a request served upon them, the claimant need not serve the application notice on the defendant and the court may deal with the application without a hearing. However, at least 14 days must have passed since the request was served and the time stated in it for a response has expired. (PD 28.5.5). Usually, however, the request should be served on the defendant at least three clear days before the date listed for the hearing of the application.

The evidence relied upon in support of the application should include evidence as to whether any response has been provided by the defendants and, if so, a description of the response.

In the example given, a request for further information is made in a case involving a claim for damages for asbestos-related disease where the defence amounts to either a mere blanket denial, or a denial with an averment that the statutory provisions are not applicable. It is a fairly common occurrence that defences in cases involving asbestos litigation, where the exposure took place a long time ago, reflect an absence of any thorough investigation of the claim. An averment that exposure did not take place as alleged and/or that the defendants deny the applicability of the pleaded regulations upon which the claimant relies are common responses.

It should be noted, however, that requests for further information should be used sparingly and not in the same way as requests for further and better particulars were used historically prior to the introduction of the CPR. In *Mcphilemy v Times Newspapers Ltd* [1999] 3 All ER 775 Lord Woolf MR indicated that he preferred the situation where parties should await simultaneous exchange of witness statements together with standard disclosure before an application for further information be made. After exchange and disclosure, the parties' respective cases should be fairly obvious. The need for extensive pleadings should thereby be reduced as often these can lead to a situation where the issues are obscured rather than thrown into relief. Therefore, requests for further information should be approached with caution as the defendants may put forward the argument that 'all shall be revealed' upon exchange of witness statements and standard disclosure.

Where requests for a clarification of facts to which one or more of the issues in the case relate, the courts will adopt a fairly strict approach in considering whether to allow requests for clarification. Fishing expeditions are discouraged, as are requests which are too vague or where the information requested cannot reasonably be provided.

When considering an application the court will have regard to the following:

(i) the likely benefit that will result if the information is given; and

(ii) the likely cost involved in providing such information and the general question of proportionality and the overriding objective to deal with the case justly.

If it is a reasonable request that requires information that would be likely to narrow the issues, result in an overall saving of costs or genuinely reveal the true nature of the case being put forward by the defendants, then the application is more likely to succeed.

NB Under practice direction to Part 18 para 5.5 where the second party has made no response to a request served upon him, the first party need not serve the application notice on the second party and the court may deal with the application without a hearing. At least 14 days must have passed since the request was served and the time stated for a response has expired.

A12.2

APPLICATION NOTICE WITH PART 'C' STATEMENT OF TRUTH

Application Notice		In the ANY TOWN COUNTY COURT	

You should provide this information for listing the application

1. How do you wish to have your application dealt with
   - a) at a hearing? ☒ } *complete all questions below*
   - b) at a telephone conference? ☐
   - c) without a hearing? ☐ *complete Qs 5 and 6 below*
2. Give a time estimate for the hearing/conference
   1 (hours) ____ (mins)
3. Is this agreed by all parties? ☐ Yes ☒ No
4. Give dates of any trial period or fixed trial date
5. Level of judge   DISTRICT
6. Parties to be served   DEFENDANT

Claim no.	
Warrant no. (if applicable)	
Claimant (including ref.)	MR A GOODCHAP
Defendant(s) (including ref.)	DODGY CORPORATEVEIL LIMITED
Date	

Note You must complete Parts A **and** B, and Part C if applicable. Send any relevant fee and the completed application to the court with any draft order, witness statement or other evidence; and sufficient copies for service on each respondent

Part A

1. Enter your full name, or name of solicitor

I (We) [STATE NAME OF FIRM] on behalf of the claimant/defendant

2. State clearly what order you are seeking and if possible attach a draft

intend to apply for an order (a draft of which is attached) that [2]

(1) The defendants do provide further information of the defence as particularised in the claimant's request for further information of the defence [DATED].

(2) The costs of and incidental to the application be the claimants's in any event.

3. Briefly set out why you are seeking the order. Include the material facts on which you rely, identifying any rule or statutory provision

because [3] the defendants have [failed to][adequately respond to] the the claimant's request for further information of the defence.

Part B

I (We) wish to rely on: *tick one box*

the attached (witness statement)(affidavit) ☐   my statement of case ☐

4. If you are not already a party to the proceedings, you must provide an address for service of documents

evidence in Part C in support of my application ☒

Signed		**Position or office held** (if signing on behalf of a firm or company)	

(Applicant)('s Solicitor)('s litigation friend)

Address to which documents about this claim should be sent (including reference if appropriate) [4]

	if applicable	
	fax no.	
	DX no.	
Tel. no. Postcode	e-mail	

The court office at Any Town County Court, Any Street, Any Place, Anytown is open from 10am to 4pm Monday to Friday. When corresponding with the court please address forms or letters to the Court Manager and quote the claim number.

N244 Application notice 04/00   © Crown copyright. Produced by infolaw 11/04

Part C

Claim No. [   ]

I̶ (We) wish to rely on the following evidence in support of this application:

The claimant, Mrs Joanne Bloggs (Widow and Administratix of the Estate of Joseph Bloggs (deceased)) makes this application for an order that the defendants do provide [further information][clarification] of the defence.

The deceased was employed by the defendants as a fitter from [RELEVANT DATES]. The claimant alleges that her late husband was exposed to asbestos either negligently and/or in breach of statutory duty by the defendants, their servants or agents and/or predecessors in title as a result of which the claimant developed asbestos related disease and subsequently mesothelioma and the claimant died on [DATE]. A claim for damages was made against the defendants and proceedings were issued on [DATE]. A defence was filed on [DATE] in which the defendants deny liability. The defendant's denial of liability makes averment that the defendants did not expose the claimant to asbestos dust or fibres either negligently or at all. However, the defendants do not further particularise the reasons for the denial of liability. The defendants further deny the applicability of the regulations pleaded in the Particulars of Claim and upon which the claimant relies.

A request for further information of the defence was served on the defendants (the Respondent) in writing stating that a response to the request should be served on [DATE]:

EITHER

No response has been received from the Defendants to date.

OR ALTERNATIVELY

The defendants have failed to adequately respond to the request for further information and attached and exhibited herewith is a copy of the claimants request for further information [AND IF APPROPRIATE A COPY OF THE DEFENDANTS RESPONSE].

The applicant respectfully requests the Court to make the order as requested together with an order for costs in the applicant's favour.

Statement of Truth

*(I believe) * (̶T̶h̶e̶ ̶a̶p̶p̶l̶i̶c̶a̶n̶t̶ ̶b̶e̶l̶i̶e̶v̶e̶s̶) that the facts stated in Part C are true

*delete as appropriate

Signed		Position or office held	[PARTNER]
	(Applicant)('s Solicitor)(̶'̶s̶ ̶l̶i̶t̶i̶g̶a̶t̶i̶o̶n̶ ̶f̶r̶i̶e̶n̶d̶)	(if signing on behalf of firm or company)	
		Date	

A12.3

REQUEST FOR FURTHER INFORMATION

IN THE ANYTOWN COUNTY COURT   CLAIM NO

BETWEEN:

MRS JOANNE BLOGGS
(WIDOW & ADMINISTRATRIX OF THE ESTATE OF JOE BLOGGS DECEASED)

Claimant

-and-

OLD BOILER ENGINEERING CO LTD

Defendant

REQUEST FOR FURTHER INFORMATION OF THE DEFENCE

Under Paragraph 2

Of the whole paragraph

REQUEST

1. Pursuant to the Civil Procedure Rules, a Defendant is required to give reasons for a denial. Please state precisely why the Defendant contends that the Regulations named could not and/or did not apply to the Deceased's employment with it.

UNDER PARAGRAPH 4

Of the whole paragraph

REQUEST

2. Please confirm that if the Claimant establishes that the Defendant was exposed to asbestos when working for the Defendant, the Defendant will admit that such was in breach of its duty of care (whether in negligence or statutory duty) to the Deceased.
3. If the Defendant contends that such exposure to asbestos would not constitute a breach of its duty to the Deceased, please specify the basis of such contention.

    (The Claimant again refers to the Civil Procedure Rules and the requirement for the Defendant to set out reasons for any denial).

The Defendant is requested to answer this Request for Further Information within 28 days of service.

DATED THIS   day of   200

A13

APPLICATION FOR DISCLOSURE AND INSPECTION OF DOCUMENTS POST-ISSUE PURSUANT TO CPR 31.12

A13.1

COMMENTARY

In an application for specific disclosure the practice direction supplementing Part 31, para 5.4 should be considered carefully before drafting the affidavit or statement of truth in support of the application. The overriding objective will be foremost in the mind of the district judge in deciding the merits of the application and the issue of proportionality and justice to the parties are important factors in determining firstly the success of the application and, secondly the scope of the order for disclosure itself.

The potential value of the claim will be a factor in determining the success or failure of the application but care should be taken in confining the ambit of the documents or classes of documents which are sought since failure to do so may fall foul of the proportionality rule. The ease with which a search can be undertaken and the number and classes of documents involved should be identified or described as accurately as possible. Lack of precision in the description of the documents or classes of documents is a common reason given for the courts' refusal to make such orders.

The court has jurisdiction under CPR 31.12 to make an order for specific disclosure at any time whether or not standard disclosure has taken place (*Dayman v Canyon Holdings Ltd* (2006) Ch D 11/1/2006). CPR 31 does not contain a restriction to the effect that specific discovery would only be ordered after standard disclosure has taken place.

The order for specific disclosure can impose up to three obligations upon the party against whom the order is made i.e. to disclose documents specified in the order, to carry out a search for documents, and to disclose documents located as a result of that search. The application can be resisted on the grounds that either disclosure, the search itself or inspection of a document would be disproportionate. In *Legal & General Asssurance Society Ltd v Taulke-Johnson* [2002] EWHC 120 an application for specific disclosure under CPR 31.12 was allowed on the basis that the disclosure was within the disclosing party's capabilities even at a late stage of the proceedings. The likely cost of the disclosure was not prohibitive and the significance of the information and documents was likely to be substantial.

The significance of the further information sought is a persuasive reason for an order for disclosure being made and therefore the issues to which the documents relate should be clearly specified within the affidavit or statement of truth.

Note that where a party claims a right to withhold inspection of documents, the mere fact that a document was confidential was not a reason for withholding inspection (see *Coflexip SA v Stolt Offshore MS Ltd* (2004) Ch D).

A13.2

APPLICATION NOTICE WITH PART 'C' STATEMENT OF TRUTH

Application Notice

You should provide this information for listing the application

1. How do you wish to have your application dealt with

   a) at a hearing? ☐ } *complete all questions below*
   b) at a telephone conference? ☐
   c) without a hearing? ☐ *complete Qs 5 and 6 below*

2. Give a time estimate for the hearing/conference
   _____ (hours) _____ (mins)

3. Is this agreed by all parties? ☐ Yes ☐ No

4. Give dates of any trial period or fixed trial date

5. Level of judge

6. Parties to be served

In the	
Claim no.	
Warrant no. (if applicable)	
Claimant (including ref.)	
Defendant(s) (including ref.)	
Date	

Note You must complete Parts A **and** B, **and** Part C if applicable. Send any relevant fee and the completed application to the court with any draft order, witness statement or other evidence; and sufficient copies for service on each respondent

Part A

1. Enter your full name, or name of solicitor

I (We) [1] on behalf of the claimant/~~defendant~~

2. State clearly what order you are seeking and if possible attach a draft

intend to apply for an order (a draft of which is attached) that [2] pursuant to CPR r 31.12 (1) the Defendants do disclose the documents or classes of documents specified in the attached schedule hereto and/or carry out a search to the extent stated in the Draft Order annexed hereto and further that the defendants shall disclose any documents located as a result of that search. because [3]

3. Briefly set out why you are seeking the order. Include the material facts on which you rely, identifying any rule or statutory provision

(1) The documents or classes of documents referred to in the schedule annexed hereto are relevant to one or more of the issues between the parties.
(2) The aforementioned documents are or have been in the possession and control of the defendants.
(3) The documents disclosed by the Defendants in their disclosure statement dated [date] are inadequate.
(4) The defendants are under a duty to carry out a reasonable and proportionate search for the documents or classes of documents listed in the schedule annexed hereto and have failed to do so.
(5) The Court has power to order specific disclosure of the aforementioned documents or classes of documents pursuant to CPR r 31.12(1).

Part B

I (We) wish to rely on: *tick one box*

4. If you are not already a party to the proceedings, you must provide an address for service of documents

the attached (witness statement)(affidavit) ☐   my statement of case ☐

evidence in Part C in support of my application ☒

Signed		Position or office held	
	(Applicant)('s Solicitor)~~('s litigation friend)~~	(if signing on behalf of a firm or company)	

Address to which documents about this claim should be sent (including reference if appropriate) [4]

		if applicable	
	fax no.		
	DX no.		
Tel. no.	Postcode	e-mail	

The court office at

is open from 10am to 4pm Monday to Friday. When corresponding with the court please address forms or letters to the Court Manager and quote the claim number.

N244 Application notice 04/00   © Crown copyright. Produced by infolaw 11/04

Part C   Claim No. [   ]

I (We) wish to rely on the following evidence in support of this application:

The claimant claims damages for personal injuries and losses sustained as a result of the work related condition namely Hand Arm Vibration Syndrome/Vibration White Finger as a result of exposure to vibration during the course of his employment with the defendants as a result of their negligence and/or breach of statutory duty.

The circumstances of the development of the claimant's conditions are [State brief facts of the claim].

It is alleged that the defendants were negligent in that they failed to reduce the periods of time for which the claimant was exposed to vibration whether by introducing a system of job rotation or limiting the amount of time the claimant was required to use relevant equipment or otherwise. It is further alleged that the defendants were negligent in that they failed to heed the incidence of vibration induced injury amongst the workforce which was identified by routine health surveillance undertaken by the occupational health department.

It is further alleged that if the defendants considered the information which would have been available from the occupational health department that the damage suffered by the claimant could have been avoided by introducing simple and sensible measures to reduce the risk of vibration damage which would not have been prohibitive in terms of either cost or efficiency. The defendants have produced documents in relation to vibration emission levels from the handheld tools which, the defendants contend, show that the level of vibration to which the claimant was exposed was not enough to require preventative measures being taken by the defendants.

The claimant contends that the risk of damage to the claimant would have been apparent to the defendants in the light of the significant incidence of HAVS symptoms amongst the workforce as identified in the occupational health records and, had the defendants taken heed of the same, reasonable precautions could have been undertaken to reduce that risk to the lowest reasonably practicable level.

I am instructed and verily believe that an identifiable and significant incidence of Hand Arm Vibration Syndrome (HAVS) existed amongst the workforce for several years before the claimant began to exhibit symptoms of HAVS.

A request for disclosure of the documents was made to the defendants on [Date]. The defendants have failed or refused to disclose those documents and have failed or refused to carry out a reasonable search for the same.

The claimant requests that the defendants be ordered to conduct a search of the occupational health records of all employees who have been employed within the department in which the claimant worked and who were exposed to vibration from the relevant handheld tools within the period from [Insert relevant dates] and which may identify those employees who have been diagnosed with HAVS or have exhibited symptoms consistent with a diagnosis of HAVS. It is further requested that those documents which are discovered as a result of that search should be disclosed to the claimant's solicitors.

It is further submitted that a search of the occupational health department records would not be disproportionate in relation to the value of the claim since the occupational health department routinely completed questionnaires described as "Hand Arm Vibration Syndrome Questionnaire". A copy of the same questionnaire in relation to the claimant which has been obtained from the claimant's occupational health record is attached herewith and exhibited as "AB1". It is submitted that such questionnaires have been completed in respect of each employee within the department and such questionnaires would be easily retrieved from each occupational health file for each employee. It is further submitted that the documents could be redacted to obliterate the identities of the employees concerned so as to avoid any potential issues of confidentiality.

It is estimated that there are approximately 37 employees currently employed with the department and that no more than 50 employees' occupational health files, including ex-employees, would be involved over the period [Insert relevant dates].

These documents are directly relevant to the issue of the level of risk of vibration damage to which the claimant was exposed and also to the issue of foreseeability of the injury to the claimant.

Cont'd.../

It is also submitted that the claimant would be prejudiced in the presentation of his claim without being given the opportunity to inspect the documents or classes of documents requested and identified in the draft order annexed hereto. It is further submitted that disclosure of the requested documents will enable the claimant to advance his case or to damage that of the defendants or that disclosure of the requested documents may lead to a chain of enquiry which has either of those consequences.

I respectfully request that the Court makes the order in the terms requested.

Statement of Truth

*(I believe) *(The applicant believes) that the facts stated in Part C are true

delete as appropriate

Signed		Position or office held	[PARTNER]
	(Applicant)('s Solicitor)('s litigation friend)	(if signing on behalf of firm or company)	
		Date	

A13.3

DRAFT ORDER

IN THE ANYTOWN COUNTY COURT   **CLAIM NO**
BETWEEN:

MR A GOODCHAP

Claimant

AND
ANYOLD IRONFOUNDERS LTD

Defendant

DRAFT ORDER

TAKE NOTICE that we wish to apply for an Order in the following terms:-

1   The Defendants shall within 28 days of the date of this Order conduct a search of all occupational health records relating to the following classes of employees;

   (i) All employees now engaged in the use of vibration tools in the fettling department, and;

   (ii) All ex-employees who were engaged in the use of handheld tools within the fettling department;

within the period January 1999 to December 2004

2   In consequence of the search, the Defendants shall within 7 days thereafter disclose to the Claimant's solicitors those documents described as 'Hand Arm Vibration Syndrome Questionnaire' in respect of the employees or classes of employees referred to in paragraph 1 (i) and (ii) above.

3   The costs of and incidental to this Application be paid by the Defendants within 14 days of the date of this Order.

Dated this   day of

Signed ……………………………………………….

Ref:

Solicitors for the Claimant

TO: The District Judge

      The Defendants

APPLICATION TO VARY CASE MANAGEMENT TIMETABLE UNDER CPR 28.4

A14.1

COMMENTARY

In a fast track case an application to vary the case management timetable must be made under CPR 28.4(1) (*see the practice direction which supplements CPR Part 28*).

If variation of the date fixed for returning the allocation questionnaire is desired then the application must be made under CPR 26.3(6)(A). An application to vary the time fixed for returning the pre-trial checklist or to vary the trial or trial period must be made under CPR 28.4(1)(a), (b) or (c). All other dates set by the court for doing any act may not be varied by the parties if the variation would make it necessary to vary any of the dates for the return of the pre-trial checklist, the trial or the trial period (see CPR 28.4(2)).

The parties may vary dates for compliance with the court order by written agreement except where this would effect the date for the return of the pre-trial checklist, trial or trial period.

Any variation that affects the trial date in particular will be closely scrutinised by the courts and compelling reasons must be given before a court will alter the trial date or trial period. One example, as is referred to in the draft application herewith, is the situation that often arises in personal injury cases where the medical evidence is incomplete because the prognosis is uncertain.

Consideration should also be given in such circumstances as to whether an application for an order for a split trial on liability.

In multi track cases an application to vary directions should be made under CPR 29.5(1). The same principles apply and the dates may be varied by agreement between the parties so long as that does not affect any of the dates referred to in CPR 29.5(1)(a) to (e) eg trial period, trial itself, pre-trial review etc (*see the practice direction which supplements CPR Part 29 para 6*).

A14.2

APPLICATION NOTICE WITH PART 'C' STATEMENT OF TRUTH

Application Notice			**In the ANY TOWN COUNTY COURT**	
You should provide this information for listing the application			**Claim no.**	AT12345
1. How do you wish to have your application dealt with				
			Warrant no. (if applicable)	
a) at a hearing?	☐	} *complete all questions below*		
b) at a telephone conference?	☐		**Claimant** (including ref.)	MR A GOODCHAP
c) without a hearing?	☐	*complete Qs 5 and 6 below*		
2. Give a time estimate for the hearing/conference			**Defendant(s)** (including ref.)	ASBESTOS SHIPPING LIMITED
_____ (hours) _____ (mins)				
3. Is this agreed by all parties? ☐ Yes ☐ No			**Date**	
4. Give dates of any trial period or fixed trial date				
5. Level of judge				
6. Parties to be served				

Note You must complete Parts A **and** B, and Part C if applicable. Send any relevant fee and the completed application to the court with any draft order, witness statement or other evidence; and sufficient copies for service on each respondent

Part A

1. Enter your full name, or name of solicitor

I (We) [1] [STATE NAME OF FIRM] on behalf of the claimant/defendant

2. State clearly what order you are seeking and if possible attach a draft

intend to apply for an order (a draft of which is attached) that [2] **The Case Management timetable set out in the Order of the Court dated [Date] be varied pursuant to CPR r 28.4**

3. Briefly set out why you are seeking the order. Include the material facts on which you rely, identifying any rule or statutory provision

because [3] **The claim has been listed for [trial][a trial period] on [Date/s]. The claim is not ready to be heard at trial since, eg the order for directions dated [Date] has not been complied with.**

Part B

I (We) wish to rely on: *tick one box*

the attached (witness statement)(affidavit) ☐   my statement of case ☐

4. If you are not already a party to the proceedings, you must provide an address for service of documents

evidence in Part C in support of my application ☒

Signed		**Position or office held** (if signing on behalf of a firm or company)	[PARTNER]
(Applicant)('s Solicitor)('s litigation friend)			

Address to which documents about this claim should be sent (including reference if appropriate) [4]

	if applicable	
	fax no.	
	DX no.	
Tel. no. Postcode	e-mail	

The court office at

is open from 10am to 4pm Monday to Friday. When corresponding with the court please address forms or letters to the Court Manager and quote the claim number.

N244 Application notice 04/00   © Crown copyright. Produced by infolaw 11/04

Part C

Claim No. | AT12345

I (We) wish to rely on the following evidence in support of this application:

The claimant makes this applications for and order for variance of the Directions given by District Judge [Name] by order dated [Date] under CPR r 28.4.

This claim has been allocated to the Fast Track.

The claim has been listed for trial the trial period has been provided for [Dates] by the Order dated [Date]. The Order provided that: [State relevant provisions within the timetable which the applicant seeks to vary].

As a result of delays in the timetable the claim will not be ready for trial since, eg witness evidence has yet to be exchanged [state reasons] OR the medical evidence on behalf of the claimant is not yet complete since [eg an accurate prognosis or diagnosis has yet to be provided].

This being an application to vary the [trial date][trial period] which the Court has fixed the matter falls to be dealt with under CPR 28.4.

The claimant respectfully requests that the Order be made in the terms sought.

Statement of Truth

* (I believe) (the Applicant believes) that the facts stated in Part C are true

**delete as appropriate*

Signed

(Applicant)('s Solicitor)('s litigation friend)

Position or office held
(if signing on behalf of firm or company)

[PARTNER]

Date

N244 Application notice 02/07

© Crown copyright. Issued by Information for Lawyers Limited   2

A14.3

DRAFT ORDER

IN THE ANYTOWN COUNTY COURT   CLAIM NO

BETWEEN:

MR A GOODCHAP

Claimant

and

ASBESTOS SHIPPING LTD

Defendant

DRAFT ORDER

Upon the Claimant and the Defendant having agreed to the terms set forth in the Schedule hereto it is ordered:-

1   The trial period listed for [*date*] be vacated and a new trial period be substituted commencing [*date*] OR:

2   The Trial date of [*date*] shall be vacated.

3   The following directions shall apply [*state proposed new directions*].

4   The costs of and incidental to this Application be costs in the case.

Dated this   day of   2006

Signed.. Signed......................................

Solicitors for the Claimant   Solicitors for the Defendant

Ref: Ref:

APPLICATION FOR SUMMARY JUDGMENT UNDER CPR 24

A15.1

COMMENTARY

CPR 24.2 permits the court to summarily dispose of cases where a party has no reasonable prospects of succeeding in the claim or defence.

Applications under CPR Part 24 for summary judgment can be made only after filing of the acknowledgment of service or a defence. They should usually be made between acknowledgement of service and filing of the allocation questionnaire. However, in some circumstances an application for summary judgment may be more likely to succeed if it is made after disclosure and exchange of witness evidence. By that time both parties have effectively nailed their colours to the mast.

In personal injury claims applications under CPR 24.2 rarely succeed since where liability is denied the Court will be reluctant to find that there is no real defence or issue which have no reasonable prospect of succeeding. Where factual disputes arise the courts are more likely to allow the issues to be heard at trial. Therefore it is difficult to envisage a situation in personal injury claims where applications under CPR 24.2 will succeed. The example given involves one set of circumstances which could give rise to a successful application.

The draft application provided here relates to a claim for damages for dermatitis caused by exposure to hazardous substances and failure by the defendants to carry out appropriate risk assessments in breach of reg 6(1) of the COSHH Regulations 1999. Regulation 6(1) imposes strict liability. The Defendant has provided no evidence of having carried out risk assessments either by way of documents or witness statements. In the absence of any evidence of risk assessments the application has been made for summary judgment under CPR 24.2.

In the example given the practitioner may consider it more prudent to 'keep their powder dry' in respect of a breach of reg 6(1) of the COSHH Regulations but the draft application provides an example of how CPR 24.2 may allow the court in such a situation to enter judgment on the basis that the defendant has no real prospect of successfully defending the claim.

Note that the issue of causation is dealt with in the application as being proven by the medical evidence although it is not a necessary requirement of CPR 24 that causation should be established. However, it is unlikely that an application in these circumstances would be successful where causation is in dispute. The example assumes that medical evidence is agreed or is not challenged by the defendants.

The hearing for an application for summary judgment is not a trial in itself. (See *Three Rivers District Counsel v Bank of England (No 3)* [2001] 2 All ER.513, HL.)

The court should consider the evidence produced by way of witness statements and also the evidence that could reasonably be expected to be available at trial. The question as to whether there is a real prospect of success should not be approached by applying the standard of proof at trial ie the balance of probabilities. (See *Royal Brompton Hospital NHS Trust v Hammond (No 5)* [2001] EWCA Civ 550, CA.)

The test which the court will apply is whether the defence has a *realistic* prospect of success as opposed to a fanciful prospect. *See Swain v Hillman & GAM* (1999) Times, 4 November 1999, CA where Lord Woolf MR stated that the words 'no real prospect of succeeding' did not need amplification and the word 'real' required the court to see whether there was a realistic rather than fanciful prospect of success. CPR 24.2 was not intended to dispense with the need for a trial where there were issues which should be considered at trial. The Judge should not conduct a mini-trial in deciding whether to exercise the power. Furthermore it was incorrect to adopt the test that the claim 'would be bound to be dismissed at trial'.

The burden of proof rests on the applicant to show that there are grounds to believe that the respondent has no real prospects of success and that there is no other compelling reason for a trial. See practice directions supplementing Part 24 and also *ED and F Man Liquid Products Ltd v Patel* [2003] EWCA Civ 472. Under Practice Direction 24.2(3) the application notice or the evidence contained in it must (a) identify concisely any point of law or provision in a document on which he relies, and/or (b) state that it is made because the applicant believes that on the evidence the respondent has no real prospect of succeeding on the claim or issue or of successfully defending the claim or issue to which the Application relates, and in either case state that the applicant knows of no other reason why the disposal of the claim or issue should await trial.

An application under CPR 24 may be combined with an application for an interim payment of damages and also with an application to strike out under CPR 3.4(2) (see commentary to A16 and A18).

A15.2

APPLICATION NOTICE WITH PART 'C' STATEMENT OF TRUTH

Application Notice

In the ANY TOWN COUNTY COURT	
Claim no.	AT12345
Warrant no. (if applicable)	
Claimant (including ref.)	MR A GOODCHAP
Defendant(s) (including ref.)	A N ENGINEERING COMPANY LTD
Date	

You should provide this information for listing the application

1. How do you wish to have your application dealt with

    a) at a hearing? ☐ } *complete all questions below*

    b) at a telephone conference? ☐

    c) without a hearing? ☐ *complete Qs 5 and 6 below*

2. Give a time estimate for the hearing/conference

    _____ (hours) _____ (mins)

3. Is this agreed by all parties? ☐ Yes ☐ No

4. Give dates of any trial period or fixed trial date

5. Level of judge

6. Parties to be served

Note You must complete Parts A **and** B, **and** Part C if applicable. Send any relevant fee and the completed application to the court with any draft order, witness statement or other evidence; and sufficient copies for service on each respondent

1. Enter your full name, or name of solicitor

Part A

I (We)[1] [state name of firm] on behalf of the claimant/~~defendant~~

2. State clearly what order you are seeking and if possible attach a draft

intend to apply for an order (a draft of which is attached) that [2]

(1) Judgment be entered for the Claimant for an amount to be decided and costs.

(2) The costs of and incidental to this application be the claimant's in any event.

3. Briefly set out why you are seeking the order. Include the material facts on which you rely, identifying any rule or statutory provision

because[3] pursuant to CPR 24.2 the Court may give Summary Judgment against the defendant on the whole of the claim on a particular issue if it considers that the defendant has no real prospect of successfully defending the claim or issue.

Part B

I-We wish to rely on: *tick one box*

4. If you are not already a party to the proceedings, you must provide an address for service of documents

the attached (witness statement)(affidavit) ☐   my statement of case ☐

evidence in Part C in support of my application ☒

Signed		**Position or office held**	[PARTNER]
(Applicant)('s Solicitor)(~~'s litigation friend~~)		(if signing on behalf of a firm or company)	

Address to which documents about this claim should be sent (including reference if appropriate)[4]

	if applicable	
	fax no.	
	DX no.	
Tel. no. Postcode	e-mail	

The court office at

is open from 10am to 4pm Monday to Friday. When corresponding with the court please address forms or letters to the Court Manager and quote the claim number.

N244 Application notice 04/00   © Crown copyright. Produced by infolaw 11/04

Part C   Claim No.   AT12345

I-We wish to rely on the following evidence in support of this application:

The claimant makes this application for an order pursuant to CPR r 24.2 that Summary Judgment shall be entered against the defendant on the issue of primary liability with the issues of contributory negligence and damages to be assessed at a later date. The claimant who is employed by the Defendants as a machine operator claims damages for personal injury and losses and expenses incurred as a result of the Defendant's negligence. It is alleged that the defendants were negligent in that they exposed the claimant to hazardous substances and thereby caused him to develop the condition of dermatitis on both hands.

It is alleged, inter alia, that the defendants were negligent in that they exposed the claimant to coolant oils which were known to be hazardous to the skin and to which the provisions of the Control of Substances Hazardous to Health Regulations (COSHH) 1999 are applicable. The Particulars of Claim alleged, inter alia, that the defendants were negligent in that they were in breach of their obligations under regulation 6(1) of the aforesaid Regulations in that they carried on work liable to expose the claimant to a substance hazardous to health without having made a suitable and sufficient assessment of the risk created by that work. Breach of regulation 6(1) COSHH imposes strict liability upon the defendants.

By their defence the defendants deny liability under regulation 6(1) of the aforementioned Regulations and aver that a risk assessment was carried out prior to the introduction of the coolant oils into the work process. This averment is not further particularised within the defence.

The claimant relies on the medical evidence of [State name] in his report dated [Date] in which he confirms that the claimant's condition has been caused by exposure to the substance to which the claimant was exposed at work. The defendants admit causation OR the defendants do not seek to rely on medical evidence. As such the issue remaining to be decided is whether the defendants were in breach of duty of care/breach of statutory duty.

Disclosure has taken place by list. The defendants have provided full disclosure of documents by way of their obligations under the Pre-Action Protocol and also by virtue of the Order of the Court [dated] in which directions for disclosure of documents were provided. A copy of the defendants' List of Documents and Statement of Truth is attached herewith and exhibited as [Number of exhibit].

Witness statements have been exchanged between the parties pursuant to the Order of the Court dated [Date].

The Court's attention is drawn to the absence of any risk assessments or documents relating to the same contained with the Defendants' list.

The Court's attention is further drawn to the witness statements upon which the defendants rely and which do not disclose any evidence that a risk assessment, either sufficient or suitable, has been carried out prior to the introduction of the aforementioned hazardous substance into the work process.

The evidential burden rests with the defendants to show that on the balance of probability a risk assessment was in fact carried out in accordance with their obligation imposed by regulation 6(1) of the aforementioned Regulations.

It is submitted that there is an absence of any documentary evidence or witness evidence to rebut the allegation of breach of regulation 6(1) COSHH Regulations 1999 and further that there is no evidence which can reasonably be expected to be available at trial to support a denial of breach of the aforementioned Regulation 1999. It is submitted that the Defendants have failed to discharge the burden of proof that a suitable and sufficient risk assessment was performed. In the circumstances the claimant will establish primary liability against the defendants. It is submitted therefore, that the defence has no real prospect of success and it is further submitted that there is no other compelling reason why this issue should be disposed of at trial.

Cont'd.../

In all the circumstances, the claimant respectfully requests that the Court shall make the order as requested together with an order for costs in the claimant's favour.

Statement of Truth

* (I believe) (The applicant believes) that the facts stated in Part C are true

delete as appropriate

Signed		**Position or office held**
		[PARTNER]
(Applicant)('s Solicitor)('s litigation friend)		(if signing on behalf of firm or company)
		Date

A15.3

DRAFT ORDER

IN THE ANYTOWN COUNTY COURT   CLAIM NO

BETWEEN:

MR A GOODCHAP

Claimant

and

A N ENGINEERING COMPANY LTD

Defendant

DRAFT ORDER

---

1. Pursuant to CPR 24.2 Judgment on primary liability be entered in the Claimant's favour against the Defendants.

2. The issue of [contributory negligence], [medical causation] [quantum] shall be left to be decided by the trial Judge at the hearing which has been listed for [*date*].

3. The Claimant's costs of and incidental to this Application be paid by the Defendants within 14 days of the date of this Order.

Dated this   day of   2006

Signed……………………………………. Signed…………………………………….

Solicitors for the Claimant   Solicitors for the Defendant

Ref: Ref:

APPLICATION TO STRIKE OUT THE DEFENCE UNDER CPR 3.4(2)(a) FOR FAILURE TO DISCLOSE REASONABLE GROUNDS FOR THE DEFENCE

A16.1

COMMENTARY

Under CPR 3.4(2) the court has an unqualified discretion to strike out a claim or defence in three distinct situations:

(a) where the statement of case discloses no reasonable grounds for bringing or defending a claim; or

(b) where the statement of case is an abuse of the court's process; or

(c) where there has been a failure by one party to comply with a Rule, Practice Direction or Court Order.

The court has an inherent jurisdiction under CPR 3.4 to strike out all or any part of a statement of case. The power can be exercised either on an application by a party, or it may be exercised by the court of its own initiative.

This commentary and application deals with a situation where both CPR 3.4(2)(a) and 3.4(2)(c) are applicable in that, firstly, under 3.4(2)(a) it is submitted that the defence discloses no reasonable grounds and under 3.4(2)(c) that there has been a failure to comply with a rule, practice direction or court order. It is to be noted that reference is made to CPR 16.5 (Contents of Defence). It is submitted that where a defence is filed which amounts to nothing more than a blanket denial, or 'holding defence' as was more common in litigation prior to the introduction of the CPR, such a defence would fall foul of CPR 16.5, breach of which would tend to bolster the application to strike out the defence under CPR 3.4(2)(c) (failure to comply with a rule, practice direction etc) (see CPR 16.5 and the Practice Direction supplementary to CPR Part 16).

An application under CPR 3.4(2) may also be combined with an application under Part 24 (Summary Judgment). There is clearly an overlap between Parts 3.4 and 24 but both give the court two distinct powers. The distinction is that striking out under CPR 3.4 is directed at the construction of the defence ie the way in which the defence is drafted, whereas Summary Judgment under Part 24 is an examination of the merits of the defence and a test of its weaknesses. The practice direction which supplements CPR rule 3.4 describes some instances in which a defence can be struck out where the court concludes that the defence discloses no reasonable grounds. Paragraph 1.6 of the practice directions refers to cases which consist of a bear denial or otherwise set out no coherent statement of facts.

However, a court will be very cautious in its approach to request to strike out to ensure that the overriding objective is observed. The court will tend to refuse an application which would require a detailed examination of documents and protracted argument (see *Three Rivers District Council v Bank of England (No 3)* [2003] 2 AC 1).

Part 3.4(2)(a) applies to statements of case which are incoherent or unreasonably vague, or while the facts set out may be coherent they do not amount in law to a defence (see Practice Direction 3, para 1.6). Part 3.4(2)(c) covers cases where non-compliance with a rule or practice direction.

The court will consider all the relevant circumstances which may include prejudice suffered by the other party. An order to strike out can be made even where the rule, practice direction or court order which has been breached makes no mention to the consequences of that breach. In fact CPR 16.5 does not mention any particular sanctions.

The court will consider all of the circumstances and may consider other sanctions falling short of a strike out eg an award of costs on the indemnity basis or by imposing an 'Unless Order' with a time within which to comply to remedy the breach or procedural fault (*Biguzzi v Rank Leisure plc* [1999] 1 WLR 1926). Where the prejudice which has resulted from the breach leaves the Court unable to deal fairly with the case the more likely it is that the statement of case will be struck out (see *Purefuture Ltd v Simmons and Simmons* 25 May 2000, unreported, CA).

Many cases fall within both CPR 3.4 and Part 24 and it is common practice to combine the striking out application with an application for summary judgment. The court may treat an application under CPR 3.4(2)(a) as if it was an application under Part 24.

Although there is no requirement under CPR 3.4(2) to produce evidence in support of an application it is advisable that any facts which require proof should be carefully considered and evidence in support should be filed and served. In the example given herewith the defence, which amounts to either a blanket denial or is incoherent or nonsensical, would stand on its own as evidence in support of the application.

An application under CPR 3.4(2) should be made at the earliest opportunity and before allocation if possible.

A16.2

APPLICATION NOTICE WITH PART 'C' STATEMENT OF TRUTH

Application Notice

	In the ANY TOWN COUNTY COURT

You should provide this information for listing the application

1. How do you wish to have your application dealt with

   a) at a hearing? ☐ ⎫

   b) at a telephone conference? ☐ ⎬ *complete all questions below*

   c) without a hearing? ☐ *complete Qs 5 and 6 below*

2. Give a time estimate for the hearing/conference
   _____ (hours) _____ (mins)

3. Is this agreed by all parties? ☐ Yes ☐ No

4. Give dates of any trial period or fixed trial date

5. Level of judge

6. Parties to be served

Claim no.	AT12345
Warrant no. (if applicable)	
Claimant (including ref.)	MR A GOODCHAP
Defendant(s) (including ref.)	ASBESTOS SHIPPING LIMITED
Date	

Note You must complete Parts A **and** B, **and** Part C if applicable. Send any relevant fee and the completed application to the court with any draft order, witness statement or other evidence; and sufficient copies for service on each respondent

1. Enter your full name, or name of solicitor

2. State clearly what order you are seeking and if possible attach a draft

3. Briefly set out why you are seeking the order. Include the material facts on which you rely, identifying any rule or statutory provision

4. If you are not already a party to the proceedings, you must provide an address for service of documents

Part A

I (We) [(1)] on behalf of the claimant/~~defendant~~

intend to apply for an order (a draft of which is attached) that [(2)] (1) pursuant to CPR r 3.4(2) the defence be struck out and judgment be entered on behalf of the claimant for damages to be assessed together with costs of the action. (2) The costs of and incidental to this application be the claimant's in any event.

because [(3)] the defendant's by their defence have failed to disclose any reasonable grounds for defending the claim. Further the defence does not comply with CPR r 16.5.

Part B

I (We) wish to rely on: *tick one box*

   the attached (witness statement)(affidavit) ☐   my statement of case ☐

   evidence in Part C in support of my application ☒

Signed		**Position or office held**	[PARTNER]

(Applicant)('s Solicitor)(~~'s litigation friend~~)   (if signing on behalf of a firm or company)

Address to which documents about this claim should be sent (including reference if appropriate) [(4)]

		if applicable
	fax no.	
	DX no.	
Tel. no. Postcode	e-mail	

The court office at
is open from 10am to 4pm Monday to Friday. When corresponding with the court please address forms or letters to the Court Manager and quote the claim number.

N244 Application notice 04/00   © Crown copyright. Produced by infolaw 11/04

Part C   Claim No. | AT12345 |

~~I~~(We) wish to rely on the following evidence in support of this application:

Statement of Truth

*~~(I believe)~~ (the Applicant believes) that the facts stated in Part C are true

delete as appropriate

Signed _____ **Position or office held** | [PARTNER] |

(Applicant)(~~'s Solicitor~~)(~~'s litigation friend~~)   (if signing on behalf of firm or company)

Date _____

A16.3

DRAFT ORDER

IN THE ANYTOWN COUNTY COURT   CLAIM NO

BETWEEN:

MR A GOODCHAP

Claimant

and

ASBESTOS SHIPPING LTD

Defendant

DRAFT ORDER

Upon hearing the Claimant and the Defendant it is ordered that:-

1. The Defence be struck out.

2. Judgment be entered for the Claimant for an amount to be decided by the Court and costs.

3. The costs of and incidental to this Application be the Claimant's in any event.

Dated this   day of   2006

Signed…………………………………… Signed…………………………………….

Solicitors for the Claimant   Solicitors for the Defendant

Ref: Ref:

APPLICATION FOR AN ORDER FOR THE ISSUES OF LIABILITY AND QUANTUM TO BE TRIED SEPARATELY PURSUANT TO CPR 3.1(2)(i)

A17.1

COMMENTARY

The Civil Procedure Rules (CPR 3) provide general powers of case management which the courts may exercise of its own initiative. Under CPR 3.1 a list of the powers is given which includes the power to direct that the issues arising in any case may be dealt with separately. For instance the issue of liability may be dealt with independently of the issue of quantum particularly in personal injury cases where the medical evidence is unlikely to be completed for some considerable time. It is quite common in personal injury cases for the issues of liability to be tried before the issue of damages where the prognosis is uncertain because continuing treatment or surgery is required.

CPR 3.1(2)(i) allows the court to direct a separate trial of any issue. Costs savings may be obtained in deciding the issue of liability at an early stage and it may also serve the interests of justice that a final assessment of damages should not be undertaken until an accurate and reliable prognosis of the Claimant's condition can be made. In cases involving more serious injuries it may be that quantification of damages cannot be meaningfully assessed. In such a case it may well be in the interests of justice and of all parties concerned to postpone the assessment of damages until the medical evidence is satisfactory and complete.

In *Parkin v Bromley Hospital NHS Trust* 4 October 2001, unreported, WL34008611 (Buckley J) where liability was admitted the assessment of damages hearing was adjourned for a period of eight months to enable an accurate assessment of quantum to be calculated. This case involved a claim for clinical negligence against the defendant NHS Trust in which a child suffered severe brain damage at the moment of birth.

In *Aden v Securicor Custodial Services Ltd* [2004] EWHC 394, QB (Eady J) the claimant developed severe psychiatric problems following an accident. The claimant applied to the court under CPR 3.1(2)(i) for an order that the issues of liability and quantum be decided at separate trials. The claimant had been detained in hospital under the Mental Health Act after developing severe psychotic symptoms. The court was requested to order a separate trial to allow the claim for damages to be assessed after he had been discharged from secure psychiatric care. The court refused the application on the grounds that it was not in the interests of justice to allow a separate trial since this would have prejudiced the defendant insurers who would be faced with liabilities which could not be quantified for an indefinite period of time.

A detailed and accurate summary of the medical evidence should be given within the statement of truth and any medical reports should be annexed and exhibited with the application.

It is also desirable that a draft list of further directions, preferably agreed with the other party, should be provided to assist the court in disposing of the issue of liability at a separate trial.

A17.2

APPLICATION NOTICE WITH PART 'C' STATEMENT OF TRUTH

Application Notice

	In the ANY TOWN COUNTY COURT

You should provide this information for listing the application

1. How do you wish to have your application dealt with

   a) at a hearing? ☐ ⎫
   b) at a telephone conference? ☐ ⎬ *complete all questions below*
   c) without a hearing? ☐ *complete Qs 5 and 6 below*

2. Give a time estimate for the hearing/conference
   _____ (hours) _____ (mins)

3. Is this agreed by all parties? ☐ Yes ☐ No

4. Give dates of any trial period or fixed trial date

5. Level of judge

6. Parties to be served

Claim no.	AT12345
Warrant no. (if applicable)	
Claimant (including ref.)	MR A GOODCHAP
Defendant(s) (including ref.)	A N ENGINEERING COMPANY LIMITED
Date	

Note You must complete Parts A **and** B, **and** Part C if applicable. Send any relevant fee and the completed application to the court with any draft order, witness statement or other evidence; and sufficient copies for service on each respondent

Part A

1. Enter your full name, or name of solicitor

I (We) [1] on behalf of the claimant/~~defendant~~

2. State clearly what order you are seeking and if possible attach a draft

intend to apply for an order (a draft of which is attached) that [2] (1) pursuant to CPR r 3.1(2)(i) the Court shall direct a separate trial on the issue of liability. (2) Further Case Management Directions be ordered in accordance with the attached draft list of directions annexed hereto. (3) Costs of and incidental to this application be costs in the case.

3. Briefly set out why you are seeking the order. Include the material facts on which you rely, identifying any rule or statutory provision

because [3] the Court has power to order a split trial by virtue of CPR r 3.1(2)(i) and by so doing it is likely that a significant costs saving will be achieved and the case will be concluded at a much earlier stage.

Part B

I (We) wish to rely on: *tick one box*

4. If you are not already a party to the proceedings, you must provide an address for service of documents

the attached (witness statement)(affidavit) ☐   my statement of case ☐

evidence in Part C in support of my application ☐

Signed		**Position or office held**	[PARTNER]
(Applicant)('s Solicitor)(~~'s litigation friend~~)		(if signing on behalf of a firm or company)	

Address to which documents about this claim should be sent (including reference if appropriate) [4]

		if applicable
	fax no.	
	DX no.	
Tel. no.	Postcode	e-mail

The court office at
is open from 10am to 4pm Monday to Friday. When corresponding with the court please address forms or letters to the Court Manager and quote the claim number.

N244 Application notice 04/00   © Crown copyright. Produced by infolaw 11/04

Part C   Claim No.   AT12345

I (We) wish to rely on the following evidence in support of this application:

The claimant claims damages for personal injuries, losses and expenses incurred as a result of injuries sustained in an accident at work on [Date].

The claimant is and was at all material times employed by the defendants.

[State brief facts of the accident/claim].

It is alleged that the defendants were negligent in that [state primary allegations of negligence].

The defendants deny liability.

Proceedings were issued on [Date].

The defence was received on [Date].

The main injuries that the claimant has suffered are [Details of injuries] and are described in the report of [Medical expert] dated [Date].

It is unlikely that the medical evidence will be completed with an accurate prognosis within the next 6 months/ 12 months. [Details of medical opinion in relation to prognosis, etc]. A copy of the medical report of [NAME] dated [DATE] is attached and exhibited herewith.

The issues with regard to liability are set out in the Particulars of Claim and Defence. It is submitted that if the claimant succeeds on liability it is more probable than not that quantum will be agreed without a further hearing.

It is further submitted that if liability were to be tried separately from and before the issue of quantum there would be a substantial or significant costs saving between the parties.

It is further submitted that the likely value of this claim is in excess of £15,000.00 and as such the claim would ordinarily be allocated to the Multi Track. In deciding the issue of liability at this early stage by means of a "split" trial should the claimant succeed on the issue of liability, the further issues of causation and quantum will be able to be narrowed to allow the court to allocate the matter to the Fast Track.

Should the Court be so minded as to grant this order it is anticipated that the hearing on liability would last no longer than one day.

The claimant respectfully requests that the Court make the order as requested together with an order for costs in the case.

Statement of Truth

* (I believe) (The Applicant believes) that the facts stated in Part C are true

**delete as appropriate*

Signed		Position or office held	[PARTNER]
	(Applicant)('s Solicitor)('s litigation friend)	(if signing on behalf of firm or company)	
		Date	

A17.3

DRAFT ORDER

IN THE ANY TOWN COUNTY COURT   CLAIM NO AT12345

BETWEEN:

MR A GOODCHAP

Claimant

and

A N ENGINEERING COMPANY LTD

Defendant

_____

DRAFT ORDER

_____

1. Pursuant to CPR 3.1(2)(i) the claim shall be listed for hearing on the issue of liability only.

2. The following directions shall apply [list appropriate directions for disclosure, witness evidence etc].

3. The costs of and incidental to this Application be costs in the case.

Dated this   day of   2006

Signed………………………………. Signed…………………………………..

Solicitors for the Claimant   Solicitors for the Defendant

Ref: Ref:

APPLICATION FOR AN INTERIM PAYMENT UNDER CPR 25.6

A18.1

COMMENTARY

The jurisdiction to order an interim payment has its basis in the Supreme Courts Act 1981 S32 and the County Courts Act 1984 s 50. The court has power to require a party to the proceedings to make an interim payment on account of any damages which that party 'may be held liable to pay to or for the benefit of another party to the proceedings if a final judgment or order of the court in the proceedings is given or made in favour of that other party' (SCA 1981 s 32 and CCA 1984 s 50).

The objective that the courts try to achieve by adopting this procedure is to provide financial relief to an impecunious claimant. However, there is no specific requirement within CPR 25 to show any hardship on the part of the claimant that would be alleviated by an interim payment. However, the court has a wide discretion that is founded in the former RSC rules to make an interim payment order 'if it thinks fit' and 'of such amount as (the Court) thinks just'. The exercise of the court's discretion is extremely wide and such considerations as financial hardship may be taken into account but that is not a prescriptive criteria and there are no limitations on the exercise of the court's discretion save for those imposed by CPR 25.7. The claimant does not have to persuade the court that the interim payment of damages is required to cater for any particular requirement or expense more than a general requirement that a Claimant ought to be paid his damages as soon as reasonably may be done (see *Stringman v McArdle and McCardell* [1994] 1 WLR 1653). The court has no interest in the purpose to which the interim payment of damages will be put (see *Campbell v Mylchreest* (1998) PIQR P20).

Generally, an interim payment will not be ordered where the size of the potential damages award is likely to be modest or where evidence in support of quantum is uncertain, eg where causation is in issue. Indeed, there may be little point in making an application for an interim payment where the claim has been allocated to the fast track bearing in mind the speed at which the timetable under a fast track case should ordinarily operate.

The conditions which must be satisfied are contained in CPR 25.7(1) and these can be summarised as follows:

(i) the Defendant has admitted liability to pay damages to the claimant; or

(ii) the claimant has obtained Judgment against the defendant for damages to be assessed; or

(iii) the court is satisfied that, if the claim went to trial, the claimant would obtain judgment against the defendant for 'a substantial sum of money'; or

(iv) where there is more than one defendant the court is satisfied that the conditions above apply and also that all of the defendants are either (a) a defendant that is insured in respect of the claim, (b) a defendant whose liability would be met under s 151 of the Road Traffic Act 1988 (or MIB) or (c) that the defendant is a public body.

In the example given, provision is made for circumstances where the claimant has either admitted liability or the claimant has obtained judgment against the defendant. In the absence of such an admission or judgment it may be difficult to persuade the court that an interim payment is appropriate particularly where there are any reservations as to the likely size of any award, causation issues or liability issues and this is especially so in cases involving multiple defendants.

The standard of proof required to be met by the claimant on an application under CPR 25.7 is that on the balance of probabilities the claimant would obtain judgment. This means more than merely 'likely to succeed' but the court is not required to be sure in the sense of being satisfied beyond reasonable doubt (see *Shearson Lehman Brothers Inc v Maclaine Watson & Co Ltd* [1989] QB 842).

Under CPR 25.9 the fact that an order has been made for an interim payment shall not be disclosed to the trial judge until all questions of liability and the amount of damages to be awarded have been decided, unless the defendant agrees. This observes the principle, much like those governing Part 36 CPR payments and offers to settle, which seeks to avoid the risk that a trial judge may be influenced by the fact of an interim payment having been made in deciding either liability or quantum.

CPR 25.8 lists further orders that the court may make to adjust an interim payment in circumstances where one defendant claims reimbursement from another defendant by way of a contribution, indemnity or other remedy (see CPR 25.8(3)) to which the interim payment relates.

An application for an interim payment may often be combined with an application for summary judgment under CPR 24 under which the court has power to make a 'relevant order'. Obviously, if summary judgment is sought on the grounds that the defence has no reasonable prospect of success it would fulfil the criteria under CPR 25.7(1)(c).

Finally, it should be noted that an application for an interim payment can be made without notice but the applicant must state within the body of the application the reasons why notice was not given (see PD 25.3).

A18.2

APPLICATION NOTICE WITH PART 'C' STATEMENT OF TRUTH

Application Notice

You should provide this information for listing the application	In the ANY TOWN COUNTY COURT	
1. How do you wish to have your application dealt with	**Claim no.**	
a) at a hearing? ☐ ⎫ complete all questions below	**Warrant no.** (if applicable)	
b) at a telephone conference? ☐ ⎭		
c) without a hearing? ☐ complete Qs 5 and 6 below	**Claimant** (including ref.)	MR A GOODCHAP
2. Give a time estimate for the hearing/conference _____ (hours) _____ (mins)	**Defendant(s)** (including ref.)	DODGY CORPORATEVEIL LIMTED
3. Is this agreed by all parties? ☐ Yes ☐ No		
4. Give dates of any trial period or fixed trial date	**Date**	
5. Level of judge		
6. Parties to be served		

Note You must complete Parts A **and** B, **and** Part C if applicable. Send any relevant fee and the completed application to the court with any draft order, witness statement or other evidence; and sufficient copies for service on each respondent

Part A

1. Enter your full name, or name of solicitor

I (We) (1) [STATE NAME OF FIRM] on behalf of the claimant/~~defendant~~

2. State clearly what order you are seeking and if possible attach a draft

intend to apply for an order (a draft of which is attached) that (2) (1) The defendants do pay the sum of [Amount] by way of an interim payment of damages to the claimant within 28 days of the date of this order. (2) The costs of and incidental to the application be the claimant's in any event.

3. Briefly set out why you are seeking the order. Include the material facts on which you rely, identifying any rule or statutory provision

because(3) pursuant to Part 25.6 the Court has power to make an order for an interim payment of damages in circumstances where the provisions of CPR 25.6 are fulfilled.

Part B

I (We) wish to rely on: *tick one box*

4. If you are not already a party to the proceedings, you must provide an address for service of documents

the attached (witness statement)(affidavit) ☐   my statement of case ☐

evidence in Part C in support of my application ☒

Signed _____ **Position or office held** [PARTNER]

(Applicant)('s Solicitor)(~~'s litigation friend~~) (if signing on behalf of a firm or company)

Address to which documents about this claim should be sent (including reference if appropriate)(4)

	if applicable	
	fax no.	
	DX no.	
Tel. no. Postcode	e-mail	

The court office at

is open from 10am to 4pm Monday to Friday. When corresponding with the court please address forms or letters to the Court Manager and quote the claim number.

N244 Application notice 04/00   © Crown copyright. Produced by infolaw 11/04

Part C   Claim No. [   ]

I (We) wish to rely on the following evidence in support of this application:

The claimant makes this application for an Order that the defendants do pay the sum of [AMOUNT] on account of damages for injuries and losses in an accident at work.

The claimant [is][was] employed by the defendants [state occupation and brief details of the accident/elements of work related condiition or disease].

A claim for damages was made against the defendant by letter dated [Date]. The defendant has responded to the claim and

(a) the defendant has admitted liability to pay damages;

(b) proceedings have been issued on [Date] and the claimant has obtained judgment against the defendant for damages to be assessed. A copy of the judgment order is attached herewith.

It is submitted that, if the claim went to trial the claimant would succeed in obtaining judgment for a substantial amount of money against the defendant. The defendant is insured in respect of this claim by [Name of insurer and policy number].

The claimants injuries are detailed as follows:

[State brief details of injury] and are fully described in the attached medical report herewith.

It is submitted that the claimant is likely to recover a sum in respect of general damages for pain, suffering and loss of amenity in the region of [State amount].

or where contributory negligence is in issue

Upon full liability being decided in the claimants favour it is likely that the sum awarded for general damages for pain, suffering and loss of amenity would be in the region of [Amount] and after a discount for contributory negligence of [State percentage/proportion] the claimant is likely to be awarded the sum of [Amount]. In addition the claimant claims special damages [State amount] and a schedule of special damage is attached herewith.

It is submitted that the level of interim payment claimed is no more than a reasonable proportion of the likely amount of final judgment.

NB ATTACH AND EXHIBIT

(1) Medical Report

(2) Schedule of Special Damages

(3) Order for Judgment against the defendants

Statement of Truth

* (I believe) (The Applicant believes) that the facts stated in Part C are true

**delete as appropriate*

Signed [   ]   **Position or office held** [PARTNER]

(Applicant)('s Solicitor)('s litigation friend)   (if signing on behalf of firm or company)

Date [   ]

A18.3

DRAFT ORDER

IN THE ANYTOWN COUNTY COURT   CLAIM NO

BETWEEN:

MR A GOODCHAP

Claimant

and

DODGY CORPORATEVEIL LIMITED

Defendant

DRAFT ORDER

1. The Defendants do pay the sum of [AMOUNT] by way of an interim payment of damages to the Claimant within 28 days of the date of this Order.

2. The costs of and incidental to the application be the Claimant's in any event.

DATED THIS   DAY OF   200

APPLICATIONS FOR PROVISIONAL DAMAGES

A19.1

COMMENTARY

An Order for Provisional Damages must specify three things, namely:

(i) the disease of type of deterioration which for the purpose of the award of immediate damages has been assumed will not occur and will entitle the Claimant to further damages if such disease/deterioration occurs at a future date;

(ii) the period within which an Application for further damage may be made;

(iii) what documentation must be filed and preserved as the case file in support of any future Applications.

In the example given a provisional award is sought in respect of an asbestos-related disease. The types of documents which must be filed are listed in the 'Schedule of Contents of Case File'.

The period within which an Application may be made has been stated as being without limit as to time. This drafting avoids any difficulties over the time period within which the future Application must be made. An alternative form of words may be used such as 'within the duration of the life of the Claimant', although it is probably safer to use the wording in this example (without limit as to time) so as to avoid any potential problems. Note that CPR 41.3 states that the Claimant may not make an Application for damages after the expiry of the period specified.

PD41 provides a model for the Judgment or Order which is also helpful.

Note that the Statement of Facts refers specifically to the evidence in support of the Application in order to fulfil the criteria for a provisional award, namely:

(i) the Particulars of Claim include a claim for a provisional award;

(ii) a description of the type of future disease or deterioration in the physical or mental condition which is envisaged;

(iii) the risk or chance of developing a more serious condition (mesothelioma, lung cancer or asbestos disease being serious by their very nature).

The future disease or deterioration must be 'serious' ie beyond that which would be the ordinary consequence of the injury complained of (see *Wilson v Ministry of Defence* [1991] 1 All ER 638). The risk or chance of developing the more serious condition must be quantifiable or measurable as opposed to being merely fanciful (see *Patterson v Ministry of Defence* (1987)).

The Court has discretion as to whether an award for provisional damages should be made instead of the normal lump sum or trial award. This discretion will only be exercised where the criteria set out in SCA 1981, s 32A and CCA 1984, s 51, are fulfilled.

If the further deterioration occurs the application for further damages should be made within the period specified in the judgment order. An extension of the period within which to make this application can be made by seeking a further order at any time (see CPR 41.2(3)). The procedure for applying for a provisional award is set out in CPR 41.3 that provides that:

(i) only one Application may be made in respect of each disease/type of deterioration;

(ii) 28 days' notice must be given in writing to the Defendants of the Claimant's intention to seek the Order;

(iii) the identity of the Defendants' insurer must be given, if known, and 28 days' notice must also be given to that insurer;

(iv) 21 days after the expiry of the notice period the Claimant must apply for directions.

A19.2

APPLICATION NOTICE WITH PART 'C' STATEMENT OF TRUTH

Application Notice

In the ANY TOWN COUNTY COURT	
Claim no.	AT12345
Warrant no. (if applicable)	
Claimant (including ref.)	MR A GOODCHAP
Defendant(s) (including ref.)	ASBESTOS SHIPPING LIMITED
Date	

You should provide this information for listing the application

1. How do you wish to have your application dealt with
   a) at a hearing? ☐ } *complete all questions below*
   b) at a telephone conference? ☐
   c) without a hearing? ☐ *complete Qs 5 and 6 below*
2. Give a time estimate for the hearing/conference
   _____ (hours) _____ (mins)
3. Is this agreed by all parties? ☐ Yes ☐ No
4. Give dates of any trial period or fixed trial date
5. Level of judge
6. Parties to be served

Note You must complete Parts A **and** B, and Part C if applicable. Send any relevant fee and the completed application to the court with any draft order, witness statement or other evidence; and sufficient copies for service on each respondent

Part A

1. Enter your full name, or name of solicitor

I (We) [1] on behalf of the claimant/defendant

2. State clearly what order you are seeking and if possible attach a draft

intend to apply for an order (a draft of which is attached) that [2] (1) Judgment be entered on behalf of the claimant for an award of provisional damages pursuant to CPR 41.2(1).

(2) The costs of an incidental to this application be the claimant's in any event. because [3]

3. Briefly set out why you are seeking the order. Include the material facts on which you rely, identifying any rule or statutory provision

The requirements of CPR 41.2(1) are fulfilled.

Part B

I (We) wish to rely on: *tick one box*

4. If you are not already a party to the proceedings, you must provide an address for service of documents

the attached (witness statement)(affidavit) ☒   my statement of case ☐

evidence in Part C in support of my application ☒

Signed _____ **Position or office held** [PARTNER]
(Applicant)('s Solicitor)('s litigation friend) (if signing on behalf of a firm or company)

Address to which documents about this claim should be sent (including reference if appropriate) [4]

	if applicable
	fax no.
	DX no.
Tel. no. Postcode	e-mail

The court office at
is open from 10am to 4pm Monday to Friday. When corresponding with the court please address forms or letters to the Court Manager and quote the claim number.

N244 Application notice 04/00   © Crown copyright. Produced by infolaw 11/04

Part C   Claim No.   AT12345

I (We) wish to rely on the following evidence in support of this application:

The claimant refers the court to the following documents attached herewith:-

(1) Agreed statement of facts.

(2) Schedule of contents of case file and copy documents.

Statement of Truth

*(I believe) (the Applicant believes) that the facts stated in Part C are true

*delete as appropriate

Signed   **Position or
                                                        office held**   [PARTNER]

(Applicant)('s Solicitor)('s litigation friend)   (if signing on behalf
                                                        of firm or company)

                                                        Date

A19.3

STATEMENT OF FACTS

IN THE ANY TOWN COUNTY COURT   CLAIM NO AT12345

BETWEEN:

MR A GOODCHAP

Claimant

and

ASBESTOS SHIPPING LTD

Defendant

STATEMENT OF FACTS

---

1. The Claimant is Albert Goodchap and he was born on [*date of birth*].

2. The Claimant was employed by the Defendants as particularised in the Particulars of Claim and Further and Better Particulars of the Particulars of Claim.

3. During the said course of the Claimant's employment with the Defendants he came into contact with asbestos as a result of which he has suffered injury, loss and damage.

4. On [*date*] the Claimant issued a Claim Form against the Defendants herein claiming damages for the said disease and alleging the cause of the disease was their negligence and/or breach of statutory duty as further particularised in the Particulars of Claim.

5. The Claimant has been medically advised that there is a risk of Mesothelioma, Lung Cancer and Asbestos Disease. The Claimant relies upon the medical report prepared by [*name of expert*] as itemised in the Schedule of Contents of the Case File.

WE AGREE THE ABOVE STATEMENT OF FACTS

Dated this   day of   2006

Signed...................................... Signed......................................

Solicitors for the Claimant   Solicitors for the Defendant

Ref: Ref:

A19.4

SCHEDULE OF CONTENTS CASE FILE

IN THE ANY TOWN COUNTY COURT   CLAIM NO AT12345

BETWEEN:

MR A GOODCHAP

Claimant

and

ASBESTOS SHIPPING LTD

Defendant

SCHEDULE OF CONTENTS OF CASE FILE

The case file herein includes the following documents:-

1. Order dated [*dated*].
2. Copy pleadings consisting of:-
    a. Particulars of Claim dated [*dated*]
    b. Further and Better Particulars of the Particulars of Claim dated [*dated*]
    c. Defence
    d. Agreed Statement of Facts
    e. Copy of the medical reports of:-

        i.   [*list all medical reports for both Claimant and Defendants*]

Dated this   day of   2006

Signed…………………………………. Signed…………………………………..

Solicitors for the Claimant   Solicitors for the Defendant

Ref: Ref:

A19.5

DRAFT ORDER

IN THE ANY TOWN COUNTY COURT   CLAIM NO AT12345

BETWEEN:

MR A GOODCHAP

Claimant

AND

ASBESTOS SHIPPING LTD

Defendant

CONSENT ORDER

Upon the Claimant and the Defendant having agreed to the terms set forth in the Schedule hereto it is ordered:-

1.   The Claimant be at liberty to enter Judgment in the sum of £[*amount*] amount by way of immediate damages upon the assumption that the Claimant will not at a future date as a result of the act or omission giving rise to the Cause of Action herein develop the following decisions:-

    a.   Asbestos-induced Mesothelioma

    b.   Asbestos-induced Lung Cancer

    c.   Asbestos-induced Bilateral Pleural Thickening causing a significant disability

    d.   Asbestosis causing a significant disability

2.   By consent it is ordered that the Claimant, if at a future date, does so develop such disease or suffers such deterioration as referred to in paragraph 1 he should be entitled to apply for further damages, without limit as to time.

3.   The sum of £[*amount*] standing in Court to the credit of this action be paid to the Claimant's solicitors forthwith.

4.   Interest up to and including the date of this Order be payable to the Defendants and any interest thereafter to the Claimant.

5.   The Defendants do further pay the Claimant's costs of this Action to be assessed if not agreed.

6. It is further directed that the document specified in Schedule 1 hereto and annexed shall constitute the case file herein and shall be lodged and preserved as material for any further assessment.

7. It is further directed that the Statement of Facts annexed hereto at Schedule 2 is agreed.

Dated this   day of   2006

Signed..................................... Signed.....................................

Solicitors for the Claimant   Solicitors for the Defendant

Ref: Ref:

APPLICATION FOR COURT APPROVAL ON BEHALF OF A CHILD ('INFANT SETTLEMENT')

A20.1

COMMENTARY

When a claim for damages is made on behalf of a child, or a person under disability, the approval of the court is required before any settlement or compromise will take effect. Until that time there is no contract between the parties. CPR 21.10(1) specifically confirms that no settlement, compromise or payment on behalf of a child (or patient) shall be valid without the approval of the court.

Where settlement is achieved before proceedings are issued the court's approval is obtained by adopting the Part 8 procedure and requesting the court to approve the settlement or compromise (CPR 21.10(2)).

The practice direction which supplements CPR 21 sets out the procedure and contents of the application (see PD21, para 6.3). The claim form must set out the facts and details of the claim, state whether the settlement is full and final or by way of compromise, and must have a draft consent order attached.

An opinion on the merits of the settlement or compromise given by counsel should almost always be supplied. PD21 para 6.3(1) does permit a solicitor acting for the child or patient to provide the opinion on the merits. However, most courts would expect the opinion to be provided by counsel.

The information which should be provided within the statement of evidence in support of the application should include the following:

(i) whether and to what extent the defendants admit liability;

(ii) the age and occupation (if any) of the child or patient;

(iii) the litigation friend's approval of the proposed settlement or compromise; and

(iv) the circumstances of the accident, any medical reports, schedules of special damage and, where liability is not admitted in full, any evidence including police reports, details of prosecutions in RTA cases etc must be provided. (See PD21 para 6.2.)

Where settlement is achieved after issue of proceedings the procedure is identical save for the fact that obviously the Part 8 procedure is not adopted.

Where the claim involves a claim for damages for future pecuniary loss see PD21.1 para 6.6 to 6.9.

If approval is given the court will give directions for the investment of the monies into the court funds. The court will require a form for the request for investment to be completed (CFO form 320). The form is usually completed by the master or district judge although some courts are idiosyncratic and may require the CFO form 320 to be completed and attached to the application notice. (See PD21.1 para 10.1.) There are specific rules for the investment of funds on behalf of patients according to the size of the settlement and these are dealt with in paragraph 11.1 and 11.2 of the Practice Direction.

Where a damages award is for a very small amount the court may order the money to be paid direct to the litigation friend to be put into a building society account, or similar account, for the child's use. Should there be any particular or specific requirements of the child to be met with any immediate payment before the award is invested the statement and draft order should set out the details.

A20.2

STATEMENT OF TRUTH

1. STATEMENT OF [STATE NAME OF SOLICITOR]

2. ON BEHALF OF THE CLAIMANT

3. NO. OF STATEMENT:

4. DATED:

IN THE ANYTOWN COUNTY COURT   CLAIM NO:

BETWEEN:

MASTER WILLIAM BLOGGS

(Suing by his Father & Litigation Friend Joseph Bloggs)

Claimant

-and-

BOTHERHAM CITY COUNCIL

Defendant

STATEMENT OF [STATE NAME OF SOLICITOR]

I, [*name of solicitor*], Solicitor for the firm of [*state name and address of firm*] will say as follows:-

1   I have the care and conduct of this action on behalf of the Claimant who is a minor represented in this action by his Father and Litigation Friend Joseph Bloggs.

2   The Claimant is a boy aged [*age*] having been born on [*date of birth*] and who sustained injuries in an accident on [*state accident date*].

3   The accident occurred [*state brief facts*] at [*state location of accident*] sustaining injury.

4   The accident occurred on the premises owned or occupied by the Defendants.

5   The Defendants have admitted liability for the accident and have agreed to pay damages to the Claimant.

6   A medical report has been obtained from [*state name of medical expert*], and is dated [*state date of report*]. A copy of the medical report are attached and exhibited to this statement and marked [*state initials of solicitor and number of exhibit*].

7   In his report [*name of medical expert*] confirms that the Claimant [*state experts confirmation of accident details and injuries*] eg the claimant, fell from a 'zip

wire' in a public playground landing on the ground and suffering a fracture to the bones in the right wrist. The Claimant was detained overnight in hospital and the fracture was thereafter treated conservatively by placing the same in a cast. Some of the Claimant's school/sporting activities were affected for a short period.

8   At the time of examination, 18 months post-accident, the Claimant has made a virtually full recovery. He had full pain free movement in the wrist. The only activity which caused any symptoms was playing guitar by reason of the need to flex maximally. However, this is described as a very minor complaint.

9   The prognosis was full resolution within 18 months of the injury. The prognosis has been borne out.

10   With regard to general damages Counsel's advice has been obtained and a copy of the advice of [*name of counsel*] of Counsel dated [*date*] is exhibited to this statement and marked [*initials and no. of exhibit*].

11   The Defendants have offered to pay the Claimant the sum of [£XXX] in respect of general damages. Special damages are claimed I the sum of [£XXX]. [There are no special damages claimed].

12   I have read the opinion of Counsel and in view of what appears therein I submit that the proposed settlement in the total sum of [£XXX] is in all the circumstances just and equitable.

13   I have provided a copy of Counsel's advice to [*state name of litigation friend*], who has informed me that [*he/she*] agrees that the proposed settlement in the sum of [£XXX] is in all the circumstances just and equitable.

14   I attach and exhibit herewith [*state initials and no. of exhibit*] a letter, form of acceptance duly signed and dated by [*state name of litigation friend*] of the Claimant confirming his agreement to settlement in the terms stated.

15   The Claimant's costs have been agreed with the Defendants in the sum of [£XXX] and I enclose and exhibit marked [*initials and no. of exhibit*] a letter dated [*date*] from the Defendant's solicitors/insurers confirming agreement to the same.

16   In the circumstances, the Court is respectfully requested to approve of the proposed settlement in the total sum of [£XXX] together with costs in the agreed sum of [£XXX].

STATEMENT OF TRUTH

I believe that the facts stated in this witness statement are true.

SIGNED..

DATED..

[Claimant's Solicitors signature]

A20.3

DRAFT ORDER

IN THE ANYTOWN COUNTY COURT   CLAIM NO:

BETWEEN:

MASTER WILLIAM BLOGGS

(Suing by his Father & Litigation Friend Joseph Bloggs)

Claimant

-and-

BOTHERHAM CITY COUNCIL

Defendant

DRAFT ORDER

BEFORE His Honour Judge/District Judge [*state name*] on   day of

UPON hearing Counsel [Solicitor] for the Claimants and Counsel [*solicitor*] for the Defendant the following terms of settlement agreed between the parties are approved by and made an Order of the Court and BY CONSENT

IT IS ORDERED that all further proceedings in this action be stayed (except for the purposes of enforcement or carrying the terms into effect) and that there be liberty to apply for that purpose and generally:

That the Defendant do pay to [the Claimant's solicitors] or Joseph Bloggs the Father and next friend of the Claimant the sum of [£xxx] on or before the   day of .

ALTERNATIVELY

The Defendant do pay the sum of [£xxx] into the Court Funds Office on or before [*date*] (Subject to a first charge under Section 16(6) of the Legal Aid Act 1988) to be invested and accumulated in the Special Investment Account pending further Order.

The Claimant's solicitor attend a hearing for further investment directions on [*date*] at [*time*] at [*address of court*] (the fund to be paid to the child on majority as [*he/she*] may request).

SUPPLEMENTARY PROVISIONS TO BE ADDED WHERE NECESSARY;

(i) (Where the claim is in respect of a Fatal Accident);-

The said sum of [£XXX] is apportioned as follows:-

(a) (Under the Law Reform (Miscellaneous Provisions) Act 1994 the sum of [£xxx]

(b) (Under the Fatal Accidents Act 1976);-

> (i)   (£xxx to the personal claim of the Claimant]
>
> (ii) (£xxx to the personal claim of the child dependant(s) [*names o*F *dependants*]
>
> The Defendant pay the sum of [£xxx] to the Claimant's (solicitors/litigation friend) on or before [*date*].
>
> (ii) (Where Court of Protection will require the appointment of a Receiver) the following should be added:-
>
> The Claimant's solicitor to apply to the Court of Protection for the appointment of a Receiver on or before [*date*] and upon such appointment being made the sum of [£xxx] (subject to a first charge under Section 16(6) of the Legal Aid Act 1988) together with any interest accrued on that sum from the date of this Order to be carried over for the Court of Protection to the credit of the Claimant there to be dealt with as the Court of Protection thinks fit.
>
> (iii) (In the case of a payment into Court) the following should be added:-
>
> (Any interest accrued up to the date of this Order on any money paid in by or on behalf of the Defendant be paid out to the Defendants solicitors)

That the Defendant do pay the Claimant his costs of this action to be assessed if not agreed [agreed in the sum of £xxx] as between the parties.

[if legal aid]

That [*the Claimants*] and [*the Defendants*] costs be taxed in accordance with regulation 107 Civil Legal Aid (General) Regulations 1989 (on the standard basis).

That on payment of the sums and costs mentioned above the Defendants be discharged from any further liability in respect of the Claimant's claim in this action.

A21

CHANGE OF SOLICITOR

A21.1

COMMENTARY

Part 42 CPR governs the rules in relation to giving notice of change of solicitor. CPR 42.3 gives the power to make an order declaring the solicitor has ceased to be the solicitor acting for a party. Where that party wishes to change its solicitor, appoint a new solicitor or where the party intends to act in person.

A solicitor may apply under CPR 42.3 for an order that the solicitor has ceased to act.

The procedure is quite simple and reference should be made to the Practice Direction supplementary to Part 42.

Essentially the notice of change must be filed with the court and served on every other party and, where appropriate, upon the former solicitor acting for the party (CPR 42.2(2)(b)).

The notice must state the new party's address for service and should be filed at court stating that the notice has been served as required by Part 42.2(2)(b).

Under CPR 42.3, which gives power to the court to make the order, a notice of the application must be given to the party for whom the solicitor is acting, unless the court directs otherwise, and the application must be supported by evidence (CPR 42.3(2).

A copy of the order must be served on every party to the proceedings. If it is served by a party or the solicitor, the party or the solicitor must file a certificate of service.

NB: Practice form N434 should be used to give notice of any change.

The application itself may be made in accordance with Part 23, ie the usual form N244 application notice may be used.

A21.2

APPLICATION NOTICE

Application Notice		**In the ANY TOWN COUNTY COURT**	
You should provide this information for listing the application		**Claim no.**	AT12345
1. How do you wish to have your application dealt with		**Warrant no.** (if applicable)	
a) at a hearing? ☐ }*complete all questions below* b) at a telephone conference? ☐ c) without a hearing? ☐ *complete Qs 5 and 6 below*		**Claimant** (including ref.)	MR A GOODCHAP
2. Give a time estimate for the hearing/conference ____ (hours) ____ (mins)		**Defendant(s)** (including ref.)	ASBESTOS SHIPPING LIMITED
3. Is this agreed by all parties? ☐ Yes ☐ No 4. Give dates of any trial period or fixed trial date 5. Level of judge 6. Parties to be served		**Date**	

Note You must complete Parts A **and** B, **and** Part C if applicable. Send any relevant fee and the completed application to the court with any draft order, witness statement or other evidence; and sufficient copies for service on each respondent

1. Enter your full name, or name of solicitor

2. State clearly what order you are seeking and if possible attach a draft

3. Briefly set out why you are seeking the order. Include the material facts on which you rely, identifying any rule or statutory provision

4. If you are not already a party to the proceedings, you must provide an address for service of documents

Part A

I (We) [1] on behalf of the claimant/defendant

intend to apply for an order (a draft of which is attached) that [2] (1) pursuant to CPR 42.3 it be declared that the solicitor acting on behalf of the claimant in this action has ceased to act on behalf of the said claimant. (2) The costs of and incidental to this application be paid by the claimant.

because[3] the claimant has: (1) withdrawn instructions OR (2) instructed an alternative firm of solicitors OR (3) [STATE ANY OTHER REASON].

Part B

I (We) wish to rely on: *tick one box*

the attached (witness statement)(affidavit) ☐   my statement of case ☐

evidence in Part C in support of my application ☐

Signed		**Position or office held**	
(Applicant)('s Solicitor)('s litigation friend)		(if signing on behalf of a firm or company)	

Address to which documents about this claim should be sent (including reference if appropriate)[4]

	if applicable	
	fax no.	
	DX no.	
Tel. no. Postcode	e-mail	

The court office at

is open from 10am to 4pm Monday to Friday. When corresponding with the court please address forms or letters to the Court Manager and quote the claim number.

N244 Application notice 04/00   © Crown copyright. Produced by infolaw 11/04

Part C

Claim No. | AT12345

I (We) wish to rely on the following evidence in support of this application:

Statement of Truth

* (I believe)(The Applicant believes) that the facts stated in Part C are true

**delete as appropriate*

Signed _____

(Applicant)('s Solicitor)('s litigation friend)

Position or office held _____

(if signing on behalf of firm or company)

Date _____

2

A21.3

DRAFT ORDER

IN THE ANYTOWN COUNTY COURT   **CLAIM NO:**

BETWEEN:

MR A GOODCHAP

Claimant

AND

ASBESTOS SHIPPING LTD

Defendant

_____

DRAFT ORDER

_____

The Applicant seeks an Order in the terms sought:

TAKE NOTICE THAT

1. It be declared that [*name of solicitor and firm*] has ceased to be the solicitor acting on behalf of the Claimant [*name*] in this action.

2. The costs of and incidental to this Application be paid by the Claimant/Claimant's solicitor be declared that the solicitor acting on behalf of the Claimant the Claimant seeks an Order in the terms sought.

Dated this   day of   2006

Signed…………………………………. Signed………………………………………….

Solicitors for the Claimant   Solicitors for the Defendant

Ref: Ref:

A22

COSTS PROCEEDINGS UNDER CPR PART 8

A22.1

COMMENTARY

These application notices provide the basic form of the application under CPR Part 8 and begin the process for recovery of costs.

In non-fixed costs cases the procedure is straightforward. If no agreement on costs can be obtained a bill should be drawn and served along with the form N252 (notice of commencement).

In the first example Part 8 proceedings are required where the claim has settled pre-issue. If the matter settles post-issue then there is no requirement for a Part 8 notice since the right to costs arises the judgment, order or award or by inter partes agreement.

The second example relates to an application for fixed costs in a road traffic accident case under CPR 45.7. This fixed costs regime applies to RTAs which occurred after 6 October 2003.

The defendants or the costs advocates on behalf of the defendants have been known to object to payment of insurance premium equivalents in cases funded by way of a conditional fee agreement or collective conditional fee agreement. In such cases an application under CPR Part 8 with reference to CPR 45.7 is appropriate.

Assessment proceedings must begin within three months of the judgment, order or award or other determination that give rise to the right to costs (CPR 47.7). A notice of commencement form N252 must be served on the other party together with a copy of the bill of costs (CPR 47.6(1)). If the other party dispute the costs then a points of dispute must be served within 21 days after service of the notice of commencement. Any reply to the points of dispute must be served within 21 days after receipt of the points of dispute (CPR 47.13).

A22.2

CLAIM FORM

**Claim Form
(CPR Part 8)**

In the ANY TOWN COUNTY COURT	
Claim No.	AT123456

SEAL

Claimant
Mr A Goodchap
[address]

Defendant(s)
Mr D Fendant
[address]

Does, or will, your claim include any issues under the Human Rights Act 1998? ☐ Yes ☒ No

Details of claim *(see also overleaf)*

The claimant brings this action under Part 44.12A of the Civil Procedure Rules for the recovery of legal costs and disbursements incurred as a result of pursuing a claim for damages for personal injuries following an accident which occurred on [Date] and for which the claimant has recovered in the sum of [Amount].

The claimant's claim for damages was settled by agreement on [Date]. It was expressly agreed by the defendants and confirmed in their letter dated [Date] that the defendants would, in addition to the payment of damages pay the claimant's costs to be assessed if not agreed. Copy correspondence between the defendant insurers, [Name], to the claimant's solicitors, [Name], dated [Date] are attached to this claim form.

The parties have failed to reach agreement in relation to the amount of the claimant's costs and the claimant seeks the following order:

		£
Defendant's name and address	Mr D Fendant	
	[address]	

Court fee	
Solicitor's costs	to be assessed
Issue date	

The court office at

is open between 10 am and 4 pm Monday to Friday. When corresponding with the court, please address forms or letters to the Court Manager and quote the claim number.

Claim No.	AT123456

Details of claim *(continued)*

1. The defendants shall pay the claimant's costs arising out of the accident on [Date] to be the subject of a Detailed Assessment if not agreed.

2. Interest shall be paid upon the claimant's costs in accordance with section 69 of the County Courts Act 1984.

3. The costs of the part 8 proceedings shall be dealt with at the Detailed Assessment Hearing.

Statement of Truth

*(I believe)(The Claimant believes) that the facts stated in these particulars of claim are true.
* I am duly authorised by the claimant to sign this statement.

Full name _____

Name of claimant's solicitor's firm [State Name of Firm]

signed _____ position or office held [Partner]
*(Claimant)(Litigation friend)(Claimant's solicitor) (if signing on behalf of a firm or company)
*delete as appropriate

[State Name and Address of Firm and Reference]

Claimant's or claimant's solicitor's address to which documents should be sent if different from overleaf. If you are prepared to accept service by DX, fax or e-mail, please add details.

A22.3

CLAIM FORM UNDER PREDICTABLE COSTS REGIME

**Claim Form
(CPR Part 8)**

In the ANY TOWN COUNTY COURT	
Claim No.	AT123456

Claimant
Mr Albert Goodchap
[address]

SEAL

Defendant(s)
Mr D Fendant
[address]

Does, or will, your claim include any issues under the Human Rights Act 1998?   ☐ Yes   ☒ No

Details of claim *(see also overleaf)*

The claimant brings this action under Part 44.12A of the Civil Procedure Rules for the recovery of legal costs and disbursements incurred as a result of an accident which occurred on [Date] for which the claimant recovered damages in the sum of [Amount].

The claimant's claim for damages was settled by agreement on [Date] and it was expressly agreed between the parties that the defendants would in addition to the payment of damages pay the claimant's costs payable under the predictive costs regime (calculated in accordance with Rules 45.9 – 45.11 of the CPR) or, in the alternative costs to be assessed if not agreed. Copies of letters from the defendant's insurers [Name] to the claimant's solicitors [name] dated [Dates] and from [Claimant's solicitor] to [Defendants' Insurer] dated [Date] are attached to the claim form.

The parties have failed to reach agreement in relation to the amount of the claimant's costs and the claimant seeks the following order:

1. The defendants shall pay the claimant's costs arising out of the accident on [Date] to be the subject of a Detailed Assessment if not agreed.
2. Interest shall be paid upon the claimant's costs in accordance with section 69 of the County Courts Act 1984.
3. The costs of the part 8 proceedings shall be dealt with at the Detailed Assessment hearing.

Defendant's name and address	Mr D Fendant [Address]		£
		Court fee	
		Solicitor's costs	to be assessed
		Issue date	

The court office at

is open between 10 am and 4 pm Monday to Friday. When corresponding with the court, please address forms or letters to the Court Manager and quote the claim number.

N208 Claim Form (CPR Part 8) 10/00   © Crown Copyright. Produced by infolaw 11/04

Claim No.	AT123456

Details of claim *(continued)*

Statement of Truth
*(I believe)(The Claimant believes) that the facts stated in these particulars of claim are true.
*I am duly authorised by the claimant to sign this statement.

Full name _____

Name of claimant's solicitor's firm [State Name of Firm] _____

signed _____ position or office held [Partner]
*(Claimant)(Litigation friend)(Claimant's solicitor) (if signing on behalf of a firm or company)
*delete as appropriate

[State Name and Address of Firm and References]   Claimant's or claimant's solicitor's address to
which documents should be sent if different from
overleaf. If you are prepared to accept service by
DX, fax or e-mail, please add details.